Women
In Theatre

Women
In Theatre

Compassion & Hope

Edited with an Introduction and Notes by

Karen Malpede

LIMELIGHT EDITIONS

New York

Third Limelight Edition June 1991
Second Limelight Edition September 1987
First Limelight Edition May 1985

Library of Congress Cataloging in Publication Data

Main entry under title:

Women in theatre.

Reprint. Originally published: New York: Drama Book
Publishers, 1983.

Bibliography: p.
Includes index.
1. Women in the theater—Addresses, essays,
lectures. 2. Feminist theater—Addresses, essays,
lectures. 3. Prose literature—Women authors.
I. Malpede, Karen.
[PN1590.W64W6 1985]   792'.088042   84-26138
ISBN 0-87910-035-4

Book design by Dennis J. Grastorf, The Angelica Studio.

Printed and bound in the United States of America.

For the generations of women,
especially
my great-aunt Etta Wheeler;
grandmother Myrtle Liebschutz
and mother Doris Isgrig,
who both acted in the theatre;
and infant daughter, Carrie Sophia,
whose wisdom will exceed whatever we have learned.

Contents

Preface

I WANTED TO MAKE A VOLUME of theoretical writings by women who, no matter what their particular craft, had created or envisioned entire theatres which, for the most part, existed outside a commercial mainstream. I have been more interested in aspiration and persistence than in fame or profit. I wanted a volume that would speak to young women of a brave heritage, reminding each of us that the theatre must be created anew by each generation and that those to whom we owe our history are those who dared to dream the dream that had not happened yet.

The editor's limitations necessarily limited selections to women who wrote in English. I had hoped to include theoretical work by Maria Irene Fornes, and by Megan Terry and Jo Ann Schmidman of the Omaha Magic Theatre, which would have filled the gap existing in the book of American women playwrights and directors who emerged during the 1960s. In each case, however, heavy production schedules intervened, and the women felt themselves unable to supply the requested texts. I had also hoped to include writings on the feminist theatre from England and Canada, but, again, the requested material was not available.

Acknowledgments

Y FRIEND Erika Duncan, novelist and critic, read the introduction many times and with her good sense and fine imagination helped me to find its final form. My editors at DBP, Judith Rudnicki and Kristen McLaughlin, pushed and prodded, inspired and led me through the maze of my own thought to a clear and reasonable presentation. All my errors are my own. During work on this book I have been lucky to enjoy the friendship of women whose minds are excellent and whose hearts are warm. I want especially to thank Dorothy Dinnerstein, Mira Hamermesh, Jean Mundy, Gloria Feman Orenstein, and Sallie Finch Reynolds. Judith Malina's courage, devotion, and art always make me give thanks. She kindly allowed me to excerpt at will from her unpublished diaries. Among the theatre people I have been fortunate to work with over the years, I would especially like to thank the actors Michele Frankel, Elia Brača, Nina Pleasants, Tom Gustin, Kathleen Masterson, Tina Shepard, Lois Weaver, and Dolores Brandon, who also first introduced me to the work of Angna Enters; the composer Roberta Kosse; and designers Kathleen Smith and Sally J. Lesser. I have made this book for students, hoping it will help lead them deeper into areas of research I have just touched upon as well as deeper into their own creative selves. I would like to thank my students Linda Hammond, Daniele Notaro, Rose Marie Caruso, Kathleen McLane, Maxine Berman, and Alice Hamers for their inquiring minds.

Burl Hash's perseverance, humor, caring, talent, and his unfailing commitment to a theatre for the people that is nonsexist, nonracist, passionate, and poetic are a continuing inspiration. He is co-founder and resident director of New Cycle Theatre.

I want to thank Ned Ryerson for his constant support and for the writer's friendship we share. Julian Beck, Karl Bissinger, Finley Schaef, Robert Reiss, and Hanon Reznikov are gentle men and wise; I thank them for their pacifism and for their art. My publisher Ralph Pine persists as an independent in a field now dominated by conglomerates. He is willing to take risks and for that and for his belief in my work, I am grateful.

The publisher Colin Smythe directed me to an unpublished essay on playwriting by Lady Augusta Gregory. Robert Nemiroff provided several unpublished letters by Lorraine Hansberry. Shirley Rich Krohn kindly gave permission to print some of the letters of Hallie Flanagan which she has donated to the Library and Museum of the Performing Arts at Lincoln Center. Elizabeth Burdick, a librarian of distinction whose theatre collection at the International Theatre Institute/U.S. is invaluable, supplied me with many references during the early stages of research. Rosamond Gilder's enthusiasm for the idea of this book helped secure permission to reprint several entries. Helen Merrill, my agent, has been consistently helpful.

Finally, I owe the deepest debt of gratitude to all the women whose work is represented in this volume. I have come to love them very much. They are the sources of compassion and of hope upon which the future of the theatre does rest.

Women
In Theatre

Why not some system that includes the good? What a discovery that would be—a system that did not shut out.

Virginia Woolf, Writer's Diary

Those poor women in my plays have entered so totally into my heart and head, that while I am striving as best I can to make the audience understand them, I almost feel like comforting them . . . but it is they who, little by little, end up by comforting me!

I put myself with them, and I ransack their emotions not out of mania for suffering, but because the communal lamentation *among women is greater and more detailed, is sweeter and more complete, than that which is granted them by men.*

Eleonora Duse, Actors on Acting

Writing is like giving birth; we cannot help making the supreme effort. But we also act in like fashion. I need have no fear of not making the supreme effort—provided that I am honest with myself and that I pay attention.

Simone Weil, Gravity and Grace

The hero of a gynocentric culture will be a woman who, after meeting Death, will return alive, become pregnant and give birth to a baby, thus freeing humanity from the bondage of outraged spirits.

Mira Hamermesh, Women & War: The Amazon Scare *(Unpublished)*

Introduction

GERMANY, THE TENTH CENTURY. The Church has banned the theatre—it is fleshly, lustful, immoral. A nun, Hrotsvitha of Gandersheim, sits alone in her cold convent cell. She is writing a play. She would write six plays in her lifetime, leaving behind the only link between Roman comedy and the medieval mystery and morality plays that would emerge several hundred years after her death.

What called this nun in her convent to her work of writing plays? What voice did she hear? Where did she find the strength to write in what has always been the most "masculine" of literary forms?

I once told an interviewer I had "locked myself into a lower east side tenement apartment," in order to be able to write my first play. Later I blushed when I read the words. They were too melodramatic. I had still had friends, and a dog I walked three times a day. Yet in a very real sense I had withdrawn from the world as I had lived in it up until then, and had had to do so. I needed the solitude in which to hear long forgotten things. "How do I know the voice inside myself is really my voice?" I wrote in the notes for the women who would act the play.

I think of Eva Le Gallienne walking in the woods alone, or with her friend Marion Evensen, learning Hamlet's lines for a production of the play she would also stage; or of Augusta Gregory at the age of fifty, surrounded by famous literary men, taking up her pen in private to write the first of fifty plays; or of Lorraine Hansberry, young and black in the 1950s, envisioning characters who "simply refuse to give up" and so bear "that sweet essence which is human dignity" for us, on towards a new world.[1]

Where did the strength come from to do these things? What voices did these women hear? How did they know the voice they heard was really theirs?

"Instead of turning away from the theatre, I have to approach it in a different way, a way frowned on by most people in the theatre, but the only way I am able to take.

"I have forgotten that I am an artist. I have forgotten that I am a woman," Judith Malina writes at the age of twenty-four as she is about to found the Living Theatre.[2]

Once you remember that you are an artist and a woman, what does this

I

mean? Centuries of male doctrines say women are unfit for works of mind and imagination. Do you approach the theatre in a different way, one that is frowned upon, perhaps, by many of the people in the theatre (who are mainly men)? Are you set upon a different path because you hear a different voice, a voice grown soft amid the storms of centuries that nevertheless validates women as creators of this age-old ritual art?

This book is a journey through a contemporary past that, although close to us in time, has been almost forgotten because so many of the works included here are out-of-print or have never before been printed. And it is also a quest for the origins of female consciousness, to learn if something sacred, which was lost, still lives, and if the work of women in theatre has been impelled and shaped by remembrance of a time when women were sanctioned to create.

The Homeric Hymn tells how—because Hades, god of the underworld, has abducted her daughter, Persephone—the goddess Demeter wanders the earth in grief for nine days and nights, abstaining from food and drink, shunning the bath. Brought as a nursemaid to the house of King Celeus, Demeter sits, her face covered with a heavy veil, refusing comfort. The hymn relates: "Thus she remained until the scheming Iambe amused her with jokes and made the holy lady smile, then laugh, softening her heart—Iambe who in later times pleased her at her rites of Mystery."[3]

Yearly Demeter's worshipers gathered in the temple at Eleusis consecrated to her, as earlier they had gathered in a sacred grove. They had to be Greek-speaking and they must never have shed another's blood. Scholars say they drank a barley drink containing the fungus ergot, a hallucinogenic sometimes used in childbirth to stimulate contractions. We do not know exactly what happened at Demeter's Mysteries; the initiates were forbidden to write of the event. But we do know they felt the presence of the goddesses Demeter and Persephone there with them, and that they lost their fear of death and gained an understanding of immortality. To say this is one thing, to experience it quite another. And it is here, to bridge the gap between the statement and its understanding, that the drama enters. The experience comes from witnessing and so partaking of an action. We can guess that at least a segment of the action was not unlike that which Iambe is said to have performed.

We can imagine the mythic scene, as the initiates may have imagined it. Before the stricken goddess, Iambe stood. Her heart cried out, in sympathy, to the mother whose daughter was lost. There is no greater grief than this, the grief of a mother for her child. Iambe stood silent, awed. Then began a slow stirring in her heart. Iambe felt her own desire for this grief to end; she felt the life inside her claim her once again. As long as Demeter is by pain immobilized, as long as the mother sits impassively, staring at the barren ground, there can be no life, no hope; the daughter, Persephone, cannot return. Iambe is seized by a sudden flow of energy, up from her bowels, from her belly, up. She throws back her head and laughs; she lifts up her skirts and dances. "She does what she wants done. Her intense desire finds utterance in an act."[4] Demeter—goddess, earth mother, eternal bringer of life and of decay—rises from her chair. Perhaps she, too, throws back her head and laughs. Then she joins Iambe in her dance. The two dance round and round, shaking their breasts, their hips, howling their strength. Because Iambe has wanted it, willed it, and finally enacted it, the goddess, herself, awakes. The life force begins to flow again. The sacred energy revives. Out of grief comes this wild ecstasy. And from the ecstasy the two women share, from the ecstasy of their sharing, Demeter activates the power that will bring her daughter back.

Demeter is the goddess wielding power over life. Iambe is the mortal serving-woman who represents the power of human action. A power mortals have and may yet use to ensure the continued fruitfulness of earth. Iambe "does what she wants done. Her intense desire finds utterance in an act."

Demeter's grief at the loss of her daughter, her joy at her daughter's return are metaphors—devised (it may well be) by women—which express the only eternal order those who live on earth and die can know. Death, lamentation, birth, exaltation—this is the sacred cycle of the life experience; the changing seasons, the growth and withering of vegetation, the birthing-dying generations all proclaim it.

The goddess's quick change of mood upon being presented with the dance reminds us of how close together grief and joy reside within the human heart, and of how fast one can often follow upon the other. Our inner, psychic seasons also reflect the cycle of death and rebirth manifest throughout the natural world. We enter the griefs of the past, the deaths and sorrows in our lives, in order to confront our part in them, to truly feel the pain which may have numbed us once. As we reexperience these griefs, we emerge free of the psychic patterns that have bound us to them. Just as there can be no spring without winter, there can be no human growth without the courage to feel deeply. There is no joy without sorrow. No self-knowledge without the pain of self-recognition.

The Greek Demeter is one among a world-wide pantheon of goddesses upon whose powers the return of fertility once was thought to depend. Each primitive culture developed its own version of the seasonal rites of death and rebirth and wove its own myth of meaning around each communal celebration. From these rituals, in which the goddess "character" and women actors played a central role, the drama first arose. A life-spirit was vanquished, interred, and mourned to rise again upon the female celebrants' insistent cries. Aside from Persephone, the lost fertility spirits were mainly the male-child consorts of the goddesses: Dionysus, Attis, Adonis, Osiris, Tammuz. Still, it is the grief and rage of each mother goddess (and of her human invokers) and her remembrance of the joys of having birthed these children (and their remembrance of their children's births) that frees the life-spirit from the hold death has.

Though divine, the goddess draws her strength from humankind. Without the women and men who put into a dance the human desire for life, the goddess who gives life would die. She would succumb to grief and die of immobility because the ones who served her with their dances and their songs had turned their hearts away, had lost the will to pleasure her, had forgot the hope that she might bless them with the mighty flow of energy connecting living beings to the changing universe.

"It is perhaps worth pointing out that in [the seasonal] ceremonies of the type we have been discussing a *major role is in fact usually played by women*," [emphasis added] Theodore Gaster writes in *Thespis*, his study of the origins of drama in the Near East.

> The rites of the Greek seasonal festival at Thesmophoria as well as of several similar festivals, were confined exclusively to women, and at the Eleusinian Mysteries, the all-night vigil was kept by women only. In the Attis cult, both in its earlier Phrygian form and later, after it had been introduced into Greece, the official personnel consisted primarily of women; while the mock burial and subsequent disinterment of Adonis was performed, says Plutarch, by women; and in the fifteenth idyll of Theocritus, it is a woman who sings the dirge, and it is women that are said to rise at daybreak and commit the "corpse" of that god to the waters. Similarly, it was women who wept for Osiris at the annual ceremonies in Egypt; and it was likewise women that bewailed Ta'uz, i.e., Tammuz, in the medieval ceremonies at Harran.[5]

Critic Rosamond Gilder explains how the goddess myths and seasonal rites arose:

> Clothed in the symbols of desired increase, the head woman of the tribe took upon herself the attributes of godhead. By costume and mimicry she became the very power she invoked, forcing it to do her bidding by the magic of her gestures. Around her, her companions enacted the dance-drama of their needs...wherever she [the Earth Mother] appeared, she was the prototype of

that first actress-priest of the primitive grove, and her attributes remained the same—the symbols of fertility—the child who dies to be reborn and the band of attendant women dancing the drama of birth and death and resurrection.[6]

The seasonal rites and their attendant explanatory myths occurred worldwide. Everywhere, it seems, the rites and myths embodied women's wild cry that life begin again. Everywhere, the grief and rage and joy of women was alone deemed powerful enough to loose death's hold. And everywhere, the drama—both classical and folk—derived from this most human wish for life: life-returning, life-begetting-life, the sole life-eternal.

"What we have to seize and to insist upon is the overpowering hold which the sense of Life, the need for Life, the essential Life-giving faculty, exercised upon the primitive religions," Jessie L. Watson writes in *From Ritual to Romance*.[7]

Gilbert Murray concurs, in his introduction to Gaster's *Thespis*, "It is hardly an exaggeration to say that when we look back to the beginnings of European literature we find everywhere drama, and always drama derived from a religious ritual designed to ensure the rebirth of the dead world."[8]

In each and every one of these life-desiring, life-affirming rituals which are the origins of drama, *women played major roles as characters, performers, and creators, as the ones who imagined the content and who wrought the form.*

Women's disappearance from the creation and performance of such rituals marked an apocalyptic change in human consciousness. Now two separate forms, tragedy and comedy, were needed to deal with the full range of human feeling which once had been expressed by the life-cult's cyclic emotional continuum. In tragedy (called "most sublime") the focus shifted from the rebirth and resurrection of a life-spirit to the battle with fate and the subsequent fall of the specific heroic man. "Tragedy which took its plots, its content from the heroic saga, from the lives and struggles of individual heroes, ended in death, because in this world the human individual knows no resurrection. Comedy is nearer to the original folk-play and finds its consummation in a revel and a marriage."[9]

Although, in the literal sense, human beings know no resurrection in this world, transformation is given us to know if we can enter our past griefs deeply enough to be able to transcend them. When mournful tragedy was split from joyous comedy, the possibilities for social change and personal transformation were greatly lessened. Tragedy and comedy support fixed social orders (which are patriarchal) and, traditionally, the only hope of overturning them has been by violence.

The separation of tragedy from comedy (and of women from acting in the theatre) coincided with another separation: that of god from humankind. Originally, as Jane Ellen Harrison explains throughout *Themis*, what was worshiped was not differentiated from the worshipers. Slowly, the human will toward individuality created a separation between the act of worship and the feelings so expressed. Specific deities emerged at the same time as human beings began to have a sense of their own specificity. In Greece, the Olympian deities were endowed with human personalities and human histories in celebration, it now seems, of the dawn of human understanding of these things. But at that moment, too, the gods and goddesses human beings had created began to live apart from human beings.[10] They dwelled on lofty Mount Olympus—like us, but untouched by us—immortal, as we are not; jealous and demanding, often. It was they who now controlled our fate. And so it was that the human race left infancy and arrived at adolescence, achieving the sense of self by first elevating and then warring with parental figures.

Over many hundreds of years, as men, who reach peak sexual potency (if not the gentleness that might please women best) in adolescence, expressed and solidified their power on earth, religious longing would consolidate into the fear/love worship of a single, masculine father-creator. "For God has now revealed Himself differently. He wills not that his faithful be one with Him, but that *they, abiding in the fear of God, retain their individuality.*"[11] (Emphasis added.)

The monotheistic God exacts obedience, judges, and punishes. Through the presence of His son, He also suffers for men and redeems them. His son, like many of the pagan life-spirits before him, was born of one immortal and one mortal parent. But unlike them, and unlike us, God's son was born of a woman who was and remained so virginal her hymen was not ruptured by the birth. The spirit entered her body and conceived a child who left as gently as his seed had come. There was no pain, no crying-out, no blood, no energy, no effort, no orgasmic ecstasy involved in giving birth to God the son. The woman who did so—gentle, good, and loving as she was—remained a vessel only. A vehicle for male will. Her own sense of power denied to her through denial of the great effort of her flesh.

The monotheistic idea, elevating one male God above all the natural world, required the separation of spirit from flesh. This most brutal separation is, perhaps, the root cause of tragedy, and no one has suffered from it more drastically than women. As King Lear says to Cordelia, his once favorite daughter:

> Better thou
> Hadst not been born than not to have pleas'd
> Me better.

Later he states the reason why women's lives depend upon complete obedience to men:

> Down from the waist they are Centaurs,
> Though women all above:
> But to the girdle do the gods inherit,
> Beneath is all the fiends':

Man's fall from grace was brought about by a woman, Eve, who tempted him with the "evil" knowledge of birth and death which the pagan goddesses had once freely imparted to their worshipers. The Virgin Mary redeems us slightly as a sex, but only insofar as we forget our sensuality, and the miraculous power inherent in it. The spirit/body split claimed by monotheistic religion has been, quite simply, ecologically and morally disastrous. Pillage of the natural world, despisal of women, and self-hatred on the part of men who "fell" from grace have been its results. Tragedy has been its most exalted dramatic form.

To alter the ethical and emotional basis of patriarchy we have to replace the idea of the fall of man with a new dramatic action, one that revives the ancient sense of each person's intimate relatedness to each other natural form at the same time as it heightens consciousness of each person's individual becoming in the world.

When women danced at the seasonal rituals, the first dramas that we know, they gave forth mighty cries. They cried in grief at the death of the life-spirit, cried in joy at its rebirth. Listen to them as they cry in mourning for the loss of their child/lover, Life. Listen to them as they cry in joy at the new birth of the consort/child. Their cries are animal, human, and divine. They utter from the bowels, belly, and the heart. Crying out like this, the grieving, or the birthing, or the celebrating woman knows she is not separate from the basest animal that lives, nor from the most exalted natural force beyond control. She is one with the slimy maggot burrowing through the decomposing corpse; one with the moon that pulls majestic waves upon the rocky shore; one with her creative self as she gives voice to songs of praise. She knows what modern man and the woman made in his image— who are forever fearing or denying God—have long forgot: flesh, spirit, nature, feeling, thought, birth, death, and decay all are one, and each one holy. All are joined in that great round which is the miracle of life's return.

Does the woman alone at her writing desk making a play, or the woman conceiving a theatre against all odds, or the woman in rehearsal, giving her ideas shape, remember that drama first arose from this great birthing, mourning, celebratory cry? Does she dream the theatre might someday become that sacred life-affirming act again? And according to her temperament and talents, does she then craft an aesthetic which pursues this dream?

The evidence, if viewed with a sympathetic eye, reveals that, yes, she does. Each woman represented in this volume, while creating within, but also on a level unacceptable to, darker and more mysterious than, the prevailing patriarchal forms, has touched the ancient life-affirming origins of theatre and has made her art from this deeply felt imperative.

Perhaps the dancers whose art was most completely censored because of the spirit/body split articulated the ancient ties most closely. Isadora Duncan wrote of the ideal woman dancer: "She will realize the mission of woman's body and the holiness of all its parts. She will dance the changing life of nature, showing how each part is transformed into the other . . . She will dance the body emerging again from centuries of civilized forgetfulness, emerging not in the nudity of primitive man, but in new nakedness, no longer at war with spirituality and intelligence, but joining them in a glorious harmony."[12]

Martha Graham knows the ancient stories and their meanings and goes to them again and again as if to the source. In her notes to *Voyage* she writes: "Night is the Time of the Goddess . . . is the Time one enters the regions of Demeter, Persephone, Isis, Mary the Mother of God, Hecate—the prostitute—Death, change—Renewal."[13]

Katherine Dunham sought the African dances of possession as if to unlock the key to her own creativity and found a dance of eros (the kind of dance Iambe danced): "They were face to face, bodies touching, both of them squatting now with arms pressed close to their sides . . . there was no sound except heavy breathing, but the chant continued and the drum, and it seemed that the air was heavy with some other heat and sound."[14]

The ancient knowledge is there, too, in the plays and in the theories of the playwrights. The tenth-century nun, Hrotsvitha of Gandersheim, explains in the preface to her collected plays: "I have been compelled through the nature of this work to apply my mind and my pen to depicting *the dreadful frenzy of those possessed* by unlawful love, and *the insidious sweetness of passion*—things which should not even be named among us."[15] (Emphasis added.) Nun that she was, she turned her fascination with earthly passion toward heavenly ends: "For the more seductive the blandishments of lovers the more wonderful the divine succour and the greater the merit of those who resist, especially when it is fragile woman who is victorious and strong man who is routed with confusion."[16]

Within the confines of the Catholic Church—which, after all, allowed her the freedom to pursue her work as no house and children would have—Hrotsvitha managed a daring feat. She reinvented drama, losing nothing of its old attachment to erotic passion, and maintaining woman as the central character. Though she separated flesh from spirit, she understood that women had to be more than men's chattel, and she saw that freedom from sexual relations with men was not too high a price to pay for freedom from the restrictions imposed upon her sex. She was even able to enlist the help of God to defy the deep misogyny of the Middle Ages. "He has given me the ability—I am a teachable creature," she insists. "He has given me a perspicacious mind, but one that lies fallow and idle when it is not cultivated."[17] So she wrote her plays and poems with His sanction (and the sanction of the same Church which had banned the theatre), while through her work she undertook to show how "fragile" woman might be victorious over "strong" man.

Nothing much had changed for women in the nine centuries which intervened before Augusta Gregory wrote in her notes to *Grania*: "I think I turned to Grania because so many have written about sad, lovely Deirdre, who when overtaken by sorrow made no good battle at the last. Grania had more power of will, and for good or evil twice took the shaping of her life into her own hands."[18] Women playwrights still faced the problem of how to show women's strength within the confines of patriarchal rule.

Augusta Gregory made her plays from the Celtic myths, legends, and stories told her by the Irish folk. True to her source, she wished to touch that region of the heart and mind where seen and unseen worlds meet. The tie to the ancient life-affirming cry is loud in all her plays. The turn from grief to joy happens in an instant, accomplished by the extreme emotion of her language. She felt the life of the people, and she knew that the popular emotions are the extreme ones, that life, when lived communally, is lived 'twixt grief and joy.

Producers and directors like Hallie Flanagan, Judith Malina, and Barbara Ann Teer have understood theatre as a socially transforming art. They have made theatre companies and evolved aesthetics around people's needs to alleviate the pains of poverty and racism.

Flanagan's Federal Theatre took shape from the needs and desires of those on relief during the Depression. "In Los Angeles," she writes, "I listened to a rehearsal of one of our orchestras in an original score being composed on the project for Shaw's *Caesar and Cleopatra*. 'I'm interested in the flute motif,' I said to the conductor. 'It's so fleeting one always wants more.' The conductor-composer smiled. 'My flutist has a tremor of the lips and can only sustain for a bar at a time. I had to compose with that in mind.' It was the job of those of us directing the project so to compose our plans and our plays that they would make assets and not liabilities out of the tremors developed through years of unemployment and despair."[19] Hallie Flanagan fashioned theatres across the land that spoke to us of what we might become.

Judith Malina's Living Theatre is centered around what she and her collaborator, Julian Beck, have named the Taxco Oath. In 1949, in Mexico, she was approached by a small beggar boy, and recorded the incident in her journal:

> I want to give him, not a few centavos, but all my care, all my devotion, to cure his eyes—to stay in Mexico and cure them all—the entire plan of my life lies open in his sore eyes.
> I screamed because I was leaving him, and I had already promised myself to him, and to do the work that I had to do for him, because in that pain and blindness he made it clear.[20]

Years later Judith Malina would perform in a bare mud patch in one of Brazil's worst slums and write:

> One year ago tonight
> We played in the Sportpalast
>   in Berlin
> For seven thousand people
> And tonight we lie in the mud
> Of an obscure favela
> Outside the airport of Sao Paulo.[21]

The large productions in the great theatres of Europe that have won her so much acclaim are but an aspect of an aesthetic whose real brilliance lies in its keen identification with the victims of oppression and its drive to make survivors of those who suffer.

Barbara Ann Teer gave up a career in the commercial theatre to found the National Black Theatre in Harlem where "revivalist rituals" are performed to free the life-force inside actors and audience. "My ancestors say there is something within—it banishes all pain." Teer explains. "That energy—that life-force—that's inside us is there. It's given, and it's in everybody. Everybody wants to experience themselves as able to generate their power and to experience the validation of that power."[22]

The critic Rosamond Gilder defined her work as a combination of "imagination and sympathy." Libertarian theorist Emma Goldman was drawn to the plays of Ibsen, Shaw, Tolstoy, Hauptmann, and even Strindberg because they inspired humankind "in its eternal seeking for things higher and better." Neither Gilder nor Goldman could be satisfied with apprehending only the evident, most likely patriarchal, values in the works they wrote about; to do so would have disgraced their own intelligence and strength. They wanted the drama to show a path toward human dignity that would include women, too. So they approached each text with the need to know its highest aspiration. Their writing becomes a model for a kind of criticism that is neither narrowly judgmental nor coldly analytical. Their work illuminates, reveals, and encourages the aesthetic and human values the critics themselves hold dear.

Throughout theatre history there have been actresses who have known it is not what female characters do, since their actions have been limited by men, so much as the inner quality of their resistance to this situation which evidences their true humanity. As actresses they could have a full sense of their own dignity only if they empathized deeply with each character they played. In a real sense, each actress staked her life upon the ability she had to bring to light in every woman that she played qualities of heart, mind, and imagination denied woman under patriarchal law. This is why Eleonora Duse could say, "those poor women in my plays . . . little by little end up by comforting me."[23]

Ellen Terry calls Desdemona "a saint," a woman who is completely uncomprehending of the deceitful ways of the world. Desdemona's unconventionality makes it as impossible for her to stop pleading for Cassio, whom she feels has been wronged, as it does for her to guess her husband's jealousy, when she knows she has been true. "A great tragic actress, with a strong personality and a strong method, is far better suited to [the part] for Desdemona is strong, not weak,"[24] Terry writes.

The "character" in history as we know it is a tragic and, finally, an isolated being, no matter how aware he or she is of social conditions, no matter how bravely or existentially social conditions are opposed. Women actors who played in plays of male history, in which women's actions in the world are truncated or subordinated to meet man's needs, had to find within themselves the means for personal/individual transcendence of their "characters'" abortive fates. The women actors freed themselves from that history through the exercise of compassion—the gift of being able to give the character's spirit those elements of strength and grace that could not yet materialize as actions in the social world. These actresses have known what it would serve us all to learn. People are potentially far nobler than any of us have yet become. By cleaving to the inner essence, the unrealized aspiration, the strength might at last be found to live that high desire out.

The theatre under patriarchy has been defined as violent conflict, the *agon*; the constant battle between the stronger and the weak; the *angst* of separation from what is meaningful in daily life. Having created the father-god, the sons soon began to rail against his harsh judgmentalness, his unavailability, his lack of compassion. The battle segments of the old seasonal rites came to be the center of this drama. There was mortal conflict between the old authority figure and the young man lusting after freedom and power. (The entire patriarchal political spectrum, from socialist revolution to monarchy to fascist dictatorship, works according to this schema—the overthrow of the old man by the young, and the mutual fear of this inevitable occurrence.)

The women represented in this book retain knowledge of another way, one that has never excluded men but which invites men to join as equals in a quest. Quite a few of them were the daughters of strong-minded artistic mothers who sanctioned and actively supported the careers of their girl-children. Fanny Kemble, Eva Le Gallienne, Isadora Duncan, Rosamond Gilder, and Barbara Ann Teer, for example, frequently acknowledge their mothers' roles in their own artistic growth. Daughters first, many of these women became the mothers of daughters and sons, the nurturers of the very life they knew must live beyond them. As mothers and/or as daughters did they remember what the goddesses and their life-spirit children taught? Battle is not the essential life-experience; birth, death, rebirth, and nurture are. The mother is biologically tied to the child; she wakes as the child wakes; her breasts ache if she refuses to give food. She has no choice but respond to the demands of another life with physical caring and, if she dare give herself over to the feeling, with a nongenital yet deeply erotic love. The rest of us have the choice to turn away, to block out the demanding cry. And we also have the choice to act in the world as if all of life has a biological claim on us which we must either heed or suffer from if we turn away.

The life-spirits were the child/consorts of the mother goddess. Her initial task was to birth them, but her primary responsibility was to give herself over to her love for them. Such vulnerability on the part of the mother goddess is worth our emulation. All of us have the choice to invoke the memories of mothering and the longing for it—which lives in us as the children we all are—and to use them in an adult way. If we become brave enough as a race to finally abandon our "needs" for punishment by, control of, and rebellion against the life-force we will be able to share the mother goddess's rage at the events which ripped her child from her, her grief at separation and death, and her joy at the reemergence of the child/lover, Life. We will join Iambe's dance.

The theatre arising from the necessity to care for life has a new quality and tone. The type of dramatic tension created by divisive conflict is replaced by a new, almost unexplored tension of sensual, erotic, and intellectual affinity between characters. The pull together, towards intimacy, is as complex, and as fraught with terror and impossibility, as is the drive toward dominance. The theatre loses nothing essential to it from this change; it gains an understanding of human nature which includes the possibility of real communication, of healing, and of hope.

This change in artistic impulse—from a will toward dominance and the alienation implicit in it, toward caring and true intimacy—is both an advance in the human race's struggle for self-realization and a return to the origins of drama and worship when, as we have seen, women led the dancing and the songs, the lamentations and rejoicing that yearly called new life into being.

Today we are threatened by a man-made nuclear power far in excess of any destructive force nature ever wrought. All glorifications of destruction have special danger now, since they lead us closer to acceptance of our own nuclear doom. If art has purpose in these days of woe, it has a hallowed purpose, unattained by any other human undertaking except the act of love. Theatre has a mandate now to overwhelm our own destructive force with our own insistent wish to live, to love. Iambe's dance must be revived in all our written, spoken, and acted works. We need to dance the dance of life until we each are grown brave enough in its exultant beat to look into each other's eyes and chant our happiness, our joy, our courage in the face of death, our wish to live. Up from the bowels, from the belly, up, Iambe's roar is heard. Only then does Demeter raise her head and smile. Only when the sharing is complete and one has seen the other's grief and given her new strength does the sacred energy revive and issue joy.

This anthology is offered as a single addition to this imperative communal quest. It is offered to those who care about the theatre and seek their own place in it with the hope that the theatre will resume its ancient function and with new actions, myths, and ritual moments bring new life into being.

KAREN MALPEDE
Brooklyn, N.Y.

Acting:
The Female Character

Fanny Kemble

Ellen Terry

Eva Le Gallienne

Angna Enters

Fanny Kemble

[1809–1893]

AN INTRODUCTION

FANNY KEMBLE WROTE a great deal about her stage life and about the nature of acting itself. In so doing, she made a significant contribution to the body of acting theory written by women which, as I become more and more acquainted with it, seems more and more to suggest an approach to acting that has been uniquely shaped by female sensibilities. The fact that much of this theory appears in the midst of autobiographies or journal entries (as well as in essays) in no way compromises its importance as original work of the mind. These writings by women are not "acting methods" thought up, as has been the fashion of late, by a single director and then transmitted to, or imposed upon, disciples, students, company members. Rather, this theory is the result of years of practical experience creating character and is most useful to other working actors and to those who would understand their art. Since it comes so directly out of personal experience, the theory is direct, precise, and full of feeling for the mysteries of theatre and life. No one but the actor devotes herself so thoroughly to the study of what it means to be an individual. No other artist expresses quite the concentration of courage which allows so total an opening-up and giving-over to another being.

The acting theories of the women represented in this book are concerned with the essential, elusive questions. How to make the material one's own. How to know another as oneself. How to *be* the person words at best can just describe. How to understand another life and then give one's own form over to that understanding.

Perhaps no great actor has agonized over the impossible demands of acting quite so much as Fanny Kemble, who called it her "impotent and unpoetical craft," a "mass of wretched mumming mimicry." She was by nature a romantic; the truth of human feelings was the deepest truth she knew. And the actor's craft, which at once relies upon that truth that mocks it, alternately dismayed, disgusted, and intrigued her.

She was born Frances Anne Kemble, third child of the noted Shakespear-

17

ean actor Charles Kemble and Marie Thérèse de Camp. Her aunt was Sarah
Siddons, whose incomparable acting Fanny Kemble describes in the selection to follow called "On the Stage." Twenty-eight members of the Kemble
family, for three generations, had earned their livings in the theatre and
though Fanny spent her childhood free of its demands, at the age of sixteen
her parents determined she should enter the profession as Juliet. They
hoped that the failing box-office receipts of the Covent Garden Theatre,
which Charles Kemble managed, might be redeemed by the introduction of
a new Kemble as a star. She was an immediate success and acting remained
her somewhat reluctant vocation for the rest of her life, interrupted only by
the years of her tortured marriage to Southern slave owner Pierce Butler.

She acted from necessity, to make money and to win for herself some
measure of independence uncommon to women of her time, but she wrote
for her own pleasure. Her passionate, sensitive nature coupled with an
analytical mind set her to writing poetry, verse plays (several of which were
produced at Covent Garden), criticism, and theory, and to keeping vo-
luminous journals.

In 1832, after Covent Garden had been given up by her father, Charles
and Fanny Kemble came to America on tour. As always, Fanny kept an extensive journal, published in 1835, from which the first two selections in
this section are taken. In America she met and married Pierce Butler, a marriage which produced the book, *Journal of a Residence on a Georgian Plantation*. Written in 1838-39, while she was mistress of Butler's rice and cotton
plantations on the Georgian sea islands, it is a vivid exposure of the ways
bondage warps both master and slave, and a clear analysis of the particularly
tragic plight of the slave woman and of her powerless and dominated white
mistress. Fanny Kemble's hatred of the miseries of slavery caused the wreck-
age of her marriage. After she wrote *Journal of a Residence* she fled her husband, though it meant leaving her two daughters in his custody until they
were old enough to join her of their own free will. Marriage behind her, she
returned to the stage to earn her living.

Kemble's persistent inquiry into the nature of a craft, the pretense of
which both infuriated and intrigued her, created the essay "On the Stage,"
which is her most concise theoretical statement. But perhaps the clearest insight into what her own acting might have been like comes from the "Notes
on Romeo and Juliet" she prepared for the benefit of an actor playing opposite her. Moment by moment she proceeds through the play, raising the
verbs of being up from the unconscious, juxtaposing feeling with feeling
until each sudden shift of meaning and intensity brings alive the full range
of emotional truth it was her greatest gift to love and strive to understand.

—K.M.

Fanny Kemble

[1809–1893]

SELECTIONS

From *The Journal of Frances Anne Butler*

The two volumes of Fanny Kemble's American *Journal* were first published in 1835. They were written between 1832 and 1834, as she toured eastern American cities with her father. None of the individual entries are dated by year. Also, most proper names were left out, for the sake, I would guess, of propriety.—K.M.

Tuesday, 6th [New York]

After dinner, Colonel_____ called, and very nearly caused a blow up between me and my father: he came preaching to me the necessity of restoring those lines of Bianca's, in the judgment scene, which were originally omitted, afterwards restored by me at Milman's request, and again cut out, on finding that they only lengthened the scene, without producing the slightest effect. My father appeared perfectly to agree with me, but added, that I might as well oblige the people. I straightforth said I would do no such thing. People sitting before the curtain must not come and tell me what I am to do behind it. Not one out of a hundred, in the first place, understand what they are talking about; and why, therefore, am I to alter my work at their suggestion, when each particular scene has cost me more consideration than they ever bestowed upon any whole play in all their lives. Besides, it would be with me and my parts, as with the old man, his son and his ass, in the fable of old; I should never have done ltering, and yet never satisfy any body, for the most universal talent I know of is that of finding fault. So, all things well considered, the New Yorkians must e'en be contented with the judgment of Miss O'Neill, my father, and their obedient, humble servant. Worked till tea-time; after tea, wrote letters till now, bedtime.

From *The Journal of Frances Anne Butler*, originally published in 1835, reissued in a facsimile one-volume edition (New York: Benjamin Blom, 1970).

Friday, 11th

Mr. ＿＿ and ＿＿ came in after the play. We had a discussion as to how far real feeling enters into our scenic performances. 'Tis hard to say: the general question it would be impossible to answer, for acting is altogether a monstrous anomaly. John Kemble and Mrs. Siddons were always in earnest in what they were about; Miss O'Neill used to cry bitterly in all her tragedy parts; whilst Garrick could be making faces and playing tricks in the middle of his finest points, and Kean would talk gibberish while the people were in an uproar of applause at his. In my own individual instance, I know that sometimes I could turn every word I am saying into burlesque (*never* Shakespeare, by the by,) and at others my heart aches and I cry real, bitter, warm tears, as earnestly as if I was in earnest.

Wednesday, 5th

At half-past five, went to the theatre. The play was *Romeo and Juliet*; the house not good. Mr. ＿＿ played Romeo. I acted like a wretch, of course; how could I do otherwise? Oh, Juliet! vision of the south! rose of the garden of the earth! was this the glorious hymn that Shakespeare hallowed to your praise? was this the mingled strain of Love's sweet going forth, and Death's dark victory, over which my heart and soul have been poured out in wonder and ecstasy?—How I do loathe the stage! these wretched, tawdry, glittering rags, flung over the breathing forms of ideal loveliness; these miserable, poor, and pitiful substitutes for the glories with which poetry has invested her magnificent and fair creations—the glories with which our imagination reflects them back again. What a mass of wretched mumming mimicry acting is! Pasteboard and paint, for the thick breathing orange groves of the south; green silk and oiled parchments, for the solemn splendour of her noon of night; wooden platforms and canvass curtains, for the solid marble balconies, and rich dark draperies of Juliet's sleeping chamber, that shrine of love and beauty; rouge, for the startled life-blood in the cheek of that young passionate woman; an actress, a mimicker, a sham creature, me, in fact, or any other one, for that loveliest and most wonderful conception, in which all that is true in nature, and all that is exquisite in fancy, are moulded into a living form. To *act* this! to *act* Romeo and Juliet! horror! horror! how I do loathe my most impotent and unpoetical craft! . . .

In the last scene of the play, I was so mad with the mode in which all the preceding ones had been perpetrated, that, lying over Mr.＿＿'s corpse, and fumbling for his dagger, which I could not find, I, Juliet, thus apostrophised him,—Romeo being dead—"Why, where *the* devil *is* your dagger, Mr. ＿＿?" What a disgusting travesty. On my return home, I expressed my entire determination to my father to perform the farce of Romeo and Juliet no more. Why, it's an absolute *shame* that one of Shakespeare's plays should be thus turned into a mockery.

From *Notes Upon Some of Shakespeare's Plays*

On the Stage

Things dramatic and things theatrical are often confounded together in the minds of English people, who, being for the most part neither the one nor the other, speak and write of them as if they were identical, instead of, as they are, so dissimilar that they are nearly opposite.

That which is dramatic in human nature is the passionate, emotional, humorous element, the simplest portion of our composition, after our mere instincts, to which it is closely allied, and this has no relation whatever, beyond its momentary excitement and gratification, to that which imitates it, and is its theatrical reproduction; the dramatic is the *real*, of which the theatrical is the *false*.

Both nations and individuals in whom the dramatic temperament strongly preponderates are rather remarkable for a certain vivid simplicity of nature, which produces sincerity and vehemence of emotion and expression, but is entirely without the *consciousness* which is never absent from the theatrical element. . . .

The combination of the power of representing passion and emotion with that of imagining or conceiving it—that is, of the theatrical talent with the dramatic temperament—is essential to make a good actor; their combination in the highest possible degree alone makes a great one.

There is a specific comprehension of effect and the means of producing it, which, in some persons, is a distinct capacity, and this forms what actors call the study of their profession; and in this, which is the alloy necessary to make theatrical that which is only dramatic, lies the heart of their mystery and the snare of their craft in more ways than one: and this, the actor's *business*, goes sometimes absolutely against the dramatic temperament, which is nevertheless essential to it. . . .

When Mrs. Siddons, in her spectacles and mob-cap, read *Macbeth* or *King John*, it was one of the grandest dramatic achievements that could be imagined, with the least possible admixture of the theatrical element; the representation of the *Duke's Motto*, with all its resources of scenic effect, is a striking and interesting theatrical entertainment, with hardly an admixture of that which is truly dramatic.

Garrick was, I suppose, the most perfect actor that our stage has ever produced, equalling in tragedy and comedy the greatest performers of both;

From *Notes Upon Some of Shakespeare's Plays* by Fanny Kemble (New York: AMS Press, 1972).

but while his dramatic organisation enabled him to represent with exquisite power and pathos the principal characters of Shakespeare's noblest plays, his theatrical taste induced him to garble, desecrate, and disfigure the masterpieces of which he was so fine an interpreter, in order to produce or enhance those peculiar effects which constitute the chief merit and principal attraction of all theatrical exhibitions.

Mrs. Siddons could lay no claim to versatility—it was not in her nature; she was without mobility of mind, countenance, or manner; and her dramatic organisation was in that respect inferior to Garrick's; but out of a family of twenty-eight persons, all of whom made the stage their vocation, she alone preeminently combined the qualities requisite to make a great theatrical performer in the highest degree.

Another member of that framily—a foreigner by birth, and endowed with the most powerful and vivid dramatic organisation—possessed in so small a degree the faculty of the stage, that the parts which she represented successfully were few in number, and though among them there were some dramatic *creations* of extraordinary originality and beauty, she never rose to the highest rank in her profession, nor could claim in any sense the title of a great theatrical artist.—This was my mother. And I suppose no member of that large histrionic family was endowed to the same degree with the natural dramatic temperament. The truth of her intonation, accent, and emphasis, made her common speech as good as a play to hear, (oh, how much better than some we *do* hear!) and whereas I have seen the Shakespeare of my father, and the Shakespeare and Milton of Mrs. Siddons, with every emphatic word underlined and accentuated, lest they should omit the right inflection in delivering the lines, my mother could no more have needed such notes whereby to speak *true* than she would a candle to have walked by at noonday. She was an incomparable critic; and though the intrepid sincerity of her nature made her strictures sometimes more accurate than acceptable, they were inestimable for the fine tact for truth, which made her instinctively reject in nature and art whatever sinned against it.

I do not know whether I shall be considered competent to pass a judgment on myself in this matter, but I think I am. Inheriting from my father a theatrical descent of two generations and my mother's vivid and versatile organisation, the stage itself, though it became from the force of circumstances my career, was, partly from my nature, and partly from my education, so repugnant to me, that I failed to accomplish any result at all, worthy of my many advantages. I imagine I disappointed alike those who did and those who did not think me endowed with the talent of my family, and incurred, towards the very close of my theatrical career, the severe ver-

dict from one of the masters of the stage of the present day, that I was "ignorant of the first rudiments of my profession." . . .

The dramatic faculty . . . lies in a power of apprehension quicker than the
disintegrating process of critical analysis, and when it is powerful, and the
organisation fine, as with Mrs. Siddons, perception rather than reflection
reaches the aim proposed; and the persons endowed with this specific gift
will hardly unite with it the mental qualifications of philosophers and
metaphysicians: no better proof of which can be adduced than Mrs. Siddons
herself, whose performances were, in the strict sense of the word, excellent,
while the two treatises she has left upon the character of Queen Constance
and Lady Macbeth—two of her finest parts—are feeble and superficial.
Kean, who possessed, beyond all actors whom I have seen, tragic inspiration, could very hardly, I should think, have given a satisfactory reason for
any one of the great effects which he produced. Of Mdlle. Rachel, whose
impersonations fulfilled to me the idea of perfect works of art of their kind, I
have heard, from one who knew her well, that her intellectual processes
were limited to the consideration of the most purely mechanical part of her
vocation; and Pasta, the great lyric tragedian, who, Mrs. Siddons said, was
capable of giving her lessons, replied to the observation, "*Vous avez dû
beaucoup étudier l'antique,*" "*Je l'ai beaucoup senti.*" The reflective and analytical quality has little to do with the complex process of acting, and is alike remote from what is dramatic and what is theatrical.

There is something anomalous in that which we call the dramatic art that
has often arrested my attention and exercised my thoughts; the special gift
and sole industry of so many of my kindred, and the only labour of my own
life, it has been a subject of constant and curious speculation with me, com-
bining as it does elements at once so congenial and so antagonistic to my nature.

Its most original process, that is, the conception of the character to be
represented, is a mere reception of the creation of another mind; and its
mechanical part, that is, the representation of the character thus ap-
prehended, has no reference to the intrinsic, poetical, or dramatic merit of
the original creation, but merely to the accuarcy and power of the actor's
perception of it; thus the character of Lady Macbeth is as majestic, awful,
and poetical, whether it be worthily filled by its pre-eminent representative, Mrs. Siddons, or unworthily by the most incompetent of ignorant provincial tragedy queens.

This same dramatic art has neither fixed rules, specific principles, indispensable rudiments, nor fundamental laws; it has no basis in positive science, as music, painting, sculpture, and architecture have; and differs from

them all, in that the mere appearance of spontaneity, which is an acknowledged assumption, is its chief merit. And yet—

> *This younger of the sister arts,*
> *Where all their charms combine—*

requires in its professors the imagination of the poet, the ear of the musician, the eye of the painter and sculptor, and over and above these, a faculty
peculiar to itself, inasmuch as the actor personally fulfills and embodies his
conception; his own voice is his cunningly modulated instrument; his own
face the canvas wheron he portrays the various expressions of his passion; his
own frame the mould in which he casts the images of beauty and majesty
that fill his brain; and whereas the painter and sculptor may select, of all
possible attitudes, occupations, and expressions, the most favourable to the
beautiful effect they desire to produce and fix, and bid it so remain fixed for
ever, the actor must live and move through a temporary existence of poetry
and passion, and preserve throughout its duration that ideal grace and dignity, of which the canvas and the marble give but a silent and motionless
image. And yet it is an art that requires no study worthy of the name: it
creates nothing—it perpetuates nothing; to its professors, whose personal
qualifications form half their merit, is justly given the meed of personal admiration, and the reward of contemporaneous popularity is well bestowed
on those whose labour consists in exciting momentary emotion. Their most
persevering and successful efforts can only benefit, by a passionate pleasure
of at most a few years' duration, the play-going public of their own immediate day, and they are fitly recompensed with money and applause, to
whom may not justly belong the rapture of creation, the glory of patient and
protracted toil, and the love and honour of grateful posterity.

Notes on *Romeo and Juliet*

[These few notes were addressed as mere suggestions to a gentleman studying the
part of Romeo, who did me the honour to consult me upon his rendering of the
part. They are neither an analysis of the play nor of the character, but mere *hints for
acting.*—F. A. K.]

ROMEO represents the *sentiment*, and Juliet the *passion* of love.

The *pathos* is his, the *power* is hers.

His first scene is mere rose-light before sunrising; the key-note to the
after *real* love and life is given in the lines,—

> *"I fear too early,"* etc.

The spirit of the balcony scene is that of joyful tenderness, and something of a sort of sweet surprise at the fervid girl-passion which suddenly wraps him round, and carries him as with wings of fire towards the level of its own intensity.

All the succeeding scenes are pervaded by the elastic spirit of joy and triumph of his secret happiness. Mercutio's death is the sudden heavy thunder-cloud in the bright sky; his own duel with Tybalt—the breaking of the lightning storm, and the falling of the bolt that strikes and shatters his green tree of life. His furious burst of uncontrolled rage and hatred is followed by the utter collapse of all passion, leaving only *consciousness*, but no *discrimination* of infinite trouble—a nightmare of indefinite abysmal misery.

The scene in the friar's cell is the sheer expression of the *violence of weakness*—haggard bewilderment. Hunted for his life by the Capulets, hidden from the pursuit of justice, *palpitating with nervous anguish,* apprehensive of instantaneous revengeful murder, expectant of inevitable sentence of death, overwhelmed with horror of his own sanguinary deed, because his victim is kinsman to his wife, filled with passionate longing and desire for the possession of that wife, for which all preparation had been made, even for that night, the spirit of the whole scene, from its beginning to its end, is summed up in the speech, beginning

"Thou canst not speak of what thou dost not feel."

Gradually, as the friar utters his concluding admonition, the vital invincible hope of youth, and the anticipation of the "joy past joy," which beckon him, rise triumphant above all the misery and culminate in the farewell.

In the parting scene in Juliet's room, she languid with passion, wan with woe, beneath his reiterated tender offering of his life to her, the throbbing of the natural desire to live,—here again his self-sacrifice is the sentiment, her selfishness the passion of love.

The opening of the fifth act is a gentle, tender, melancholy ecstasy, a blending of exquisite memories and hopes in a pervading atmosphere of sadness.

After the news of Juliet's death, one *blasphemous* outburst of mad agony follows, and then the iron gloom of utter despair, the blackness of darkness, the absolute *possession* by misery of his whole being, *through which* his dwelling on the details of the apothecary's existence, his one or two sobs of tenderness:—

> *"Hast thou no letters to me from the friar?*
> *Well, Juliet, I will lie with thee to-night."*

his farewell to Balthasar, his warning to Paris, his recognition of him after killing him,—all are lingering and broken touches of the sweet, tender, pathetic nature, choked with the bitterness of his fate, and breaking through the settled, sullen, savage hardness of his despair.

I am not careless, as I may have appeared to you, of the value of the text of Shakespeare; but, poet, philosopher, and playwright as he was, your dealings with him are in the latter capacity only. You need not be afraid of eliminating the two nobler elements of his works; omit what you will, that is *impossible*.

Remember too, that his *inspiration*—and I use the word advisedly—did not protect him from the errors of his time and place. As for occasional breaking of his lines, my excitement the other evening made them more frequent than they really were; and a good musician should know how to redeem a faulty line, in some measure, by his utterance.

Ellen Terry

[1847–1928]

AN INTRODUCTION

LIKE FANNY KEMBLE, Ellen Terry was born into a theatrical family; and, like her, she was an inveterate writer of prose (though not of fiction). A book of memoirs, a series of lectures on Shakespeare, and a now famous correspondence with George Bernard Shaw all attest to the fine quality of her mind and to her grace of spirit.

Her parents, Benjamin and Sarah Ballard Terry, were actors who toured Britain, bringing their small children with them. Three sisters, Marion, Kate, and Florence, also made acting their profession. Ellen Terry's first acting job came at the age of eight when actress Nelly Kean, wife and collaborator of Charles Kean, chose her to act the part of Mamillius in Shakespeare's *The Winter's Tale*. She learned her craft from Mrs. Kean, who once slapped her sharply because she had not shown sufficient anguish as the child Arthur in *King John* when the executioners came to bind him. "I was taught that day that if we would express emotion naturally in the supernatural language of great dramatic poetry, we must first imagine the emotion in our own terms."[1]

It was often said of Ellen Terry that she spoke Shakespeare's words as if they were her own. She once told the actor Henry Irving that Shakespeare was the only man she had ever truly loved. Certainly he was the only man whose own ambitions never seemed to interfere with hers (for it is really a striking fact how few women have actually managed full, creative lives in the theatre at the same time as they were married). Terry remained a Shakespearean actor, between marriages, from childhood until her old age, and such was the quality of her understanding that she did in fact seem to be on the most intimate terms with each of Shakespeare's characters. At his Tercentenary in 1916 she praised him as "My friend, my sorrow's cure, my teacher, my companion, the very eyes of me."[2]

At the age of sixteen, Ellen Terry had married the middle-aged painter Frederick Watts, who shipped her home abruptly once he realized he could not mold her into quite the creature he desired. Despondent and confused, she turned to a study of Shakespeare for solace and picked up her acting career where it had left off. A liaison with the architect Edward Godwin caused her to give up her profession again for six years. When that relationship ended, leaving her with two young children to support, she returned to the stage. In 1878, after having achieved major recognition for her portrayal of Portia in *The Merchant of Venice*, she became Henry Irving's leading actress at the Lyceum Theatre, a collaboration that lasted nearly thirty years.

Irving was in the business of mounting scenically elaborate, cut-and-pasted, Victorianized versions of Shakespeare, but under his management Terry acted many of the great roles she desired and achieved her stature as the first woman of the English stage. She was a great admirer of Irving's acting and a close companion of Irving's. The two must have developed a stunning stage rapport, working together for so long, sharing their love for a single, supreme dramatist. It was a time of great acting. Terry and Irving were at their peaks; so were Eleonora Duse and Sarah Bernhardt, women whose genius is also attested to in the following excerpts from Terry's memoirs concerning the acting at the Lyceum.

Around 1903, after the partnership with Irving had ended, Terry turned to the modern drama of Ibsen, Shaw, and J. M. Barrie. She acted Cicely Wyngate in *Captain Brassbound's Conversion,* the play Shaw had written especially for her, drawing his character study from the material in her letters to him since, up to the time rehearsals began, the two correspondents had never really met. She produced Ibsen's *The Vikings at Helgeland* and acted the role of Hjördis. The mise en scène was by her son, Gordon Craig. She was Alice in Barrie's *Alice-Sit-by-the-Fire.* But her greatest success of these years was in *The Merry Wives of Windsor.*

When Bernard Shaw first saw Ellen Terry act, before she began her collaboration with Irving, he felt she was "the woman for the new drama which was still in the womb of time, waiting for Ibsen [and, I'd add, for Shaw] to impregnate it."[3] For the next thirty years Shaw kept up his irritation at the "exasperating waste of talent" he thought Terry's work with Irving was.

Yet, by temperament, Terry was more suited to Shakespeare than to Shaw's urbanity or Ibsen's haunted conversation. She loved the beauty of Shakespeare's poetry, both what she called its "word music" and the challenge of extreme emotions. She was lithe and quick on stage. "The nervous athleticism behind her voice" (Shaw's phrase) exactly suited her to Shakespeare's verse. The new realism, she felt, had a depressing effect upon the audience. It probably also had a repressive effect upon her since it forced her to keep her passions beneath the surface, only hinting at their turbulence through the tensions of conversation. To an actress of her quickness of voice and movement such restraints upon expression seemed unnatural and unpleasant. Ellen Terry never became the great interpreter of the modern realistic drama Shaw had picked her out to be.

Toward the end of her life, she again turned to Shakespeare, creating a one-woman theatre of sorts made of readings of lengthy passage from the plays interwoven with her discourses on the nature of the characters. She had always been extremely close to her daughter, Edith Craig, who had grown up to be a suffragette and a producer of feminist plays. Edy's housemate was Christopher St. John, a woman writer who collaborated with Terry on the *Lectures on Shakespeare* and published them in 1931, after Terry's death. St. John also edited the Terry-Shaw correspondence and a new edition of Terry's memoirs to which she added several biographical chapters. St. John was the translator of the plays of Hrotsvitha, and in 1914 Ellen Terry appeared as the Abbess in Hrotsvitha's *Paphnutius*, produced by her daughter, Edy.

The *Lectures on Shakespeare*, especially those on the "Triumphant" and "Pathetic" women, were performed by Terry with great success all over England, America, and Australia. Plans for a world tour were cut short by the start of World War I and by Terry's advancing age. In the *Lectures*, the problems she had faced at the Lyceum, when her interpretation of a role differed from Irving's, were gone. Aided by St. John, she was at last free to apply her own woman's mind and imagination to Shakespeare's characters. Her interpretations are strong, fresh, and strikingly contemporary. "Shakespeare," she writes, "is one of the very few dramatists who seem to have observed that women have more moral courage than men."

—K. M.

Ellen Terry

[1847–1928]

SELECTIONS

From *The Story of My Life*

Acting at the Lyceum

My greatest triumph as Desdemona was not gained with the audience but
with Henry Irving! He found my endeavours to accept comfort from Iago so
pathetic that they brought the tears to his eyes. It was the oddest sensation
when I said "Oh, good Iago, what shall I do to win my lord again?" to look
up—my own eyes dry, for Desdomona is past crying then—and see Henry's
eyes at their biggest, luminous, soft and full of tears! He was, in spite of
Iago and in spite of his power of identifying himself with the part, very
deeply moved by my acting. But he knew how to turn it to his purpose: he
obtrusively took the tears with his fingers and blew his nose with much feeling, softly and long (so much expression there is, by the way, in blowing the
nose on the stage), so that the audience might think his emotion a fresh
stroke of hypocrisy. . . .

Desdemona is not counted a big part by actresses, but I loved playing it.
Some nights I played it beautifully. My appearance was right—I was such a
poor wraith of a thing. But let there be no mistake—it took strength to act
this weakness and passiveness of Desdemona's. I soon found that, like Cordelia, she has plenty of character.

Reading the play the other day, I studied the opening scene. It is the
finest opening to a play I know.

How many times Shakespeare draws fathers and daughters, and how little stock he seems to take of *mothers*! Portia and Desdemona, Cordelia,
Rosalind and Miranda, Lady Macbeth, Queen Katherine and Hermione,
Ophelia, Jessica, Hero, and many more are daughters of *fathers*, but of their
mothers we hear nothing. My own daughter called my attention to this fact

From *The Story of My Life* by Ellen Terry (London: Hutchinson, 1908). Reissued with additional biographical chapters as *Ellen Terry's Memoirs*, Christopher St. John, editor (New York: G.
P. Putnam's Sons, 1932). Copyright © 1932, G. P. Putnam's Sons.

quite recently, and it is really a singular fact. Of mothers of sons there are plenty of examples: Constance, Volumnia, the Countess Rousillon, Gertrude; but if there are mothers of daughters at all, they are poor examples, like Juliet's mother and Mrs. Page. I wonder if in all the many hundreds of books written on Shakespeare and his plays this point has been taken up?. . .

"Are you affected by adverse criticism?" I was asked once. I answered then and I answer now, that legitimate adverse criticism has always been of use to me if only because it "gave me to think" furiously. Seldom does the outsider, however talented, as a writer and observer, recognise the actor's art, and often we are told that we are acting best when we are showing the works most plainly, and denied any special virtue when we are concealing our method. Professional criticism is most helpful, chiefly because it induces one to criticise oneself. "Did I give that impression to anyone? Then there must have been something wrong somewhere." The "something" is often a perfectly different blemish from that to which the critic drew attention.

Unprofessional criticism is often more helpful still, but alas! One's friends are to one's faults more than a little blind, and to one's virtues very kind! It is through letters from people quite unknown to me that I have sometimes learned valuable lessons. During the run of *Romeo and Juliet* someone wrote and told me that if the dialogue at the ball could be taken in a lighter and *quicker* way, it would better express the manner of a girl of Juliet's age. The same unknown critic pointed out that I was too slow and studied in the Balcony Scene. She—I think it was a woman—was perfectly right!

On the hundredth night, although no one liked my Juliet very much, I received many flowers, little tokens, and poems. To one bouquet was pinned a note which ran:

> "To Juliet,
> As a mark of respect and Esteem
> From the Gasmen of the Lyceum Theatre."

That alone would have made my recollections of *Romeo and Juliet* pleasant. But there was more. At the supper on the stage after the hundredth performance, Sarah Bernhardt was present. She said nice things to me, and I was enraptured that my "vraies larmes" should have pleased and astonished her! I noticed that she hardly ever moved, yet all the time she gave the impression of swift, butterfly movement. While talking to Henry she took some red stuff out of her bag and rubbed it on her lips! This frank "making up" in public was a far more astonishing thing in the 'eighties than it would be now. But I liked Miss Sarah for it, as I liked her for everything.

How wonderful she looked in those days! She was as transparent as an azalea, only more so; like a cloud, only not so thick. Smoke from a burning paper describes her more nearly! She was hollow-eyed, thin, almost consumptive-looking. Her body was not the prison of her soul, but its shadow.

On the stage she has always seemed to me more a symbol, an ideal, an epitome than a *woman*. It is the quality which makes her so easy in such lofty parts as Phèdre. She is always a miracle. Let her play 'L'Aiglon,' and while matter-of-fact members of the audience are wondering if she looks *really* like the unfortunate King of Rome, and deciding against her and in favour of Maude Adams who did look the boy to perfection, more imaginative watchers see in Sarah's performance a truth far bigger than a mere physical resemblance. Rostand says in the foreword to his play, that in it he does not espouse this cause or that, but only tells the story of "one poor little boy." In another of his plays, *Cyrano de Bergerac*, there is one poor little tune played on a pipe of which the hero says:

"Écoutez, Gascons, c'est toute la Gascogne."

Though I am not French, and know next to nothing of the language, I thought when I saw Sarah's *L'Aiglon*, that of that one poor little boy too might be said:

"Écoutez, Français, c'est toute la France!"

It is this extraordinary decorative and symbolic quality of Sarah's which makes her transcend all personal and individual feeling on the stage. No one plays a love scene better, but it is a *picture* of love that she gives, a strange orchidaceous picture rather than a suggestion of the ordinary human passion as felt by ordinary human people. She is exotic—well, what else should she be? One does not, at any rate one should not, quarrel with an exquisite tropical flower and call it unnatural because it is not a buttercup or a cowslip.

I have spoken of the face as the chief equipment of the actor. Sarah Bernhardt contradicts this at once. Her face does little for her. Her walk is not much. Nothing about her is more remarkable than the way she gets about the stage without one ever seeing her move. By what magic does she triumph without two of the richest possessions that an actress can have? Eleonora Duse has them. Her walk is the walk of the peasant, fine and free. She has the superb carriage of the head which goes with that fearless movement from the hips—and her face! There is nothing like it, nothing! But it is as the real woman, a particular woman, that Duse triumphs most. Her Cleopatra was insignificant compared with Sarah's—she is not so pictorial.

How futile it is to make comparisons! Better far to thank heaven for both these women.

EXTRACT FROM MY DIARY

Saturday, June 11. 1892.—"To see 'Miss Sarah' as Cléopâtre (Sardou superb!). She was inspired! The essence of Shakespeare's Cleopatra. I went round and implored her to do Juliet. She said she was too old. She can *never* be old. 'Age cannot wither her.'

June 18.—"Again to see Sarah—this time *La Dame aux Camélias*. Fine, marvelous. Her writing the letter, and the last act the best.

July 11.—"*Telegraph* says 'Frou-frou' was 'never at any time a character in which she (Sarah) excelled.' Dear me! When I saw it I thought it wonderful. It made me ashamed of ever having played it."

Sarah Bernhardt has shown herself the equal of any man as a manager. Her productions are always beautiful; she chooses her company with discretion, and sees to every detail of the stage-management. In this respect she differs from all other foreign artists that I have seen. I have always regretted that Duse should play as a rule with such a mediocre company and should be apparently so indifferent to her surroundings. In *Adrienne Lecouvreur* it struck me that the careless stage-management utterly ruined the play, and I could not bear to see Duse as Adrienne beautifully dressed while the Princess and the other Court ladies wore cheap red velveteen and white satin and brought the pictorial level of the performance down to that of a "fit-up" or booth.

From *Four Lectures on Shakespeare*

From *The Triumphant Women*

An actress does not study a character with a view to proving something about the dramatist who created it. Her task is to learn how to translate this character into herself, how to make its thoughts her thoughts, its word her words. It is because I have applied myself to this task for a great many years, that I am able to speak to you about Shakespeare's women with the knowledge that can be gained only from union with them.

Wonderful women! Have you ever thought how much we all, and women especially, owe to Shakespeare for his vindication of woman in these fearless, high-spirited, resolute and intelligent heroines? Don't believe the anit-feminists if they tell you, as I was once told, that Shakespeare had to endow his women with virile qualities because in his theatre they were always impersonated by men! This may account for the frequency with which

From *Four Lectures on Shakespeare* by Ellen Terry, edited with an introduction by Christopher St. John; first published 1932; reissued 1969 by Benjamin Blom, New York.

they masquerade as boys, but I am convinced that it had little influence on Shakespeare's studies of women. They owe far more to the liberal ideas about the sex which were fermenting in Shakespeare's age. The assumption that "the woman's movement" is of very recent date—something peculiarly modern—is not warranted by history. There is evidence of its existence in the fifteenth century. Then as now it excited opposition and ridicule, but still it moved! Such progress was made that Erasmus could write: "Men and women have different functions, but their education and their virtues ought to be equal." He was shocked at the ignorance of young ladies of rank in the Low Countries. They were not nearly as well educated as their contemporaries in France, Italy and England. The scholarship of Lady Jane Grey, who at thirteen could read Plato in the original; of Mary Stuart, who at sixteen delivered an extempore oration in Latin; of Queen Elizabeth who made translations of the classics, was not exceptional in the class of society which received any education at all. Vives, the Spanish tutor of Katharine of Aragon, who accompanied her to England, urged, like Erasmus, that girls should be given as good an education as boys. Then, as now, some people thought this most undesirable. What use was learning to a woman? It might even have the dreadful result of making her less attractive to a man! The masculine dislike of the intellectual woman is expressed by the critic of Vives who wrote:

"From a braying mule and a girl who speaks Latin good Lord deliver us!"

That women were teased about wanting to "wear the breeches" is clear from an Italian caricature, dated 1450, which represents some fashionable ladies of the period struggling awkwardly to pull on men's trunk-hose!

Much more could be said to emphasise the point that the real women in Shakespeare's time inspired his general conception of femininity, but I am conscious that it is about time I "cut the cackle" and came to "the 'osses," that is, to Beatrice, Portia, and Rosalind, and the other heroines in my "triumphant" group. Yet there is one bit of cackle I am unwilling to sacrifice. I must read a contemporary description of a great lady of the Renaissance period, Margaret of France, because it might have been written about Shakespeare's Beatrice:

"Her eyes are clear, and full of fire; her mouth is fine—intellectual with something of irony, of benevolence, and of reserve. A singular countenance where the mind and the heart both rule."

Beatrice to the life! Her brilliant mind has a strong deep heart for its consort. Her cousin Hero criticises her for being too much under the sway of her mind:

> *Her wit*
> *Values itself so highly that to her*
> *All matter else seems weak.*

Her uncle Leonato endorses this criticism when he tells Beatrice that she will never get a husband if she is so shrewd of her tongue. Yet when her heart speaks seriously, Beatrice listens seriously and obeys its commands.

"By my troth a pleasant-spirited lady," says Don Pedro. The actress who impersonates Beatrice should remember that testimonial. Beatrice's repartee in her encounters with Benedick can easily be made to sound malicious and vulgar. It should be spoken as the lightest raillery, with mirth in the voice, and charm in the manner. . . .

The wonderful scene [in the church] throws such a flood of light on Beatrice's character that an actress has little excuse for not seeing clearly what kind of woman she has to impersonate. Yet however it may be now, there is evidence that in the past she was not taken seriously enough. Even in the church scene I have just read to you the idea was to make her indignation rather comic. When I first rehearsed Beatrice at the Lyceum I was told by Mr. Lacy, an actor of the old school who was engaged by Henry Irving to assist him in some of his early Shakespearean productions, of some traditional "business" which seemed to me so preposterous that I could hardly believe he really meant me to adopt it. But he was quite serious. "When Benedick rushes forward to lift up Hero after she has fainted, you 'shoo' him away. Jealousy, you see. Beatrice is not going to let her man lay a finger on another woman." I said, "Oh, nonsense, Mr. Lacy!" "Well, it's always been done," he retorted, "and it always gets a laugh." I told him then that not only was it impossible for *me* to do such a thing, but that it was so inconsistent with Beatrice's character that it ought to be impossible for any actress impersonating her to do it! I came off victorious in that tussle with Mr. Lacy, but was defeated in another with Henry Irving over a traditional "gag" at the end of the church scence. I had omitted this gag, "Kiss my hand again," when I had first played Beatrice in the provinces, and I was appalled at finding that I was expected to say it at the Lyceum. My tongue refused to utter the obnoxious words, impossible to the Beatrice of my conception, for many rehearsals. Then one day Henry said: "Now I think it is about time to rehearse this scene as we are actually going to play it, so, Miss Terry, we must please have the gag." I did not like to show any insubordination before the company, so with a gulp, I managed to obey, but I burst into tears! Henry was most sympathetic, I remember, but would not budge. I went home in a terrible state of mind, strongly tempted to throw up my part! Then I reflected that for one thing I did not like doing at the Lyceum, there would probably be a hundred things I should dislike doing in another theatre. So I agreed to do what Henry wished, under protest.

I have played Beatrice hundreds of times, but not once as I know she ought to be played. I was never swift enough, not nearly swift enough at the Lyceum where I had a too deliberate, though polished and thoughtful Benedick in Henry Irving. But at least I did not make the mistake of being arch and skittish, and this encourages me to think I could have played Rosalind well.

I have been Beatrice! Would that I could say "I have been Rosalind." Would that the opportunity to play this part had come my way when I was in my prime! I reckon it one of the greatest disappointments of my life that it did not! In my old age I go on studying Rosalind, rather wistfully, I admit.

From *The Pathetic Women*

The part of Desdemona gives an actress far more difficult problems to solve. I know no character in Shakespeare which has suffered from so much misconception. The general idea seems to be that Desdemona is a ninny, a pathetic figure chiefly because she is half-baked. It is certainly the idea of those who think an actress of the dolly type, a pretty young thing with a vapid innocent expression, is well suited to the part. I shall perhaps surprise you by telling you that a great tragic actress, with a strong personality and a strong method, is far better suited to it, for Desdemona is strong, not weak.

There is something of the potential nun in her. She is more fitted to be the bride of Christ than the bride of any man. Shakespeare implies this in the lines:

> *So opposite to marriage that she shunned*
> *The wealthy curled darlings of our nation.*

Her virginal heart is profoundly moved by the meeting with Othello. Unlike the wealthy, curled darlings, this is a man who has suffered many distressful strokes. The story of his life rouses her compassionate interest. As Othello says:

> *She lov'd me for the dangers I had pass'd,*
> *And I lov'd her that she did pity them.*

Whereas the handsome faces of curled darlings had seemed ugly to Des-

demona because their minds were ugly, Othello's face seemed fair to her because his mind was fair.

> *I saw Othello's visage in his mind,*
> *And to his honours, and his valiant parts*
> *Did I my soul and fortunes consecrate.*

Desdemona does not use the word "consecrate" idly. Love to her is a sacrament.

I have said she is a woman of strong character. Once she has consecrated
herself to Othello, she is capable even of "downright violence" of all the conventions for his sake. But I think by nature she is unconventional. Othello's
doubts that she is chaste are usually made to seem absolutely monstrous in
the theatre, because Desdemona's unconventionality is ignored. She is not
at all prim or demure; on the contrary, she is genially expressive, the kind of
woman who being devoid of coquetry behaves as she feels. Her manner to
Cassio might easily fertilize the poisonous seed of suspicion Iago has sown in
Othello's mind. The pertinacity with which she begs Othello to reinstate
Cassio does not strike me as evidence that she is a rather foolish woman,
lacking in insight. Let an actress give a charming "I'm really not asking
much of you" tone to Desdemona's suit to her husband, and a very different
impression will be produced. Her purity of heart and her charity (charity
"thinketh no evil") are sufficient explanation of her being slow to grasp the
situation. It is not until she has been grossly insulted and brutally assaulted
that she understands. Her behaviour from that dreadful moment should
surely convince us that she is not a simpleton, but a saint. . . .

"O, who hath done this deed?" cries the distraught Emilia ... when she
finds Desdemona near to death, and the innocent victim of Iago's devilish
plot, with a supreme effort of the love which does not seek its own, whispers
faintly the chivalrous falsehood:

> *Nobody; I myself. Farewell:*
> *Commend me to my kind lord.*

Yes, it may be true. Desdemona may have taken her own life. Emilia is
pondering this, I think, as she holds her dear mistress in her arms, and then
seeing she is dead, lays her back on the disordered bed. She hears Othello's
voice saying, "Why, how should she be murdered?" and although she answers "Alas, who knows?" I think she means: "*You* know!" She is beginning
to blaze. "You heard her say herself it was not I." "She *said* so," oh yes! And

Emilia moves away from the deathbed, with the enigmatic remark: "I must needs report the truth." Othello seizes her by the arm:

> *She's, like a liar, gone to burning hell!*
> *'Twas I that killed her.*

Emilia has plenty of courage. She is alone with a murderer, a crazy murderer. It is to this that jealousy has brought the noble Moor. She must know that she risks her life by angering him, but she does not care. The slur on the dead woman makes her reckless.

> *O the more angel she*
> *And you the blacker devil!*

. . .She know no fear. How she shames the fearful, those who fear the opinion of the world, or fear to make themselves ridiculous, or fear the consequences, and so are silent in the defence of truth.

> *I, peace!*
> *No! I will speak as liberal as the north;*
> *Let heaven, and men, and devils, let them all,*
> *All, all, cry shame against me, yet I'll speak.*

It is significant that the chivalrous champions of the honour of the living Hero, as of the dead Desdemona, should both be women! Significant, and original. Shakespeare is one of the very few dramatists who seem to have observed that women have more moral courage than men. . . .

Juliet, I once read, but where I cannot remember, is the first sign of a change in Shakespeare's ideas about women. This is something to ponder. It seems to be true that up to the period of his first tragedy, his women characters reveal a certain antagonism to the whole sex.

Think of Adriana in *The Comedy of Errors*, of Katherine in *The Taming of the Shrew*. They don't inspire us with love or admiration. The hysterical Lady Anne in *Richard III* is frankly a study of feminine weakness. Helena in *All's Well that Ends Well*, and Julia in *Two Gentlemen of Verona* belong to the "doormat" type. They bear any amount of humiliation from the men they love, seem almost to enjoy being maltreated and scorned by them, and hunt them down in the most undignified way when they are trying to escape. . . .

What was the cause of the change which drew Shakespeare to the creation of great-hearted, great-minded, lovable women? There is a theory, and a very plausible one, it seems to me, that when he first came to London and began writing comedies, he was still smarting under the disillusionment of his own unfortunate marriage. The women characters are either like the unamiable shrew that his wife was, or like the patient Griselda that he thought she ought to have been!

Then Mistress Mary Fitton came upon the scene, a fine creature in spite of that fault she had to excess, and the "powerful might" of her vivid personality widened and intensified the vision of the man who loved her. . . .I am attracted by this theory, but I have to warn myself and you of the danger of becoming obsessed by any *one* theory about Shakespeare! The web of life, he tells, us, "is of a mingled yarn," and this is true of the web of life in his plays. Mary Fitton is only one strand in it. If we believe the legend of his passionate love for Mary Fitton—and why should we not, since there is no smoke without fire?—we shall think it extremely probable that she was the begetter of many of those touches of aristocratic pride, of brilliant spirits, of witty speech, in his portraits of women. It says much for Shakespeare—and for her too—that in spite of the unfortunate and unhappy outcome of his devotion, he was not embittered. With one notable exception, Cressida, the women in the plays of his maturity afford evidence of this.

Eva Le Gallienne

[1899–   ]

AN INTRODUCTION

THERE WAS ONCE a popularly priced repertory company in this country where the acting was first-rate, the house almost always full, and where the best contemporary plays from Europe and America shared the stage with classics. Located on Fourteenth Street, near Sixth Avenue (where a discount store now stands, next to the U.S. Armory), and called the Civic Repertory Theatre, it was the work of one woman, Eva Le Gallienne, whose dedication to acting led her to become an actor-manager of excellence.

By 1926, twenty-seven-year-old Le Gallienne had achieved enough prestige as a Broadway actress to found her own theatre downtown. Realizing that neither she nor the theatre could truly develop in the commercial world, she used her hard-won acceptance there to secure the subsidized repertory situation in which both artists and audiences could stretch and grow.

"I was predatory and ruthless. No rich person was safe in my presence. . . I never failed to make it clear that these sums were gifts, neither loans nor investments; there could be no hope of repayment or profit. The Civic was designed as a subsidized theatre; only in this way, it seemed to me, could popular prices be combined with the necessary high standard of production, and the policy remain stable and safe from compromise."[1]

The acting company, to which the young writer May Sarton belonged, as well as the famous Russian actress Alla Nazimova, earned modest salaries. Le Gallienne lived in the attic and worked her way downstairs each morning, through administrative offices and property, costume, and scene shops, until she reached the stage for the start of rehearsal.

She made her own translations of Ibsen's plays, whose female characters were among her favorite roles. She produced Susan Glaspell's *The Inheritors* and *Alison's House,* which won the Pulitzer Prize; *Peter Pan,* in which she flew out over the audience as Peter; a fanciful *Alice in Wonderland,* in which she played the White Chess Queen; the first Chekhov play in English on the American stage; the first Giraudoux play in the U.S.

Le Gallienne was artistic director; Helen Lohman, theatre manager;

Aline Bernstein designed nearly all the settings; Marion Evensen acted in many plays. Mary Louise Bok was the major patron. The Civic Repertory was a theatre created and maintained by women.

In the six years of its existence, the Civic Rep produced thirty-four plays. Le Gallienne directed thirty-two of them and starred in nearly all. Several times commercial managers sought to move these productions uptown to Broadway, where they might begin to make a profit. Le Gallienne always refused. She was, in fact, more practical; she understood that the repertory system upon which she depended for artistic success is itself dependent upon the dedication of artists determined to work outside the marketplace.

Ticket prices at the Civic Rep ranged from $.35 to $1.50. The audience, which also depended upon a subsidized theatre to provide it with the art it craved, was discerning, large, and loyal. When, after five seasons, Le Gallienne decided to close the theatre for a year, to give herself time to think, audience members buried the stage in flowers, then stood outside the building refusing to go home until Le Gallienne answered their chants with a promise to return. (The year off was a torturous one for her, as she was severely burned in an accident at her home in Connecticut that fall.)

She did return, if only for another year, before the Depression ironically forced the closing of this people's theatre because its private patrons were no longer willing or able to contribute, and because the federal government had reneged on its promise of support. Although Le Gallienne tried to keep the company together by touring, this plan, too, proved impracticable after a few seasons. In 1935 she relinquished her position as actor-manager and struck out on her own.

Periodically, throughout the rest of her career, Le Gallienne would bring together groups of actors to stage classics, including *Hamlet,* in which she played the title role. With Cheryl Crawford, a founder of the Group Theatre, and Margaret Webster she attempted to establish another ongoing repertory company, but the venture did not last beyond a season. In 1977, sixty-five years after her career began, she toured in *The Royal Family* after a successful season on Broadway; the following year she acted in a film and in the summer of 1980 she was preparing a new role for the stage.

Although she is too consummate a woman of the theatre not to have been involved in every aspect of production, including scene design and play translation, Le Gallienne is first of all an actress. She writes about acting with the same clarity and poetic insight with which she has pursued it on the stage. In her gemlike book on Eleonora Duse, who was one of her early mentors, Le Gallienne describes Duse's intentions as an actress in words that must surely evidence her own:

The first part of her task—that of gaining absolute control over the externals of her craft—she achieved comparatively early in her career, but the second part—that of learning to summon at will emotions which were not her own but those of the characters she chose to interpret—she never ceased to work on.

She worked to enrich the resources of her mind and spirit; to deepen her perception; sharpen her imagination; widen her understanding; develop a power of concentration so intense that it could translate a mental image into reality—could make it felt, and heard, and seen. These were the means by which Duse "lived her roles"; she actually became these women—she did not force them to become her.[2]

Eva Le Gallienne has published two, currently out-of-print, autobiographies, *At 33* and *With a Quiet Heart*. Each of these volumes is full of wisdom about the art of acting and dedication to the theatre. In the following excerpts from *With a Quiet Heart,* Le Gallienne details the government's failure to provide a subsidy for the Civic Rep and shares her insights about acting Ibsen's Rebecca West and Shakespeare's Hamlet. In the chapter on her production of *Hamlet* she also introduces Uta Hagen, an actor whom Le Gallienne was as generous to at the beginning of her distinguished career as Duse once was to Le Gallienne at the start of hers.

—K.M.

Eva Le Gallienne

[1899–   ]

SELECTIONS

From *With a Quiet Heart*

The "New Deal"

During our appearance in Washington, D.C., Mrs. Franklin D. Roosevelt came to a performance of *Alice in Wonderland*. She is a Carroll fan and was most charming about our production; she seemed to feel we had succeeded in capturing the real quality of *Alice*. I had never had the honor of meeting Mrs. Roosevelt before, and when I walked out on the stage to greet her after the final curtain, still wearing my grotesque White Queen costume, I was immediately struck by her rare charm of manner and her deep humanity. She seemed to me very tall, and I couldn't help thinking how much handsomer she looked in person than her pictures would lead one to expect. She very graciously invited me to tea at the White House during our stay in Washington. The tea was happily not a social function; we sat upstairs in her sitting room and had a quiet talk. Her daughter and one or two intimates of the family circle dropped in now and then, but beyond that we were left to ourselves. I told her something of the problems I was faced with. She was tremendously sympathetic and seemed genuinely interested in the work we were attempting to accomplish.

She felt the President might be interested too, and suggested that I submit an outline to him, explaining my dream of creating repertory theatres, similar to the Civic, in important key cities throughout the counry. She told me of his concern for creating employment, and that in his scheme artists of all sorts, including workers in the theatre, were to be considered. The creating of some ten or twelve permanent repertory companies would involve the stable employment of around a thousand people, particularly as my plan included free schools connected with each of the suggested centers.

From *With a Quiet Heart* by Eva Le Gallienne (New York: Viking, 1953). Used with permission.

I was much encouraged by my talk with Mrs. Roosevelt, and immediately set to work to put on paper a comprehensive outline of this scheme so dear to my heart. I mailed it to the President. Shortly afterward I received an invitation to lunch at the White House. The President himself expressed an interest in discussing my plan with me. . . .

Mr. Roosevelt spoke of my plan with appreciation and approval, but he told me he did not find it comprehensive enough. He wanted to create employment for many more theatre people—for all the theatre people, in fact, who were unable to find work. At the time the WPA was already functioning in certain fields, and his idea was to expand it to the theatre. He spoke at some length and in considerable detail, and I listened with pleasure to his beautiful voice, noticing the ease with which he clothed his thought with appropriate and compelling words. But I could not bring myself to agree with his point of view. It seemed to me to be the antithesis of mine. His project was primarily humanitarian; his aim was not so much to bring fine theatre to the people but to provide actors and other theatre workers, *regardless of their talents*, with work. He was not particularly concerned with standards of achievement; his concern was to create opportunities for all actors to make a living. It was a fine and noble design, but one, I felt, that would inevitably encourage mediocrity at best. It is obvious that in the theatre, as in all other fields, there is a large proportion of workers, devoid of talent, who, through a pathetic and misguided love for their profession, persist in it, unwilling to face the fact that God has made them totally unfit to serve it.

My dream, on the other hand, was to create people's repertory theatres throughout the country, staffed by the very best craftsmen procurable for their respective jobs. I felt that in order to foster a theatre-mindedness in the American public comparable to that in European countries, it was mandatory to bring them the highest possible standard of performance. The subsidized state theatres of Europe employ only the most efficient workers. It is a hard-won honor to be a member of such organizations as the Comédie Française, the Moscow Art Theatre, the Vienna Burgtheater—even the Kongelige-Teater in little Denmark. Such institutions, far from giving refuge to the incompetent and the unfortunate, are designed as strongholds of the very best standards and traditions in theatrecraft.

Such a point of view must seem hard and ruthless in contrast to President Roosevelt's desire to alleviate hardship and misery. But the service of art in any form cannot be soft or easy; it is a mistake to look for kindness or pity there. *"Aus meinen grossen Schmerzen, mach ich die kleine Lieder,"* says Heine. If one's aim in life is to live in comparative comfort, ease, and contentment, one should not meddle with the arts; they are ruthless masters and demand sterner stuff.

The President listened to what I had to say. I suppose it was temerity on my part to disagree with him, but I felt so strongly in this matter that I had to say what I thought. He referred me to Harry Hopkins, the gentleman on my right, and asked me to think over and discuss with him the possibility of my heading the National Theatre Division of the WPA.

I was aware that the President was doing me a great honor in considering me for such an important post, but, disagreeing as I did with the basic concept of the entire scheme, I felt I would be unable to do a good job in this most difficult and demanding position.

Harry Hopkins and I left the White House together. We were no sooner settled in the taxicab, and had not yet left the White House grounds, when he turned to me and said, "Dear Miss Le Gallienne, you should learn to play politics."

"That's one thing I never *have* learned to do," I answered, "and I'm not sure that I want to."

"If you would just learn to play politics," he continued, "you could get millions out of the old man.". . .

In spite of the fact that I could not bring myself to consider heading the WPA Theatre Division, I felt that, since so many millions were about to be spent on theatre work, it might be possible to arrange for a modest sum to be allocated to the continuance of the Civic Repertory Theatre. . . .

I mentioned all this to Harry Hopkins, and he very sympathetically agreed that something should be done to insure the survival of the Civic Repertory. He told me he would call me up in Chicago, where I would be laying-off the week before Christmas, and asked me to be in readiness during that week to return to Washington for further conference with himself and some of his colleagues in the New Deal. He was most cordial and assured me that I had good grounds to hope for some government aid in my struggle to keep the Civic Repertory Theatre alive.

I rejoined the company in Cincinnati and, the following week, went on to Chicago. Mr. Hopkins was as good as his word; he telephoned me as he had promised, and a few days later I went back to Washington.

I spent a busy day there, In the morning I had a conference with the Secretary of Labor, Madame Perkins. She was interested in learning details of labor conditions in the theatre. I did my best to answer her questions, and some of the facts revealed seemed to surprise and startle her. Nowadays the situation would undoubtedly surprise and startle her even more.

That afternoon I had a long talk with Mr. Hopkins. It was determined that I should ask for a yearly subsidy of one hundred thousand dollars, which I felt would permit me to add four or five new productions each season to our existing repertory and also make one or two improvements I had long had in mind. It was arranged that I should make this request that evening at a dinner at which some of Mr. Hopkins' colleagues were to be present.

This dinner took place in a private dining room at the Mayflower Hotel. I had expected it to be in the nature of a business conference, but, like many similar "conferences" in the honeymoon days of the New Deal, it was more in the nature of a party. There must have been close to twenty people there, prominent members of the Brain Trust, most of them accompanied by their wives, or by secretaries of the female sex. It was a gay and animated gathering. We all had a great number of cocktails before sitting down to a very excellent dinner, and to my surprise drinks were served all during the meal; I had always thought of official dinners in the United States as being strictly washed down with ice-water. I couldn't help thinking of Chekhov's line in the last act of *The Three Sisters*, when the old nurse delightedly tells Irina what a fine life she is now leading: ". . .I have a room to myself, and a bedstead. . . all at the government expense!"

Most of these people were young, all of them eager, excited, enthusiastic, tremendously alive. They felt they were rebuilding the world, and perhaps, in a way, they were. There could be no question of their sense of dedication, their ardent desire to better the lot of their fellow men. Everything seemed possible to them, and anything that promised to distribute the goods of this world more evenly and indiscriminately seemed to them desirable; they did not examine the ways and means too closely.

I have never been what is known as a good mixer. I am not comfortable in a crowd, and at first I got the impression that some of the people present thought me aloof and a bit stand-offish. They all seemed to know each other very well, and I felt rather like the lone outsider at a family gathering. But gradually the conversation got around to the problems of the Civic Repertory Theatre and whether or not it was deserving of New Deal support. The consensus seemed to be favorable, and my answers to innumerable questions seemed to make a fairly good impression. The discussion finally focused on the exact sum of money I would require. I mentioned the hundred thousand dollars a year that Mr. Hopkins and I had decided on as adequate. I explained how I had arrived at this particular figure. Again I answered question after question, some eminently intelligent, others showing complete ignorance of the problem at hand.

Dinner had been over for some time, and Mr. Hopkins went into a huddle with some of his colleagues at the far end of the room, while the rest of us lingered over our coffee and made polite conversation.

At last Mr. Hopkins and the other gentlemen returned and sat down at the table again. I was asked whether I could manage on a subsidy of ninety thousand dollars. I was rather surprised at this sudden desire for economy and wondered, in view of the huge sums of money that had been bandied about in the general conversation, why ten thousand dollars should seem of such great importance. However, I conceded that ninety thousand would certainly enable me to save the Civic from foundering.

I was then told, with much good will and evident pleasure from all concerned, that I could definitely count on this sum, and that I should by all means return to my work with a light heart and make arrangements for the renewal of my lease on the old Fourteenth Street Theatre.

The party broke up, and Mr. and Mrs. Hopkins started to drive me back to my hotel. We were all in rather a convivial mood, and he suggested that we go on to the Maisonette Russe to hear some gypsy music. But the thought of being regaled with *"Ochy Chornaya"* in every conceivable key and tempo was more than I could bear, so instead we went back to the Hopkins's apartment, where Mrs. Hopkins made us some more coffee, and where Mr. Hopkins persuaded me to read aloud Wordsworth's "Ode: Intimations of Immortality," which we had discovered was practically our favorite poem.

When he finally dropped me off at the Carlton Hotel, Mr. Hopkins's last words to me were a solemn promise to send me the very next day an official confirmation of the proposed subsidy for the Civic Repertory Theatre, so that I might in all confidence make arrangements for the continuance of the work.

This was the last I ever heard on the subject. I never received another word from Mr. Hopkins, nor could I succeed in getting an answer to a single letter I subsequently wrote to him.

It is scarcely to be wondered at that, ever since, I have listened to talk of possible government subsidy with a very large grain of salt.

Acting Ibsen

Rosmersholm is fascinating stuff. I had made a new translation from the Norwegian, since this is one of Ibsen's plays that has suffered most from William Archer's Victorianism. We were all of us constantly amazed at the timeliness of the theme: the scenes between Rosmer and Kroll might have been conversations between Roosevelt and Hoover; it was really startling.

The character of Rebecca West is an extraordinary psychological study. How well Ibsen knew the female of the species! It must have been the insight of genius, for, as far as one knows, there were not many women in his life. Yet when one thinks of the remarkable diversity of such characters as Nora in *A Doll's House*, Hilda Wangel in *The Master Builder*, Mrs. Alving in

Ghosts, Hedda and Mrs. Elvsted in *Hedda Gabler*, Ella Rentheim and Gunhild Borkman in *John Gabriel Borkman*, Gina in *The Wild Duck*, Ellida Wangel in *The Lady from the Sea*—to mention but a few—his deep knowledge and acute observation of the female heart and mind are little short of miraculous. No wonder so many actresses have been drawn to Ibsen's plays. His gallery of women offers the same satisfying challenge to the actress that Shakespeare's incomparable gallery of men offers to the actor. There is no need for embroidery or invention; these people are living human beings, and the actor has only to open the doors of his mind and allow them to take over; the less he interferes the better. These plays do demand of an actor, however, tremendous concentration, as well as a sensitive, flexible instrument, and he must be capable of really listening and really thinking; merely pretending to listen and to think is not enough. Ibsen's plays are like icebergs; the major substance lies below the surface, and an actor's inner performance is the most important part of it. The line of thought must be kept unbroken—both on and off the stage—from the rise of the curtain to the very end of the play. Actors unused to playing Ibsen find this sustained concentration extremely tiring; yet without it, I am convinced, a successful performance is impossible.

Ibsen requires, it seems to me, a style of acting that might be described as "heightened realism." His plays bridge the gap between the artificial theatricality of Scribe and Brieux and the relaxed naturalism of Chekhov and his numerous followers. Ibsen is always a little larger than life and demands from his interpreters a corresponding stature, but it is a stature perhaps more of the brain than of the heart. Where Chekhov creates a series of moods and relies on the actor to fill them and realize them in tangible form, with all the resources of heart, human understanding, and technical invention at his command, Ibsen presents one with a clear and undeviating pattern, which it is the actor's job thoroughly to understand and absorb and to interpret with the utmost faithfulness.

Of all Ibsen's women Rebecca West in *Rosmersholm* makes perhaps the greatest demands on the player's power of concentration. For the first two acts Rebecca listens, watches, thinks, but rarely speaks. It is not until the middle of the third act that she begins to reveal herself in words, and then the intricate inner pattern is gradually unfolded: her passion for Rosmer; her murder of Rosmer's wife—achieved obliquely and by the use of mental suggestion, of psychological persuasion, but a murder none the less; her horrified realization of her incestuous relations with her own father; the gradual weakening of her will to power, of her almost pathological ego, through constant association with the purity and nobility of Rosmer's spirit, until at last she finds herself no longer capable of using the forces of evil and sees her insane passion, with all its violence and terror, transformed into a pure and selfless love. All these factors suddenly burst through the calm, reserved surface of the woman, and the darkest, most secret corners of her mind and soul are ruthlessly exposed.

But the vociferous turbulence of the last two acts must spring from a constantly sustained line of thought and feeling underlying the brooding stillness of the acts preceding. Without this preparation, Rebecca's sudden outburst seems no more than a display of theatrical fireworks. By far the most difficult part of the job lies in the first and second acts; if the actress has played them well, the rest follows inevitably. . . .

Acting Hamlet

At the age of sixteen, soon after I started work in the theatre, I made a list of the parts I was determined to play before turning forty. It was by no means a modest list, and I kept it strictly to myself. I saw no reason for courting ridicule, but there was never the slightest doubt in my mind that my aim would be achieved. So convinced was I of this that I spent a great part of my time studying these various roles, thinking about them, preparing myself for the day when I should actually be called upon to play them.

The list follows:

Hilda Wangel in *The Master Builder*
Hedda in *Hedda Gabler*
Peter in *Peter Pan*
Juliet in *Romeo and Juliet*
Marguerite Gautier in *Camille*
The Duc de Reichstadt in *L'Aiglon*
Hamlet in *Hamlet*

At thirty-eight, with only two years to go, I decided to keep faith with myself and tackle Hamlet. All the other parts on the list I had played many times, and Hamlet seemed to me to come under the head of unfinished business.

During the summer of 1936 Mr. Langner had spoken to me about playing it in Westport, but—although I had worked on the part on and off for many years—I didn't feel quite ready for it then, and also the fact of Westport's being so close to New York City deterred me. I knew that for many years there had been no precedent in this country for a woman's playing Hamlet, and realized that the idea might be received with decided skepticism, not unmixed with ridicule. In Europe the situation was different;

there had been many women Hamlets in Germany, Scandinavia, Russia, and France. The most famous French woman Hamlet was of course Sarah Bernhardt, but as recently as the early thirties Marguerite Jamois had played the part with great success at Baty's Théâtre Montparnasse in Paris. However, since the idea was foreign to our American point of view, I felt I would rather try it out in a more secluded spot than Westport, where I would be out of range of curiosity-seekers from Broadway and would be able to get a clearer audience-reaction.

Mr. Raymond Moore, at that time manager of the Cape Playhouse at Dennis, Massachusetts, expressed an interest in the production, and plans were made to present the play there in August. As soon as this was definitely settled I set to work in earnest.

Since I had long dreamed of playing Hamlet, I was already very familiar with the lines, but I wanted them to become so part of me that each thought and emotion must find expression in those particular words as simply and inevitably as though they had just sprung from my own consciousness. I wanted to eliminate all sense of having learned them. As a rule I never study the lines of a part beforehand. As the inner structure of my performance grows and takes shape, the words are gradually absorbed and become a part of the whole. And the average words one speaks on the stage are well within one's own range of expression and vocabulary; the thoughts and emotions are conveyed in sentences one might easily hit upon oneself. But Shakespeare speaks with the tongue of angels; no ordinary mortal could hope to clothe his feelings in such a cloak of glory. The lines themselves are easy enough to learn, but it is not enough just to know them; they must become an integral part of one's way of thinking. One must breathe them, live them, absorb them into one's very blood, and then one may perhaps be able to speak them as though they were in truth one's very own.

If one thinks of Hamlet as a man in his thirties, the idea of a woman's attempting to play the part is of course ridiculous. But Hamlet's whole psychology has always seemed to me that of a youth rather than of a mature man. His melancholy, his thoughts of suicide, his hero-worship of his father, his mercurial changes of mood, and above all his jealous resentment at his mother's second marriage, are touching and understandable in a boy of nineteen, whereas in a man of thirty they indicate a weak and vacillating nature in no way admirable or attractive. . . .

It would be rare indeed to find a young actor in his teens, or even in his early twenties, capable of sustaining and projecting this many-faceted, arduous role. No matter how clearly he might understand it and feel himself akin to it, it is doubtful if his instrument would be powerful and resilient enough to translate his theories into practice. It is undoubtedly mainly for this reason that Hamlet is almost always presented as a mature man; and it is also for this reason that actresses have frequently undertaken to play the part. But it must be remembered that such performances can be acceptable only if the theory of Hamlet s youth is kept in mind. It is possible for an actress at the height of her powers to give the impression of being a boy, while having at her command all the craft, range, force, and subtlety which such great roles require. This has always been true of Rostand's *L'Aiglon*, which, with a few insignificant exceptions, has always been played by women; also De Musset's Lorenzaccio, and—in a very different mood—Barrie's Peter Pan. . . .

Every morning I set off on long rambles through the woods and fields of Weston, with my copy of *Hamlet* in my pocket. Often Marion Evensen accompanied me on these journeys and patiently cued me hour after hour. The evenings were spent perfecting the stage model. A young scenic-artist, Michael Weightman-Smith, was staying down at my old cottage, and together we worked out every detail of the production. I wanted the play to move swiftly, with no scene-waits and only one intermission. I had evolved a practical scheme that would permit this, and Michael Smith contributed the necessary decoration. The play was to be played in the Viking period; I took this idea from the King's lines in Act IV, Scene 3:

> *And, England, if my love thou hold'st at aught—*
> *As my great power thereof may give thee sense,*
> *Since yet thy cicatrice looks raw and red*
> *After the Danish sword, and thy free awe*
> *Pays homage to us—*

To enhance the crudeness of violence of the North of that period, we limited our colors to every conceivable shade of red, set off by black and varying shades of gray. To achieve the desirable roughness and sturdiness of texture, we decided to weave all the materials for the principal costumes ourselves, and both looms were put to work. A professional weaver in the neighborhood was put in charge of the largest loom, and Michael Smith, Marion Evensen, and I took turns at the smaller one, producing countless yards of various kinds of fabric. Some we wove in color, some Michael Smith dyed to the exact shade required. Even had we been able to buy such stuffs ready-made, the cost would have been far beyond the range of our slim budget; and besides, there was something wonderfully satisfying in producing for ourselves these rugged materials that conformed so completely to the ideas we had in mind. When, after weeks of work, we shipped the fruits of our labors to Hélène Pons, who was to execute the costumes, we glowed with pride at her appreciation of them, of the way they responded to her drapes and pleats and folds. Later, when many actors had to wear them on hot summer evenings, the epithets bestowed upon them were less flattering; their weight and substance were almost too authentic for modern comfort.

It was not easy to cast a play like *Hamlet*, even adequately, for a week's engagement in a summer theatre. Some of my old faithfuls from the Civic rallied round me, and I was lucky in finding a few talented young people who were eager for the chance. The problem of an Ophelia was difficult. I have rarely seen the part well played, even under the best of circumstances; I have seen it played only once to my complete satisfaction. Several young actresses read for me, but none of them had the quality I sought for, and the few that approached it were either unavailable or too expensive.

I then remembered a young girl I had seen some months before; she had written to me early in the year, requesting an audition. Her father was a professor at the University of Wisconsin; her mother was a singer and a fine musician; and both were willing that she should take up a stage career, but wanted the advice of an expert before finally committing themselves to full cooperation. They promised the child to send her to New York for a few days if she could persuade me to see her and give my opinion of her talent.

My first impulse was to refuse. I had given so many hundreds of auditions in connection with the free school at the Civic, and there is always a formidable number of young people who imagine themselves destined for greatness in the theatre, demanding help and encouragement. I was loath at that time to break my serenity, but there was something about this letter that intrigued me. The handwriting alone was full of character and individuality—an increasingly rare thing nowadays, when most young people seem incapable of writing at all. The phrasing of the letter too was striking; it was forthright, honest, and simple, and the choice of words was intelligent and original; one felt a personality there. So, in spite of my reluctance, I found myself answering in the affirmative.

One day in March the girl took the train to Westport and presented herself at my house. She was very young—only just seventeen—a tall, rather gawky creature, by no means pretty, but with a face that one remembered, large hands and feet, and the shy ungainly grace of a young colt. She was obviously very nervous but made a gallant attempt to conceal it. She had been born in Germany and spent her early childhood there, so her first selection was a scene from a play of Schiller's, which she spoke in German. I told her I was not sufficiently familiar with the language to judge her fairly in that medium. She then switched to English, which she spoke without an accent, and played the end of the trial scene from Shaw's *St. Joan*.

I was puzzled by her. She spoke Joan's speech quite badly; the effect was artificial and stilted, it was forced and unnatural, and yet I sensed in her an inner truth that very occasionally filtered through in a word or a look. I was disapponted in her reading, but for some reason I felt she was worth giving a little time to. I was ruthlessly honest with her, told her that I didn't believe a word of Joan's speech, talked to her about it, gave her a few pointers, and asked her to think it over for an hour. I left her to herself in the Blue Room and went about my business. At the end of an hour I returned, and she played the scene for me again.

The improvement was startling. Though the execution was clumsy and monotonous, it was no longer a piece of stilted elocution. The truth that had glimmered so faintly in the first reading now blazed up strongly, and the over-all effect was strangely moving. I felt that here was a real talent, crude and groping, but obviously sensitive to direction: the immediate change that my criticism had brought about was proof of that. The girl listened gravely to what I had to say, thanked me politely, and went off to catch her train. I watched her as she walked down the path to the taxi that was to take her to the station. There was something touching in that youthful, gallant little figure, so full of purpose.

In 1951, I went to a Theatre Guild opening in New Haven. It was the first night of Margaret Webster's production of *St. Joan* by Bernard Shaw. I had the joy of watching that same girl play that same scene. Her fourteen years of tireless work, her constant development as an artist and as a human being, were revealed in a performance of power and beauty, honesty and radiance, that held the audience spellbound and had them cheering at the end. The name of the girl is of course Uta Hagen, a name which I feel certain will rank among the truly great names of our theatre.

So, back in 1937, it was of little Uta Hagen that I thought when the problem of casting Ophelia threatened to become insuperable. I wrote to her parents and suggested that they allow her to come East and try out for the part. I made no promises, but said I would coach her for a week and then make my decision. She arrived full of eagerness, hope, and determination. What she lacked in experience she made up in a natural instinct for the theatre, in freshness and sincerity, and above all in a complete singleness of purpose. I made up my mind to take a chance on her and let her play the part.

Several of the principals came out to Westport prior to the official rehearsals, and we did much preliminary work there. My little cottage was completely "sold out"; it was practically a case of "standing room only." A few people, including Uta, stayed at Cobb's Mill, about a mile down the road. It was a busy, happy time. The looms were still hard at work turning out materials, and our professional weaver had quite a time eluding the many offers of unskilled labor thrust upon her; each actor wanted to weave a bit of his own costume. Uta turned out to be quite good at it and actually succeeded in weaving most of the stuff for her own dress.

At last the day came to move to Dennis and start work there. . . .

We had only two weeks of rehearsal, and we worked day and night. We were all of us too eager and excited to pay much attention to such things as Equity rulings; an official of that august body would have found it hard to prevent us from working beyond the eight hours allotted by law. I'm afraid I've always been something of a rebel as far as that's concerned. I dislike being told how long I may work; if there's a job to be done, and well done, one can't be bothered to count the hours.

Giorgio Santelli had joined us in Dennis, and James Harker, who played Laertes, and I worked for an hour each morning on our duel, under Giorgio's supervision, and another hour each evening. Giorgio had planned a most exciting fight, but it was a tricky one, and he kept us hard at it. It was terribly hot weather, and any superfluous fat we may either of us have possessed rolled off with the sweat, until we were both of us reduced to shadows.

The night of the dress rehearsal came, and it was on this occasion that I, for the first and last time, really "saw Ophelia plain." The sacred fire struck, and the child Uta was transported to a region which I well knew she would not set foot in again for many years to come. The company was electrified by her performance; they crowded round her after the rehearsal and overwhelmed her with excited praise. She seemed dazed, as though just awakened from a trance, and then, quite suddenly, she fainted.

I shared the actors' feelings about her performance, but I understood so well what had taken place that I felt I must prepare her for the certain disillusionment of the nights to come. As Bernhardt would have said, *"Dieu était là"*—God was there. But even with such a great actress as Bernhardt in her prime, such occasions were rare, and, "God" failing, she had infinite resources to fall back on that could make "God's" absence at least endurable. I knew how lonely, helpless, and lost Uta would feel, left to struggle on her own.

She listened patiently and with respect while I told her not to be surprised and disappointed if her subsequent performances failed to equal, or even approach, her inspired playing at dress rehearsal. However, I don't think she believed me. I knew how she felt; I had often been through the same thing. I remembered particularly my playing of Juliet's farewell scene in a preliminary rehearsal at Tree's Academy, at the age of fifteen. I too had been lifted up by some mysterious power that swept through me and transformed me and left me dazzled and bewildered and wildly happy; but it was many years before this magic power took hold of me again. When it happens it is an overwhelming experience; I've often thought it may be similar to what mystics describe as a "state of grace." Novices are sometimes favored with this sort of revelation, but it is only after years of discipline and prayer that it occurs with any frequency, and only the most spiritually evolved can hope to summon it at will.

The next night, after the opening, little Uta sat sobbing in her dressing room. She had given a good performance, indeed an amazing one for such an inexperienced child. Her father and mother, and her brother too, were all there from Wisconsin to see her make her debut; their faces glowed with happiness and pride. But God had not been there, and, in spite of all their loving praise, Uta felt alone, abandoned, and discouraged. The next day she kept saying to me, "What happened? Why couldn't I do what I did the night before? It seemed so easy then!" All week she played conscientiously and well; she tried hard and gave the very best she was capable of giving, but the heavens were closed, and God remained silent.

That was a thrilling week at Dennis; I shall never forget it. The theatre was crowded every night. I was aware that many people came out of curiosity, expecting to see a freak performance, a ridiculous sort of stunt; quite a number, I suspect, came prepared to scoff. But when the curtain fell at the end of the play, the silence for several moments was electric, and then the storm of applause broke loose and the shouts and "bravos" brought tears to my eyes. I have seldom been so happy, though I found the eight consecutive performances almost unbearably exhausting.

I was proud of the production; it had fire and pace and great excitement. Although the acting was uneven, there were some excellent performances. George Graham was a particularly good Polonius, and later played the part in Margaret Webster's production with Maurice Evans. Howard Wierum was a sympathetic Horatio, Donald Cameron an impressive Ghost, Marion Evensen a fine Gertrude, and I liked Victor Thorley as Fortinbras. Thomas Gomez promised at rehearsal to be a wonderful Claudius, but somehow his actual performance proved disappointing.

In spite of the distance from New York, several theatre managers came up to look us over. Two of them offered to take over the production. Mr. Lee Shubert wanted me to play a limited engagement on Broadway, to be followed by a long tour throughout the country. I shall always be ashamed that I had not the courage to accept this offer. Cowardice has never been among my major failings, but on this occasion I was a coward. I was not afraid of playing the part, could I have been left in peace to play it, and I had no fear of the public's reaction. But the thought of all the fuss and commotion and publicity, the quips of the columnists, the storm of controversy that a "female Hamlet" would in all likelihood provoke, filled me with dismay. I didn't feel strong enough to face it. For the first time in my life I felt vulnerable; perhaps I was growing up. Perhaps the ordeal by fire, while strengthening me in one way, had weakened me in another. Perhaps if both John Gielgud and Leslie Howard had not played Hamlet the preceding season, I might have felt different about it—at this moment it seemed particularly daring for a woman to step in and provoke inevitable comparisons. Perhaps, above all, the prospect of having to play the part eight times a week for several months appalled me, and this was probably the decisive factor in my refusal. If I could have played Hamlet in repertory, I think I might have been persuaded—perhaps, perhaps! At all events, I decided against it, and it is one of the very few decisions in my life that I have occasionally regretted. To play Hamlet for a week and then never again is like having a glimpse of a wonderful country without ever being allowed really to explore it. However, brief as it was, the glimpse was wonderful, and I am eternally grateful for it.

Angna Enters

[1907–   ]

AN INTRODUCTION

A NGNA ENTERS'S SOLO mime theatre, the Theatre of A. E., was the first of its kind since ancient Rome. Its outlines, impulses, and intentions have been preserved in the many drawings and costume sketches she has made, and in the notes for, descriptions of, and theories pertaining to her compositions that fill three autobiographies and the discursive work, *On Mime*. And so, though the quickening of life rhythms that happens when performer and audience breathe together in the space is no longer ours to have, enough remains to give us a strong sense of this unique one-woman theatre in which the arts of painter, designer, dramatist, and actor-dancer are combined.

Enters's earliest influences were Cubism, the writings of James Joyce and Gertrude Stein, whose work she saw in the pages of Margaret Anderson's *Little Review*, the new music of Stravinsky, and the modern dance of Ruth St. Denis (which her work was in some ways a rebellion against because, she thought, modern dancers "moved too much"). From the avant-garde, Enters learned that creation of new forms was not only permissible, it is, in many ways, essential to the emergence of a clear voice.

As a student at the Art Students League, her inability to find a satisfactory "purpose" for her painting had led her to study dance, thinking movement would help her understand line. Then movement became line as she started to create in mime. "When I began what I thought of as a search for *purpose* in painting it now seems in retrospect to have led naturally to mime, as in this medium I had a definite point of view. This was to convey the salient behavior of human beings, each within his own realm of time and place."[1]

In 1924, sharing the evening with other young artists, Enters premiered the first eleven of her "dance form" compositions. By 1926 she was able to have an evening to herself. She invested twenty-five dollars of her own money in the production, printing and distributing flyers to people selected from the New York telephone directory as living in the vicinity of the theatre she rented. The program was a success, paying back the initial investment and winning for her the critical notice on which she began to build reputation and career. For the next thirty years she toured the American and European continents, performing and building her repertoire, painting and writing. Often her musical collaborator Madeleine Marshall was with her.

Her compositions cover an enormous range of time—from Greek to medieval to Renaissance to modern—and subject matter—from Catholic saints and boy cardinals to victims of the Inquisition; aristocratic, peasant, and bourgeois women and girls in all manner of pursuits. As a woman, women and sometimes boys were the characters she portrayed. The masculine presence in her stage world is secondary, seen through its effect upon the women in her pieces as they relate to, remember, wait for, or run from (imagined) men. All her character studies, while carefully constructed around the feeling of a particular age, were meant to reveal timeless, universal traits. Though her initial inspiration and liberation came from the avant-garde, Enters's own sensibility is classical (by which I do not mean antiquated but, rather, concerned less with questions of form than with the essence of human *being* and *becoming*).

"Modern art," she writes, "did not *create* form and I do not see where its recognitions of form are more perceptive, or superior. . . . Painting, as form, is more difficult when you work with a human face than a jug. It is to me quite symbolic that a majority of great painters were concerned with living human beings, and that certain workers in the modern movement are so concerned with *nature morte.*"[2]

It is as theorist and practitioner of the art of character creation that Enters's writing has enduring, illuminating interest for dramatists and actors both. Her life-long search for the "classic-line," a term borrowed from painting, might be translated as her understanding of character as "psyche in motion." She strove to give the inner human essence a physical form through which it could be seen and comprehended by the audience. She wanted, that is, to reveal the most intimate feelings of an individual life to the company of the living.

In this attempt her own personality played scant part. Her work, though intensely personal because she chose and executed it all, was not meant as personal expression. Rather, it expressed the actor's will and the wish, timeless and for all time, to experience the mystery of human life by the selfless act of becoming so available to another presence that it animates one's own.

—K.M.

Angna Enters

[1907–]

SELECTIONS

From *Angna Enters: On Mime*

Overture

Mimesis is the representation of reality by means of actions, with or without words. It is that form of theatre in which the actor-as-dramatist delineates characters *of his own creation.*

The mime is not an imitator. He enlarges, emphasizes, particularizes, comments on the character he portrays. It is as though images in the creator's memory, or flashes of vision, acting as catalytic agents, suddenly decide to have a being of their own. Then the creator-as-performer has to release these images to take their own shape, using whatever theatre forms are necessary to their realization.

In that sense, these images-become-characters are symbols: symbols natural to the reality of performer and audience; characters who are our brothers and sisters in whatever time, place, or theme—in the sense, say, that Madame Bovary is a character created by Flaubert and is also an individual unto herself, part of our collective imagination.

In mime, communication with the outside world is made by means of gesture-symbols.

These symbols are the result of the crystallization of experiences all men and women are heir to. They are a kind of semaphoric code—gesture, smile, glance, reflective thought, or physical action—by which we understand one another.

Mime is the oldest and the youngest means of dramatic expression, and the most generally universal. It lends itself in the theatre to every form, yet it retains its own form.

It is an elusive art, as its expression is entirely dependent on the imagination of the performer in the re-creation of his view of the character each time he performs.

Mime—or pantomime—is not the one best means of theatre expression. It is best only for that for which there are no words or for which too many words would be required.

THE MIME AND THE POET

The mime and the poet have this in common—the image. The mime consolidates his image through nuances of expression, for which words are at most symbols; the poet transmits his image in the association of words in composition.

The viewers of the mime capture his meaning within the elasticity of their own understanding, just as the hearers of the poet relate each image to individual experience.

There are nuances of human exchange in which mime is the most direct medium of communication, and there are word images which mime can never approximate. The mime and the poet additionally have this in common: their *purpose,* and its relationship to music.

The *meter* of the mime to his image is as composed as that of a poet to his.

PAST AND PRESENT

Mime is a many-sided medium, and what I give here is but one mime's approach to that medium. My approach is that in mime one can present images of women and men in characteristic personal moments of their being in contrapuntal relation to a particular moment in time, and at the same time crystallize a kind of similarity in human behavior down through the ages. As I wrote some years ago, my purpose is:

To give personal form to a general experience.

To make the present visible by using it to telescope what in the past was then present. It was necessary to see the past through the present, for we see what has been in terms of our own being in the present.

Thus the past would emerge as present, disclosing the essential continuity of the nature of man. The modes, manners, and rhythms were merely masks, beneath which were the old familiar universal faces of man and woman.

A mode or manner can be concrete as a stone, which when dropped in the sea of human behavior makes a whirlpool in which is swallowed a whole generation and, in time, a civilization.

Yet there always is a thread with that past. In painting it is "the classic line" which emerges as "modern." And in modes and manners it is always human behavior which emerges as contemporary. Of course every age considered itself modern—even when it didn't think about it.

Topical telescoping of the past in terms of the present was characteristic of the Greek dramatists when they retold the sacred myths in terms of their own time. Very faint was the allegory to the political tyrannies, social foibles, and idiocies of their own day.

Using a past period as a mirror one might succeed in seeing—in showing—one's own time.[*]

THE CLASSIC LINE
(Journal note—8th June, 1933)

Am tormented by elusive abstraction known as the "classic line." What is it? No matter how much one reads about it, or sees it, or recognizes it in others' achievements, it remains the unknown so far as one's own work is concerned. It is the true and perfect and variable line of life no matter how it is employed. One must find it for oneself like a child learning to walk. Applying it literally to a drawing one discovers that if one had a perfect photographic eye and could draw a figure exactly as though one had measured it, or placed a string around the form of the body, that it inevitably would be a dull lifeless drawing. The important thing is not the exact outline, but a line which suggests the fullnesses, thinnesses, the forms and solids which make each figure itself. All this theorizing is a release—a kind of cutting away of "tradition"—to one's instinctive approach.[**]

Aside: From Whence?

On tour the TV interviewer asked, "Tell me, how do you get your ideas?" This question is often asked by the press and others, although the phrase more often is: "From where?"

One ought to be prepared with some short, reasonably adequate response, but I am always caught unawares and find myself at a loss. I say "at a loss" because the question seems to presuppose that there is a succinct explanation—a methodical route easily retraceable by others. The truth is that I do not go in search of ideas. I do not know where they hide and must wait for them to find me. When they do come, I accept or reject them or, not immediately grasping their portent, lay them aside to lie in the womb that is memory until some spark causes them to fecundate. Sometimes an idea

---

[*]From Angna Enters, *Silly Girl: A Portrait of Personal Remembrance* (Boston: Houghton Mifflin, 1944).

[**]From Angna Enters, *First Person Plural* (New York: Stackpole Sons, 1937).

materializes as if it were a sudden spring shower let loose from an accumulation of thought clouds; at other times it may strike as a sudden gale which, on a fine bright day, blows up from nowhere.

To this interviewer, being again unprepared to meet what experience should have taught was an inevitable question, I committed the unpardonable sin of television and radio: I sat stricken in silence. My inquisitor, happily, was equal to the situation and came to my rescue. "You mean," she said, "that you are just sitting minding your own business and an idea comes and hits you on the head?"

I confessed that it was the perfect answer, and said that I wished I could have thought of it myself.

We laughed in mutual understanding—her perception undoubtedly stemming from her own inability to account for similar sensations—those vagrant thoughts and intuitions which sometimes consolidate into definite form.

Later, remembering this exchange, it seemed to me that the question so often arises because of the popular but mistaken notion that mime involves a process by which the performer goes about with a memory-camera, photographing interesting subjects encountered on travels far and near; or, for lack of a selective eye, translates into mime portraits of characters discovered in history, drama, or literature. Although these are legitimate, if somewhat limiting, sources of material, I do not function in this manner. I do not claim mine is the better route; but mine, though more complex, is the natural one for me. Like a poet, novelist, or dramatist, I become interested in the aspect of a mood or some facet of human behavior, and am led, largely through intuition, to invent a character who will best symbolize what I wish to convey. This character, whatever its visual form, whether abstract or literal, represents not only itself but the age and society in which it lives. The genesis of any character remains a constant in my memory, so that each time I perform it is as though it were revealing itself to me for the first time. I never lose interest in its potentialities, and I take it for granted that the viewer watches with the same obsession with the character that I too have.

Aside: The Air is a Solid

I have no way of knowing how other performers effect projection of their idea—or character—but for me this is a tactile thing, which I shall endeavor to explain.

I have heard here and there of a theory that performers must develop a sense of freedom in space. That is, they must feel unhampered by a fearful sense of being stranded alone in a strange void, the void of the stage itself, which extends out into space occupied by the audience.

My own feeling about space is quite the opposite. To me the air is a solid, but an elastic solid, comparable to the clay prepared by the modeler before he begins his work. It is a resilient medium, on which I can imprint my meaning; and beyond that, it has curious electric properties—it carries the intention of this imprint outward, in a kind of telegraphic code—in a message to myself as the entire audience from myself as the instrument of the character performed.

To me, this is no obscure, esoteric theory, but tangible reality.

I must try to clarify this by saying that, as mime, and apart from the character, I am a dual personality. That is, I exist both as the instrument through which the character reveals him-her-or-itself and as the one and only audience beyond the footlights. It is to me, as alter ego, that the character reveals himself. That others are present is only incidental, and their responses are no more than repercussions resulting from the spark of communication between the character and myself.

When I, acting as the physical instrument through which the character reveals himself, make a gesture—any movement, even a glance or a smile—I have a tactile sense of its engraving an indelible imprint on the air, no matter how fleeting the impulse which sends it forth.

This is not so abstruse as it may first seem, for to everyone, images of movements and their meanings remain in memory long after they have transpired. We remember the flight of a bird long after it has disappeared from sight. Thus to me the air is not space, but a tangible and sympathetic medium in which to imprint the image of my imagination—an image which I hope the beholder will continue to experience in memory just as the voyager after his trip experiences as though still present the color and sparkle of the sea, the feeling of its surges, and the thoughts brought on by speculation on the contents of its fearsome depths.

Let me hasten to add that I do not consider my perception, as audience to the character, greater than that of other viewers; but I do assume that whatever fascinates me about the aspects of any character I perform may arouse interest in them. I am totally devoid of any talent for conjecturing what may please an audience and can only, like Carmen, sing to please myself.

Criticism
Sympathy & Imagination

Emma Goldman

Rosamond Gilder

Emma Goldman

[1869–1940]

AN INTRODUCTION

I F ANARCHIST, feminist, antimilitarist Emma Goldman possessed an understanding of the importance of drama rare among modern-day radicals, she also possessed qualities of sympathetic entry into works of art all too rare among critics. Unlike the objective, distanced, judgmental critic, Goldman reveals herself, her own desires, dreams, and fears as fully as she does each play she writes about. And so she understands, with an immediacy the purely academic critic denies, how it is that art directly affects life. Drama, she knew, is political by its nature. Since the play takes place in a public forum (the theatre) and always concerns individual characters in relationship to social/spiritual/economic forces, it is always either in support of the status quo or it envisions another way. The better the drama the more astutely political it is going to be, since it confronts the deepest of the personal sufferings brought about by the inequities of social life.

Published in 1914, *The Social Significance of the Modern Drama* includes essays on nineteen playwrights from Scandinavia, Germany, England, Ireland, and Russia. Much of this work was undertaken in the years 1901–1903 when Goldman was living anonymously as "Miss Smith" in New York City and practicing as a nurse-midwife. She had been forced into hiding by her ouspoken sympathy for Leon Czolgosz, the young assassin of President McKinley (not for his act, but for his plight). As the most well known anarchist in the country, and nearly the only person courageous enough to care about the torture Czolgosz was enduring, she was hounded and harassed into the underground. Alone, she took refuge in the great plays of the period, finding in them the hope that was not then in her life.

Goldman's autobiography, *Living My Life,* is now a classic of the form; her essays on anarchism and women's liberation have had seminal influences on the New Left and current feminist movements. In these writings, and in the lectures she delivered to working women and men before she was deported in 1919, she makes her love of the drama frequently known. Goldman was of Russian Jewish parentage. Like many eastern European immigrants to these shores she brought a close familiarity with great contemporary and classic art. (In the early years of this century, one could hear entire plays recited from memory in the cafes of the Lower East Side.) Goldman was convinced that a people without a vibrant, living culture could not find the strength of heart, mind, or imagination to build the new world in the shell of the old. Her book of essays on the drama, which has been out-of-print for many years, was intended to acquaint Americans with those who, to her mind, were the greatest of contemporary European dramatists, so that this country, too, might begin to develop a tradition of respect for drama of social transformation.

Perhaps the most startling essay in the book concerns Strindberg. In it the feminist Emma Goldman embraces the self-defined misogynist. She enters his work with the same care for his intents as she had for those of Ibsen or Shaw. Once more her sympathetic entry serves her well. Her analysis of Strindberg is as compelling as her ability to feel and think along with all those who suffered and who spoke their truth.

While this type of nonjudgmental, illuminating criticism—arrived at through a sympathetic entry into a work of art—reveals a great deal about the artist, it reveals a great deal about the critic, too. Self-revelation is, in fact, how such criticism is accomplished. The critic makes herself vulnerable to the work, allowing it to touch the primal fears and desires inside herself. Emma Goldman understands Strindberg as she does because she, too, was a child brutalized by a mother unfulfilled. By rendering herself vulnerable to the artist's own obsession, the critic becomes capable of being deeply moved. Only then can she partake in the healing energy of art, and only then can the critic share with us her own sense of the work as powerful and transformative.

—K.M.

Emma Goldman
[1869–1940]

SELECTIONS

From *The Social Significance of the Modern Drama*

Foreword

The modern artist is, in the words of August Strindberg, "a lay preacher popularizing the pressing questions of his time." Not necessarily because his aim is to proselyte, but because he can best express himself by being true to life.

Millet, Meunier, Turgenev, Dostoyevsky, Emerson, Walt Whitman, Tolstoy, Ibsen, Strindberg, Hauptmann, and a host of others mirror in their work as much of the spiritual and social revolt as is expressed by the most fiery speech of the propagandist. And more important still, they compel far greater attention. Their creative genius, imbued with the spirit of sincerity and truth, strikes root where the ordinary word often falls on barren soil.

The reason that many radicals as well as conservatives fail to grasp the powerful message of art is perhaps not far to seek. The average radical is as hidebound by mere terms as the man devoid of all ideas. "Bloated plutocrats," "economic determinism," "class consciousness," and similar expressions sum up for him the symbols of revolt. But since art speaks a language of its own, a language embracing the entire gamut of human emotions, it often sounds meaningless to those whose hearing has been dulled by the din of stereotyped phrases.

On the other hand, the conservative sees danger only in the advocacy of the Red Flag. He has too long been fed on the historic legend that it is only the "rabble" which makes revolutions, and not those who wield the brush or pen. It is therefore legitimate to applaud the artist and hound the rabble. Both radical and conservative have to learn that any mode of creative work, which with true perception portrays social wrongs earnestly and boldy, may

From *The Social Significance of the Modern Drama* by Emma Goldman (Richard G. Badger Press, 1914).

be a greater menace to our social fabric and a more powerful inspiration than the wildest harangue of the soapbox orator.

Unfortunately, we in America have so far looked upon the theatre as a place of amusement only, exclusive of ideas and inspiration. Because the modern drama of Europe has till recently been inaccessible in printed form to the average theatre-goer in this country, he had to content himself with the interpretation, or rather misinterpretation, of our dramatic critics. As a result the social significance of the Modern Drama has well nigh been lost to the general public.

As to the native drama, America has so far produced very little worthy to be considered in a social light. Lacking the cultural and evolutionary tradition of the Old World, America has necessarily first to prepare the soil out of which sprouts creative genius.

The hundred and one springs of local and sectional life must have time to furrow their common channel into the seething sea of life at large, and social questions and problems make themselves felt, if not crystallized, before the throbbing pulse of the big national heart can find its reflex in a great literature—and specifically in the drama—of a social character. This evolution has been going on in this country for a considerable time, shaping the widespread unrest that is now beginning to assume more or less definite social form and expression.

Therefore, America could not so far produce its own social drama. But in proportion as the crystallization progresses, and sectional and national questions become clarified as fundamentally social problems, the drama develops. Indeed, very commendable beginnings in this direction have been made within recent years, among them *The Easiest Way*, by Eugene Walter, *Keeping Up Appearances*, and other plays by Butler Davenport, *Nowadays* and two other volumes of one-act plays, by George Middleton—attempts that hold out an encouraging promise for the future.

The Modern Drama, as all modern literature, mirrors the complex struggle of life—the struggle which, whatever its individual or topical expression, ever has its roots in the depth of human nature and social environment, and hence is, to that extent, universal. Such literature, such drama, is at once the reflex and the inspiration of mankind in its eternal seeking for things higher and better. Perhaps those who learn the great truths of the social travail in the school of life, do not need the message of the drama. But there is another class whose number is legion, for whom that message is indispensable. In countries where political oppression affects all classes, the best intellectual element have made common cause with the people, have become their teachers, comrades, and spokesmen. But in America political pressure has so far affected only the "common" people. It is they who are thrown into prison; they who are persecuted and mobbed, tarred and deported. Therefore another medium is needed to arouse the intellectuals of this country, to make them realize their relation to the people, to the social unrest permeating the atmosphere.

The medium which has the power to do that is the Modern Drama, because it mirrors every phase of life and embraces every strata of society—the Modern Drama, showing each and all caught in the throes of the tremendous changes going on, and forced either to become part of the process or be left behind.

Ibsen, Strindberg, Hauptmann, Tolstoy, Shaw, Galsworthy, and the other dramatists contained in this volume represent the social iconoclasts of our time. They know that society has gone beyond the stage of patching up, and that man must throw off the dead weight of the past, with all its ghosts and spooks, if he is to go foot free to meet the future.

This is the social significance which differentiates modern dramatic art from art for art's sake. It is the dynamite which undermines superstition, shakes the social pillars, and prepares men and women for the reconstruction.

Strindberg

"The reproach was levelled against my tragedy, *The Father*, that it was so sad, as though one wanted merry tragedies. People clamour for the joy of life, and the theatrical managers order farces, as though the joy of life consisted in being foolish, and in describing people as if they were each and all afflicted with St. Vitus's dance or idiocy. I find the joy of life in the powerful, cruel struggle of life, and my enjoyment in discovering something, in learning something."

The passionate desire to discover something, to learn something, has made of August Strindberg a keen dissector of souls. Above all, of his own soul.

Surely there is no figure in contemporary literature, outside of Tolstoy, that laid bare the most secret nooks and corners of his own soul with the sincerity of August Strindberg. One so relentlessly honest with himself, could be no less with others.

That explains the bitter opposition and hatred of his critics. They did not object so much to Strinberg's self-torture; but that he should have dared to torture *them,* to hold up his searching mirror to *their* sore spots, that they could not forgive.

Especially is this true of woman. For centuries she has been lulled into a trance by the songs of the troubadours who paid homage to her goodness, her sweetness, her selflessness and, above all, her noble motherhood. And though she is beginning to appreciate that all this incense has befogged her mind and paralyzed her soul, she hates to give up the tribute laid at her feet by sentimental moonshiners of the past.

To be sure, it is rude to turn on the full searchlight upon a painted face. But how is one to know what is back of the paint and artifice? August Strindberg hated artifice with all the passion of his being; hence his severe criticism of woman. Perhaps it was his tragedy to see her as she really is, and not as she appears in her trance. To love with open eyes is, indeed, a tragedy, and Strindberg loved woman. All his life long he yearned for her love, as mother, as wife, as companion. But his longing for, and his need of her, were the crucible of Strindberg, as they have been the crucible of every man, even of the mightiest spirit.

Why it is so is best expressed in the words of the old nurse, Margret, in *The Father*: "Because all you men, great and small, are woman's children, every man of you."

The child in man—and the greater the man the more dominant the child in him—has ever succumbed to the Earth Spirit, Woman, and as long as that is her only drawing power, Man, with all his strength and genius, will ever be at her feet.

The Earth Spirit is motherhood carrying the race in its womb; the flame of life luring the moth, often against its will, to destruction.

In all of Strindberg's plays we see the flame of life at work, ravishing man's brain, consuming man's faith, rousing man's passion. Always, always the flame of life is drawing its victims with irresistible force. August Strindberg's arraignment of that force is at the same time a confession of faith. He, too, was the child of woman, and utterly helpless before her.

THE FATHER

The Father portrays the tragedy of a man and a woman struggling for the possession of their child. The father, a cavalry captain, is intellectual, a freethinker, a man of ideas. His wife is narrow, selfish, and unscrupulous in her methods when her antagonism is wakened. . . .

Critics have pronounced *The Father* an aberration of Strindberg's mind, utterly false and distorted. But that is because they hate to face the truth. In Strindberg, however, the truth is his most revolutionary significance.

The Father contains two basic truths. Motherhood, much praised, poetized, and hailed as a wonderful thing, is in reality very often the greatest deterrent influence in the life of the child. Because it is not primarily concerned with the potentialities of character and growth of the child; on the contrary, it is interested chiefly in the birthgiver—that is, the mother. Therefore, the mother is the most subjective, self-centered and conservative obstacle. She binds the child to herself with a thousand threads which never grant sufficient freedom for mental and spiritual expansion. It is not necessary to be as bitter as Strindberg to realize this. There are of course exceptional mothers who continue to grow with the child. But the average mother is like the hen with her brood, forever fretting about her chicks if they venture a step away from the coop. The mother enslaves with kindness—a bondage harder to bear and more difficult to escape than the brutal fist of the father.

Strindberg himself experienced it, and nearly every one who has ever attempted to outgrow the soul strings of the mother.

In portraying motherhood, as it really is, August Strindberg is conveying a vital and revolutionary message, namely, that true motherhood even as fatherhood, does not consist in molding the child according to one's image, or in imposing upon it one's own ideas and notions, but in allowing the child freedom and opportunity to grow harmoniously according to its own potentialities, unhampered and unmarred.

The child was August Strindberg's religion—perhaps because of his own very tragic childhood and youth. He was like Father Time in *Jude the Obscure*, a giant child, and as he has Laura say of the the Captain in *The Father*, "he had either come too early into the world, or perhaps was not wanted at all."

"Yes, that's how it was," the Captain replies, "my father's and my mother's will was against my coming into the world, and consequently I was born without a will."

The horror of having been brought into the world undesired and unloved, stamped its indelible mark on August Strindberg. It never left him. Nor did fear and hunger—the two terrible phantoms of his childhood.

Indeed, the child was Strindberg's religion, his faith, his passion. Is it then surprising that he should have resented woman's attitude towards the man as a mere means to the child; or, in the words of Laura, as "the function of father and breadwinner"? That this is the attitude of woman, is of course denied. But it is nevertheless true. It holds good not only of the average, unthinking woman, but even of many feminists of today; and, no doubt, they were even more antagonistic to the male in Strindberg's time.

It is only too true that woman is paying back what she has endured for centuries—humiliation, subjection, and bondage. But making oneself free through the enslavement of another, is by no means a step toward advancement. Woman must grow to understand that the father is as vital a factor in the life of the child as is the mother. Such a realization would help very much to minimize the conflict between the sexes.

Of course, that is not the only cause of the conflict. There is another, as expressed by Laura: "Do you remember when I first came into your life, I was like a second mother?. . . I loved you as my child. But. . . when the nature of your feelings changed and you appeared as my lover, I blushed, and your embraces were joy that was followed by remorseful conscience as if my blood were ashamed."

The vile thought instilled into woman by the Church and Puritanism that sex expression without the purpose of procreation is immoral, has been a most degrading influence. It has poisoned the life of thousands of women who similarly suffer "remorseful conscience"; therefore their disgust and hatred of the man; therefore also the conflict.

Must it always be thus? Even Strindberg does not think so. Else he would not plead in behalf of "divorce between man and wife so that lovers may be born." He felt that until man and woman cease to have "remorseful consciences" because of the most elemental expression of the joy of life, they cannot realize the purity and beauty of sex, nor appreciate its ecstasy, as the source of full understanding and creative harmony between male and female. Till then man and woman must remain in conflict, and the child pay the penalty.

August Strindberg, as one of the numberless innocent victims of this terrible conflict, cries out bitterly against it, with the artistic genius and strength that compel attention to the significance of his message.

Rosamond Gilder

[1891–   ]

AN INTRODUCTION

THE FIRST WOMAN PLAYWRIGHT in Europe was a woman, the tenth-century Benedictine nun Hrotsvitha of Gandersheim. Hrotsvitha's plays on Catholic themes provide the only links beween the Roman comedies of Terence, whose forms she sought to purify with the new morality, and the emergence of the medieval mystery plays in the twelfth century. Yet Hrotsvitha is often dismissed as a freak curiosity. It's said that her plays were never staged. Samuel Johnson's infamous misogynist platitude comparing a woman preacher to a dog who walks on two legs, "You don't expect them to do it well, it's surprising they do it at all," is often quoted about her.

It has taken another woman, Rosamond Gilder, to treat the story of Hrotsvitha and her playwriting work with the serious critical acumen each demands. Because Gilder has paid attention to the merits of the work, she comes to the conclusion that the plays *were* staged, else how could they have been so stageworthy? And because she refuses to see Hrotsvitha's plays as simply a freak phenomenon, she delves into questions of their influences and origins, finding that other women taught, encouraged, and inspired Hrotsvitha. The link between the Greco-Roman dramatic tradition and Hrotsvitha's work, she discovers, is the Empress Theophano, who brought knowledge of the drama to Gandersheim from Constantinople, where theatre was still sanctioned by the Church.

"Sympathy and imagination" are the qualities Gilder says are necessary to arrive at an understanding of Hrotsvitha's work. They also give her criticism a life that extends beyond judgment, description, and even illumination into the realm of the theory of art, where the art of criticism finds its own voice.

In the opening passages of her essay, Gilder equates the medieval Catholic Church's fear of the theatre with its fear of women, intimating the early, essential connection between the beginnings of drama and the pagan societies in which women's creative power was revered. Later, as she discus-

75

ses Hrotsvitha's plays individually, Gilder explains sadism as the fascination of those who repress erotic energy, foreshadowing what is a central feminist understanding. Then she remarks upon Hrotsvitha's language, quoting from the plays to show the writer's "ability to convey profound feelings" simply and directly. Again, it seems to me, Gilder touches upon a crucial strength of women's writing throughout time.

From 1924 to 1948 Rosamond Gilder was assistant editor, drama critic, and then editor of *Theatre Arts Monthly*, the magazine founded by Edith Isaacs. In 1931 Gilder published *Enter the Actress*, from which this essay is taken; it was reissued in 1961, and is a classic text of theatre history.

—K. M.

Rosamond Gilder

[1891–   ]

SELECTION

From *Enter the Actress*

Hrotsvitha, A Tenth-Century Nun

THE FIRST WOMAN PLAYWRIGHT

Although the early Christian Church welcomed to its bosom certain re-
pentant actresses, it was on the whole the mortal enemy of the theatre. The
war between Church and stage has been long and bitter, particularly in the
early days when the theatre represented the last entrenched camp of
paganism, and as such was the subject of virulent attack and condemnation.
The Church desired nothing less than the complete annihilation of its
enemy, and in this, by the close of the fourth century, it had largely succeeded. It is therefore not a little diverting to find that the first woman of
any importance in the history of the theatre in Europe is a Benedictine nun.
From the darkest of the dark ages of the theatre, as well as of Western civilization, the work of only one playwright has come down to us intact. The six
plays of Hrotsvitha of Gandersheim stand alone, bridging the gulf between
Seneca and the *Representatio Adae*, between the Latin tragedy of A.D. 65,
and the French mystery play of the twelfth century of the Christian era.
Whatever plays were written and acted, whatever playwrights, actors and
impresarios flourished during these centuries, Hrotsvitha's comedies alone
have survived in their complete and original form. Hrotsvitha the Nun, devout daughter of the Church that sought to destroy the theatre, Hrotsvitha,
"German religious and virgin of the Saxon race," Hrotsvitha, the "strong
voice of Gandersheim," confined in a remote convent and following the
rules of a strict religious order, is yet the first woman of the theatre, the patron saint of the motley followers of Thalia and Melpomene.

The curious anomaly that has placed this devout and dedicated nun of Europe's darkest period in the hierarchy of notable playwrights of all time, grows only more interesting as it is more closely studied. Every circumstance of time and place, of surrounding atmosphere, of education and of outlook would, at first glance, make such a phenomenon seem impossible, so impossible, indeed, that historians of the drama have almost unanimously dismissed Hrotsvitha as, artistically, a "sport," without literary or spiritual issue, and therefore of slight importance. Other scholars, more pedantic than accurate, have classed her plays as forgeries, solving the problem presented in her work by denying that she had ever existed. Unfortunately for those who prefer simple classifications and sweeping statements to the vagaries of actual events, this last assumption is untenable.

The manuscript of Hrotsvitha's collected writings, discovered by Conrad Celtes in the Benedictine monastery of Saint Emmeran, Ratisbon, in 1492 or '93, and now reposing in the Munich Library, is authentically of the tenth century. Celtes published his find in 1501, embellishing the book with woodcuts which have been attributed to Dürer. The most interesting of these pictures is the frontispiece, which shows Hrotsvitha presenting her manuscript to Otto II, with the Abbess Gerberga leaning protectingly over the kneeling nun. Not to be overshadowed by his protégée, Celtes included a companion picture of himself, in which he in turn is shown in the act of presenting the first printed edition of Hrotsvitha's works to his own liege lord. The most important modern edition of the plays is that of Charles Magnin, who, in 1845, published the plays in the original Latin with a complete French translation and a biographical and critical study of Hrotsvitha's works. There are several recent English translations of the plays, so that Hrotsvitha has at last come into her own. Her existence has not only been established beyond a doubt, but her curious and delightful contribution to the literature of the theatre has become part of the heritage of the stage. With the venerable scholar Henricus Bodo, first commentator on the writings of the Nun of Gandersheim, we who read her plays for the first time will be tempted to exclaim, "Rara avis in Saxonia visa est!"

In order to appreciate fully the strength of that impulse for expression in dramatic form which must have impelled Hrotsvitha in her choice of so extraordinary a medium, we must realize what sort of world surrounded her and appreciate some of the handicaps with which she was burdened. She lived at the parting of the ways, a time of stress and strain between the collapse of the old order and the birth of the new. Europe, beaten upon by Northmen, Magyars, and Saracens, had at last repelled these marauders and won a respite from invasion. The crumbling Roman Empire had fallen apart, and a Saxon Emperor ruled a turbulent and disorganized band of feudal barons in the West. With the increasing power of the Christian Church, the last vestiges of the theatre in Italy had disappeared. It had split into its component parts, and bands of mimes, jugglers, dancers, and buffoons earned a precarious livelihood by traveling from place to place entertaining bored women and war-worn, brutish lords in the great halls of their feudal castles. The Roman theatre buildings themselves, scattered throughout Italy and Southern France, had been turned into donjon keeps—fortified castles for the protection of each man against his neighbor. The old order of the Roman world was destroyed and a new order had not yet come to take its place.

The Church itself was distracted with schisms and heresies, and its fight against paganism, in the theatre and elsewhere, was hardly more bitter than its internal conflicts. Wars, famines, and plagues completed the sufferings of the unfortunate lower orders, creating a universal chaos that has made this period seem to historians the most miserable that has afflicted the Western world. In such troubled and violent times, the convents and monasteries, which were growing up throughout Europe, were almost the only centers of culture and education that existed. The Christian Church, while doing its utmost to discredit the iniquitous literature of the pagans, was at the same time beginning to preserve it, and to act as guardians of the precious manuscripts which, in Europe at least, were all that remained as witness of past intellectual glories.

The fate of the women of the Dark Ages was necessarily harsh. A period which depended almost exclusively on its fighting men for survival had little interest in the development of the more peaceful arts and small time for the amenities of living. A woman at the time when Hrotsvitha lived was, in the eyes of men, a weak and foolish creature, useful only for the transmission of property, and the production of offspring. In the eyes of the Church, she was something more sinister than this. The venom with which the Church Fathers attacked the theatre was only surpassed by the vitriolic intensity with which they damned the female of the species and all her natural functions. Only one hope of redemption was held out to the unfortunate creature who through Eve's original weakness had brought sin and sorrow into the world. She must renounce this mundane existence and all its so-called pleasures, and vow herself to an eternal chastity, a virginity in this world mitigated by the hope of a spiritual union with the Beloved Bridegroom in the world to come.

The alternative careers which presented themselves to a woman such as Hrotsvitha in the year of grace 950 were strictly limited. She must either consent to be married off by her nearest male relative to some strong-armed warrior-baron who would acquire her property and her person simultaneously, and who would exercise a complete and unquestioned control over her whole future existence, or she might enter a religious order, where the questionable privilege of serving an earthy lord would be exchanged for the sure joys of a heavenly dedication. More compelling still, the convent gave her an opportunity for immediate intellectual development, the companionship of men and women keenly interested in the things of the mind, and the peaceful security of an ordered existence, nowhere else to be found. Monastic life, though physically restricting, was along certain lines intellectually liberating, and offered many of the inducements that college and career hold out to the young girl of today.

The Abbey of Gandersheim would be particularly attractive to an eager and enterprising mind such as Hrotsvitha's. It was an oasis in a turbulent world, a center of light and learning, of hope and peace, in the midst of danger and damnation. Founded in 850 by Ludolph, Duke of Saxony, it had already in Hrotsvitha's day acquired a unique literary and aristocratic tradition. Its abbesses were drawn from the imperial family of Saxony and held their fief directly from the King. They provided men-at-arms for their overlord, struck coins bearing their own image, and exercised all the rights and privileges of feudal barons. The close connection between the Imperial Court and the Abbey of Gandersheim brought it into the full current of the intellectual development of the day, and there is little reason to doubt that Hrotsvitha entered it the more eagerly because she knew that there she would be under the guidance of nuns who were as famed for their learning as they were for their piety.

Exactly when Hrotsvitha entered the Abbey of Gandersheim is not known, nor is there any record of her life before she took the veil. The dates of her birth and death, her family name, and all the details of her life are equally obscure, but in the brief forewords with which she enlivens her collected writings, we have a vivid impression of this extraordinary nun whose fate it was to play so unexpected a role in the history of the theatre. In thus inaugurating the delightful custom of writing prefaces to her plays, Hrotsvitha has given us what knowledge we have of her personality and her methods of work. She tells us that she was older than the Abbess Gerberga, who was born in 940, and from certain references in the texts of her poems, it is evident that she lived into the first years of the eleventh century, probably entering the convent about 960 when she was in her early twenties. She was undoubtedly of gentle birth, for Gandersheim was an aristocratic institution, welcoming the daughters of barons and lords, and presided over by an imperial princess. Moreover, her plays show familiarity with the amenities of life in the world beyond the cloister, and her education itself in an almost illiterate age attests her social standing. If, as her biographers believe, she was twenty-two or three when she took the veil, she had perhaps already experienced some of the joys and sorrows of that world which she renounced in her vows, but which, as her writings testify, she never entirely forgot.

On entering the convent, Hrotsvitha began her studies under the "learned and gentle novice-mistress, Rikkarda," but evidently she soon outstripped her teacher, for it is the Abbess Gerberga herself who introduced her to the classic literature which was to inspire her most famous work. She had other teachers as well, very possibly some learned monks and clerics from neighboring monasteries; but it was in secret, and in those quiet moments which must have been difficult to secure in the carefully apportioned and supervised routine of a nun's existence, that she began her writing. "Unknown to all around me," she explains in the preface* to her first poems, "I have toiled in secret, often destroying what seemed to me ill written, and rewriting it. . . . Up to the present I have not submitted the work to any experts, much as I needed their advice, for fear that the roughness of the style would make them discourage me to such an extent that I might give up writing altogether." Though young "both in years and learning," Hrotsvitha showed already a notable self-reliance. Even in this preface, her humility, the proper attitude of a woman and a nun, is mitigated by her very sense of her own deserts: "Although [Latin] prosody may seem a hard and difficult art for a woman to master, I, without any assistance but that given by the merciful grace of Heaven, have attempted in this book to sing in dactyls." The grace of Heaven is, of course, an inestimable blessing, and a nun must under all circumstances give credit to God for what there is of good in her work, but Hrotsvitha lets us see between the lines, and there we find a conscientious and hard-working artist who is justly proud of her efforts and of the products of her pen.

Hrotsvitha's first work was a collection of poems in praise of the Virgin Mary and of a number of saints and martyrs of the Faith. Most of the poems are founded on the tales and legends of the Greek Church, the sources of which were at first accepted wholeheartedly by Hrotsvitha, but which were beginning to fall under the ban of certain elements in the Western Church. Hrotsvitha, however, had a sufficiently good opinion of her own work to preserve these poems even when the authenticity of their sources was ques-

---

*The quotations from Hrotsvitha's prefaces and plays are taken from *The Plays of Roswitha*, translated by Christopher St. John.

tioned, proving once again her independence of judgment and decision of character.

The Martyrdom of Saint Pelagius is the most interesting among these early poems because it illustrates the sort of contact with the outside world which was possible even in a convent. This tale was told to Hrotsvitha herself by an eyewitness of the event, a Spaniard who came from the very town where Pelagius met his death. It is not surprising that martyrdoms and miracles, with all the horrors that attend them, should seem subjects of intense interest and importance to the poetess of Gandersheim, when traveling strangers could regale her with first-hand descriptions of such events. It is illuminating also to note in passing that the artistic necessity of contrasting good with bad was already present to the young nun, who did not hesitate to describe the criminal advances that were made to the beautiful young man Pelagius by his Saracen captor. His unwillingness to submit to such "abominable practices," or to accept the life of ease which would have accompanied such submission, makes his death all the more edifying. Young as she was when she wrote these poems, Hrotsvitha showed none of that ignorance which later ages have often mistaken for innocence. She knew the ways and the weaknesses of the flesh as well as the strength of the spirit, and no false prudery interfered with her frank descriptions of scenes and events which to a modern mind might seem somewhat Rabelaisian. The medieval point of view, as shown in its legends as well as its art and literature, had a tendency toward realism of detail rarely equaled even today.

The only other poem of particular interest in this first effort of the young poetess, is the *Fall and Conversion of Theophilus*, in which she tells a tale later to become the root legend of Germany's greatest drama. The story of Theophilus is one of the most popular in medieval literature and concerns the priest who sells his soul to the Devil in order to obtain worldly advancement. Ruteboeuf, one of the earliest French dramatists, made use of it in his one extant play, and as the basis of Goethe's *Faust*, it has become a classic of world literature.

With this collection of poems, Hrotsvitha established herself definitely as the poet laureate of Gandersheim. Her superiors were well pleased with her accomplishments, and from this time forward her fame as a scholar and a poet spread among the learned and accomplished prelates and laymen of the Saxon Court. To her was entrusted the task of writing a panegyric to the Ottos, and her *Carmen de gestis Oddonis* is important even today as an historic document and is quoted in the Encyclopedia Britannica. It was written at the instigation of the Abbess Gerberga and is dedicated to her by Hrotsvitha in a charming preface in which she describes herself as "one of the last of the least of those fighting under your ladyship's rule." Singled out for the honor of recording the deeds and accomplishments of the Imperial House, Hrotsvitha had won for herself a position of distinction. Her fame had spread beyond the convent walls and her audience was no longer restricted to her fellow nuns. The panegyric of the Ottos was read by the Court and commented on by Archbishop William, one of the leading prelates of the day, while the plays are definitely submitted to the judgments of "certain learned and virtuous men, patrons of the book."

Her prefaces show that Hrotsvitha thoroughly appreciated the recognition she had won, though she never lost sight of what one might term the religious amenities. Her feminine tact was not blunted by her years of conventual life, and she could turn a complimentary phrase with a skill only comparable to that of the preface writers of a later and more sophisticated age. Her own words alone can do justice to the delicate balance she maintained between justifiable pride and graceful humility, between self-assurance and disarming modesty. The Preface and Epistle which precede the most interesting of her productions, her six plays, is an excellent example of her style:

"To think that you, who have been nurtured in the most profound philosophical studies, and have attained knowledge in perfection, should have deigned to approve the humble work of an obscure woman," she exclaims in her epistle to her patrons, and then, mindful of an even higher authority, she adds: "You have, however, not praised me, but the Giver of grace which works in me, by sending your paternal congratulations and admitting that I possess some little knowledge of those arts, the subtleties of which exceed the grasp of my woman's mind. Until I showed my work to you, I had not dared to let any one see it except my intimate companions. I came near abandoning this form of writing altogether, for if there were a few to whom I could submit my compositions at all, there were fewer still who could point out what needed correction and encourage me to go on. . . . I know that it is as wrong to deny a divine gift as to pretend falsely that we have received it. So I will not deny that through the grace of the Creator I have acquired some knowledge of the arts. He has given me the ability to learn—I am a teachable creature—yet of myself I should know nothing. He has given me a perspicacious mind, but one that lies fallow and idle when it is not cultivated. . . . That my natural gift might not be made void by negligence, I have been at pains, whenever I have been able to pick up some threads and scraps from the old torn mantle of philosophy, to weave them into the stuff of my own book. . . that the creator of genius may be the more honored since it is generally believed that a woman's intelligence is slower.

In the humbler works of my salad days, I gathered up my poor researches in heroic strophes, but here I have sifted them in a series of dramatic scenes and avoided through omission the pernicious voluptuousness of pagan writers."

So for the greater glory of God, and with much "sweat and fatigue," Hrotsvitha fashioned the six plays which have brought her a kind of immortality she may not have foreseen, but which, judging by the glimpses we have of her personality, she would have been far too human not thoroughly to have enjoyed.

In telling us what she does of herself in her prefaces, Hrotsvitha unfortunately stops short of certain vital details. She attributes her interest in the dramatic form to her readings from Terence, but she fails to say what other influences led her to adopt so un-Christian a vehicle for her highly Christian teachings. She speaks of showing her productions to her companions, but does not tell us in so many words whether they performed the plays in the great hall of the Abbey of Gandersheim or possibly even in the church itself, or whether her comedies were purely literary exercises for her own entertainment. In consequence the learned scholars have disagreed violently on these points, in the end leaving the decision open to the reader who cares to study the plays with sympathy and imagination. One of the most careful students of Hrotsvitha's work, Charles Magnin, whose 1845 edition restored some of the invaluable stage directions, omitted by Conrad Celtes in his first transcription of the manuscript, is convinced that Hrotsvitha's plays were acted. The assumption that they were not performed is based largely on the fact that no other plays, religious or secular, have come down to us from tenth-century Europe.

The earliest dramatic dialogue recorded in the theatrical history of the West is the Easter trope, the *Quem Quaeritis* described in the *Concordia Regularis* of Saint Ethelwold, and dated about 965 or 975. This is nothing more than an adaptation of the liturgy, the first step toward the dramatic presentation of religious teaching and far indeed from the elaborate plots and characterizations of Hrotsvitha's comedies. The first authentic mystery play, the anonymous *Representatio Adae*, did not appear until two hundred years after her day. It has therefore seemed much simpler to many scholars to decide that Hrotsvitha was merely doing an exercise in Latin composition than to believe that she could have been moved to write and probably stage real plays at a time when no one else was doing it. This conclusion overlooks two very important factors, the influence of the Greek Church and the Greek tradition on a remarkably enterprising and independent spirit, and the dramatic viability of the plays themselves.

When Hrotsvitha entered the Abbey of Gandersheim, Otto I was still on the throne, but Otto II was Emperor during most of her lifetime. This Saxon prince was deeply interested in the intellectual development of his country. He turned to the older civilizations and particularly to Constantinople as to the seat of culture and refinement, and the Hellenistic influence was brought to his Court by ambassadors and delegates from the East. In 972, he married Theophano, daughter of the Eastern Emperor Romanus II, and this Greek princess assumed an important position in the social and political life of the Saxon Court. The Abbey of Gandersheim was so intimately connected with the Court that when it was decided that Sophia, eldest daughter of Otto and Theophano, must take the veil, the reluctant princess was sent to Gandersheim. Sophia did not wish to become a nun. She had an eye for more worldly honors and a mind capable of government. When her brother Otto III came to the throne, he summoned her to his side to help him. Later Sophia returned to the fold, became abbess in her turn, and undertook various measures to prove her equality with other princes of the Church.

While Sophia was still a novice and a young nun, the Empress Theophano often visited the Abbey, and Hrotsvitha, accredited bard of the Imperial family, was undoubtedly granted special privileges which brought her into contact with the Greek princesses and their attendant train. From such sources she would have learned at first-hand the fascinating story of the war waged in Constantinople between the Orthodox Church and the theatre. In her remote Saxon convent, where such a thing as a play had never been seen, Hrotsvitha must have listened avidly to the accounts of spectacle-loving Constantinople told by the homesick exiles who had followed their princess into the barbarous North.

The tradition of the Greek Church at this time showed two distinct and contradictory attitudes; that epitomized by Saint Chrysostom, who in the fourth century poured out the vials of his wrath and of his sublime eloquence on all that remotely concerned the stage, and that typified by the writing of Gregory Nazienzen and the Apollinari, who, when Julian the Apostate prohibited the teaching of the Greek classics to the followers of Christ, attempted to preserve the Greek literary forms for their people by re-writing the Old Testament as an Homeric epic, and the New along the lines of the classic drama. Other devout Christians made similar attempts with even less success if we can judge by the fact that, of the large body of these Christianized Greek tragedies, only a few fragments have survived.

In Hrotsvitha's day many must still have been in existence, though it is very doubtful that she ever saw them even in manuscript. We do not even know whether she could read Greek, but her constant use of Greek tales and legends as sources for her plots proves her familiarity with the literature of the Greek Church. Though she could not by any possibility have seen a play acted, the mere existence of these Byzantine dramas was enough to encourage her in her efforts. Her failure to acknowledge in her preface so venerable a precedent as that created by these Christian dramas is easily understood when we glimpse the tangled web of heresies and schisms with which the whole history of the early Church is overlaid. It was safer to recognize the pagan Terence as her prototype than to refer to the Christian sanctions of the theatre, tainted as they were by the black heresy of Arius and the triumphs of the hated Iconoclasts.

Hrotsvitha, however, must in her own mind have found ample justification for looking with tolerance upon the drama. The Empress Theophano could have told her of the astonishing truce that had been called in the age-long battle between Church and stage. One of the most extraordinary incidents in the whole history of the Church is the compromise brought about in the year 990 by Theophylactus, Patriarch of Constantinople, a member of the Empress' own family. This reverend prelate, uncle of Romanus II, Theophano's father, and head of the Orthodox Church, actually introduced the theatre into the bosom of the Church itself, permitting professional actors, actesses, and dancers from the Hippodrome to perform in Saint Sophia, and contenancing all sorts of dramatic amusements, even to the wildest buffooneries. Theophano herself loved the stage. Her father had been a devotee of the Hippodrome, her son Otto III attempted to reestablish the theatre in Italy, and her influence may in some measure account for the curious turn taken by Hrotsvitha's genius.

It does not require too wild a flight of the imagination, to picture the nuns of Gandersheim eagerly preparing to welcome their royal guest with a form of entertainment particularly dear to her heart and one of which she had been completely deprived since her departure from Constantinople. The Abbess Gerberga would not have been unwilling to show the foreign Empress that Saxony could produce a poet worthy of respect and that the resources of Gandersheim were equal to the task of presenting so sophisticated a form of entertainment as a drama. What more appropriate theme could have been chosen for the diversion of a Greek princess than Hrotsvitha's first play, *Gallicanus*, which sings the praises of Constance, daughter of Constantine, and reflects, in the story of the conversion of Gallicanus, the more famous conversion of Constantine himself, first of Christian Emperors and founder of the Empire in the East.

Hrotsvitha's avowed purpose of glorifying the "laudable chastity of Christian virgins" is here clothed in a panoply of royal pomp. The scenes laid in the court of Constantine, the crowded battlefields, the streets of Rome, the audience hall of Julian the Apostate, offered ample opportunities for the display of all the beautiful vestments, the colorful copes and chasubles, the treasures of silk, embroidery, and plate with which the sacristy of a wealthy convent would be supplied. Possibly the armor needed for the contending forces of Romans and Scythians was contributed by the knights-at-arms attached to the Abbey. With what ardor the young nuns and novices would have thrown themselves into the task of making costumes and learning their parts! If we judge the tenth century by later medieval custom, the scenes presented before the audience gathered in the Hall of the Abbey, or, as Philarète Chasle believes, in the nave of the Church itself, would not have been devoid of dignity, even of a certain splendor. Hrotsvitha's first effort in dramaturgy is not as skillful as her later plays, but no one who has accepted Shakespeare's sketchy battle scenes, nor the detached and episodic structure of his chronicle plays, need scorn Hrotsvitha's naive introduction of two contending armies on one stage, or her shorthand method of deciding the fate of a tremendous encounter in twenty-five lines of dialogue. *Gallicanus,* for all its faults, would have been an effective pageant to unroll before a queen.

Hrotsvitha, in all her plays, follows with pious faith the details of the legends which she dramatizes, but her originality is evident in the skill with which she succeeds in infusing personality into the lay figures of her tales. Constantine, whom she makes weak and vacillating in order to bring out the strength and even the holy guile of his daughter Constance; Julian the Apostate, who bids his soldiers remind the Christians of their own teachings about renouncing worldly goods while they are stripping them of all they possess; John and Paul, almoners of Constance, who are not above a little judicious prevarication while they go about the Lord's work—all these have a distinct character of their own. In Constance we see the outlines of a real individual, modeled on the lines of those "royal personages" Gerberga, Theophano, and Sophia, whom Hrotsvitha had the privilege of knowing intimately. Constance, receiving the daughters of Gallicanus and offering a fervent and thoroughly orthodox prayer for their salvation, might be the Abbess herself receiving a distinguished postulant; just as the arguments between John, Paul, and Julian the Apostate reflect the pious and at the same time scholastic disputations so typical of medieval theology.

Hrotsvitha's plays must necessarily be approached with sympathy and understanding, for they are expressed in an idiom alien to our modern point of view. They are all short—running from five to six hundred lines of concentrated dialogue broken into scenes of varying length by the transcribers of the original manuscript. At first glance, they seem naive, crude, two-dimensional. Everything appears on one plane with little attempt at rounding out of contours. Especially is this true of *Gallicanus* and of the two martyr plays, *Dulcitius* and *Sapientia*. In them Hrotsvitha has been absorbed in her didactic mission. They are preachments rather than plays, and yet even here her native dramatic instinct has not been completely subdued; a character, a scene, a bit of dialogue comes out with startling clarity. *Dulcitius* is particularly interesting in that it contains the one intentionally comic scence in Hrotsvitha's plays.

The legend turns on the strange hallucinations that overcame the Roman Governor, Dulcitius, when he attempted to rape three Christian maidens committed to his tender care. Making his way into the Palace kitchen, where he thinks the prisoners are confined, he embraces the pots and pans under the illusion that he is indulging in a night of love, to the immense amusement of the maidens themselves who watch the proceedings through a keyhole. The dramatic effect of having his would-be victims recount to each other the grotesque antics of the demented Governor, while the sound of crashing pans off stage emphasizes the excitement, is excellent. Dulcitius's reappearance, covered with soot and his clothes in rags, making futile attempts to convince his own soldiers of his identity, is cleverly worked out. The scene is obviously meant for visual presentation and is a striking example of Hrotsvitha's eye for stage effects.

In the heroic virgins of *Dulcitius* and the other martyr plays, Hrotsvitha has painted a variety of religious fanatic for whom she had apparently very little sympathy. They have none of the royal dignity of Constance, the wisdom of Sapientia, the charm of Drusiana, Mary, or Thaïs. Whether consciously or not, Hrotsvitha presents the women who have been touched by sin far more sympathetically than she does the immaculate virgins who defy their tormentors and fly straight to heaven in a blaze of unfelt torments and complacent glory. The three martyrs of *Dulcitius* have all the objectionable characteristics of the type, but they are saved from complete smugness by their amusement over the Roman Governor's absurd misadventure. Dulcitius, it is to be remarked, disappears suddenly from the story, the laughter he has provoked making him unsuitable as an instrument for really impressive martyrdom. His successor in the office of executioner dispatches two of the maidens in short order, but with the third, Irena, he argues at length, and is, of course, worsted in dialectics as he is frustrated in his design of humiliating and defiling her.

Hrotsvitha's preoccupation, in all her plays, with the glories of virginity must be taken as the hallmark of her profession. In a community of dedi-

cated nuns it was natural, indeed inevitable, that this aspect of their tribute
to God should be presented in all its beauty and nobility, and that all its
ramifications should be of palpitating interest. Undoubtedly also,
Hrotsvitha obtained a certain release for her own emotional suppressions by
elaborating these pictures of carnal dangers and the pitfalls of the flesh.
These scenes, wherein holy virgins, refusing advantageous offers of marriage, are dragged off to brothels to be "abominably defiled," or are attacked
by brutal soldiers and escape only by miraculous intervention, are the product of a mind that may have denied, but has not forgotten, the "sinful lusts
of the flesh." Hrotsvitha's plays illustrate very vividly the process of psychic
compensation which is so striking a feature of medieval monastic literature.

In *Dulcitius,* as in her last play, *Sapientia,* Hrotsvitha gives expression to a
vein of sadism which is also associated with certain aspects of repression. She
positively revels in the lurid and suggestive details of her torture scenes in a
way which has led some critics to brand these plays as completely unactable.
When we remember the enthusiasm with which such scenes were presented
in later medieval mystery plays, as evidenced by the records, and by such
pictures as that of the martyrdom of Saint Apollonia by Jean Fouquet,
Hrotsvitha's exursions into the horrific are less surprising. We are today
more squeamish about physical manifestations of the sort on our stage, but
the nuns of Gandersheim were nourished in a sturdier school. They were
suckled on tales of torture and martyrdom, and the more boiling oil, fiery
furnaces, severed limbs, and bleeding wounds a tale provided, the greater
the thrill. Hrotsvitha was not unwilling to write penny-dreadfuls of the
sort, nor could a more edifying and intimately comforting spectacle be imagined than that of these pure young girls taunting and defying Emperors
and all the strength of embattled masculine paganism while their faith prevented them from feeling the pain and ignominy to which their bodies were
subjected. We may turn with repugnance from scenes in which Sapientia's
children are scourged by the centurions, but we should not in our disgust
forget that one of the most popular scenes ever presented on the American
stage was that of the scourging of Uncle Tom, as well as, curiously enough,
the death and ascension of little Eva, a child almost as objectionable in her
way as any of Hrotsvitha's smug young heroines.

Again and again, even in these two martyr plays, which seem to us the
least actable of Hrotsvitha's works, little strokes of dialogue vividly suggest
the stage picture, as in the opening of the third scene in *Sapientia,*
when Antiochus says to the Christians, "That is the Emperor you see there,
seated on his throne. Be careful what you say to him"; or, in another scene
when Sapientia is encouraging her horde of infant martyrs, "Oh, my dearest

little ones, My beloved children! Do not let this narrow prison sadden you."
In a phrase or two, Hrotsvitha sets the stage, and one need only imagine
that attending groups of nuns, dressed as courtiers, executioners, Roman
matrons, followers, or slaves, rounding out the scenes with the actions
suggested in the text, to realize that the plays are eminently actable.

Dulcitius is the only play containing obviously comic scenes, yet all of
them, even the most terrible, are redeemed from sadness by the faith which
animates their author. To understand Hrotsvitha's spirit, it is necessary to
remember that Catholicism, even medieval Catholicism, with all its de-
monology, its horrors and damnations, was essentially a happy religion.
The promise of future blessedness compensated for much present suffering,
and the little martyrs could giggle like any other children, though in the
presence of an executioner. "What are you muttering there?" one of the latter exclaims in exasperation. "Behave yourself and do not laugh!" The constant complaint of their persecutors is that the Christians are laughing at
them, making fools of them. Not only do the Christians triumph by their
holiness, but they outargue and outwit their tormentors at every turn.

Hrotsvitha makes uses of these opportunities to air her own scholarly
accomplishments, and we find discourses on mathematics and music inter-
jected into the most unlikely situations. She feels it necessary, however, to
make some apology for these excursions into what the Emperor Hadrian in
one of her plays brands as "intricate and unprofitable dissertations." "It
would be unprofitable," Hrotsvitha's Sapientia answers, "if it did not lead
us to appreciate the wisdom of our Creator, Who in the beginning created
the world out of nothing. . . and then, in time and the age of man, formu-
lated a science which reveals fresh wonders the more we study it."

The Sapientia who formulates this apologia for the pursuit of knowledge
may well be taken as representing the Nun of Gandersheim in her later
years. Hrotsvitha's intellectual hunger is so evident, her eagerness to know
and learn so palpable, both in her plays and prefaces, that we cannot fail to
see in such sentiments as these her own excuses for enthusiasms which in a
woman and a nun of the Dark Ages needed some measure of explanation.
The stately, nobly born, and extremely intelligent Sapientia is Hrotsvitha
in the full flower of her maturity and success, devoting her life to the service
of God, and the creations of her genius to his everlasting glory.

A more tender and humanly touching Hrotsvitha is revealed in her fourth
play, *Abraham*. It is not a martyr play, nor is it overburdened with too many
"threads and scraps from the torn mantle of philosophy." In a series of swift
and straightforward scenes it tells the story of Mary, niece of the hermit Abraham, who at the tender age of eight dedicates herself to Christ. After

many years spent in solitary prayer and meditation under the care of Abraham, she is seduced by a passing stranger. In shame and horror she flees from the hermitage and abandons herself to a life of sin. Abraham follows her, and by his love and his exhortations brings her back to God.

The scenes in the brothel where Abraham, disguised as an ordinary traveler, has gone to find his niece, are handled with extraordinary delicacy and charm. At first Abraham is shown talking to the innkeeper, asking for food and lodging and for the company of the beautiful girl with whom he is "already in love" from the description he has heard of her. Mary comes in, but does not recognize her spiritual father, who with an effort conquers his emotions and continues to play his part. Hrotsvitha's treatment of this scene is particulary sensitive, and though it is almost impossible to capture the quality of her writing in a few lines, this, and the following recongnition scene give some idea of the sincerity and directness of her style, as well as her ability to convey profound feeling in a few lines. The innkeeper greets her boisterously—"Luck comes your way, Mary! Not only do young gallants of your own age flock to your arms, but even the wise and venerable come to you."

MARY: It is all one to me. It is my business to love those who love me.
ABRAHAM: Come nearer, Mary, and give me a kiss.
MARY: I will give you more than a kiss. I will take your head in my arms and stroke your neck.
ABRAHAM: Yes, like that!
MARY: What does this mean? What is this lovely fragrance, so clean, so sweet? It reminds me of the time when I was good.
ABRAHAM (*aside*): On with the mask! Chatter, make lewd jests like an idle boy! She must not recognize me or for very shame she will fly from me.
MARY: Wretch that I am! To what have I fallen! In what pit have I sunk!
ABRAHAM: You forget where you are! Do men come here to see you cry?
INNKEEPER: What's the matter, Lady Mary? Why are you in the dumps? You have lived here two years and never before have I seen a tear, never heard a sigh or a word of complaint.
MARY: Oh, that I had died three years ago before I came to this!
ABRAHAM: I came here to make love to you, not to weep with you over your sins.
MARY: A little thing moved me, and I spoke foolishly. It is nothing. Come, let us eat and drink and be merry, for, as you say, this is not the place to think of one's sins.

After eating supper, they go into the bedroom where the scene continues.

MARY: Look! How do you like this room? A handsome bed, isn't it? Those
    trappings cost a lot of money. Sit down and I will take off your shoes.
    You seem tired.
ABRAHAM: First bolt the door. Someone may come in.
MARY: Have no fear, I have seen to that.
ABRAHAM: The time has come for me to show my shaven head and make
    myself known! Oh, my daughter, oh, Mary, you who are part of my soul!
    Look at me. Do you not know me? Do you not know the old man who
    cherished you with a father's love, and wedded you to the Son of the King
    of Heaven?
MARY: God, what shall I do! It is my father and master Abraham!
ABRAHAM: What has come to you daughter!
MARY: Oh, misery!. . .
ABRAHAM: Why have you thrown yourself down there? Why do you lie
    on the ground without moving or speaking? Get up, Mary, get up, my
    child and listen to me!
MARY: No, no, I am afraid, I cannot bear your reproaches.
ABRAHAM: Remember how I love you, and you will not be afraid. . . . .
    The mercy of Heaven is greater than you or your sins. Let your sadness be
    dispersed by its glorious beams. . . .

And so on, until Mary is convinced of God's love and forgiveness and returns to the desert, riding on Abraham's horse, "that the stony road should
not hurt her delicate feet."
    With *Paphnutius*, the play immediately following *Abraham*, Hrotsvitha
handles the same theme, that of the conversion of a harlot, in an entirely different manner. *Paphnutius* is the story of Thaïs, the first dramatic presentation of this old and still popular legend. In it Hrotsvitha shows her increasing ability to differentiate character and the art with which she can develop
her material. When the hermit Paphnutius goes to Alexandria in the hope
of saving a lost soul by converting the famous courtesan Thaïs to the true
faith, he, too, like Abraham, dons worldly attire, and, armed with piety
and the necessary gold pieces, ventures into a house of sin in pursuit of his
worthy purpose. Both plays are surprisingly, if naively, realistic, for both
hermits boldly demand the most intimate favors of their would-be converts,
and Hrotsvitha does not hesitate to introduce her godly men into the bed-
chambers of these prostitutes. When Paphnutius demands of Thaïs that she
take him into a secret room, she shows him her bedroom. "How would you

like a bedchamber fragrant with perfumes, adorned as for marriage? I have such a room. Look!"

The dramatic effect of both conversions is, of course, greatly heightened by the fact that they occur at the very moment when these erring women are engaged in their evil trade—but, though the scene is the same, the whole treatment is radically different. Abraham is throughout the gentle old man, disguising his emotion with difficulty and finally revealing himself in words of kindness and gentle exhortation. Paphnutius, on the other hand, makes a very creditable lover. Young and handsome, he woos Thaïs in words he must have learned elsewhere than in his desert hermitage, but when he begins to admonish her, all gentleness disappears. Fire and brimstone, terror and grief, are the lot of one as confirmed in evil, as hardened and as profligate as Thaïs the Harlot. Hard as Mary's life of penitence, prayer, and fasting may seem to us, it has not the revolting cruelty of the fate to which Paphnutius condemns the unfortunate Thaïs.

Here again Hrotsvitha's eye for realistic detail spares us no aspect of the plight in which Thaïs found herself when she was condemned to pass what remained of her life walled into a narrow cell which had no opening save one tiny window. She shrinks with fastidious disgust from the filth which, to the medieval ascetic, was far nearer godliness than the perfumed cleanliness of a decadent Roman civilzation. It is no wonder that the unfortunate penitent died shortly after her release. But Thaïs's end is all the more edifying because of her great penitence—and this picture of physical suffering was no doubt considered highly edifying by Hrotsvitha's contemporaries, whatever it may seem to us today. Evidently also Hrotsvitha's surprising excursions into houses of ill fame were forgiven by her spiritual pastors and masters in view of the good work she was accomplishing in these unholy places. As her preface proves, she justified her treatment of such subjects by the moral effects of their teachings, but when we read the plays themselves, we cannot help thinking that Hrotsvitha enjoyed these voyages outside the convent walls, and that in her heart of hearts she loved the sinners she painted far more than she hated their sins.

Hrotsvitha must have found some difficulty in justifying all her expeditions into forbidden territory, for this surprising nun was bold enough to write at least one love story. In the preface of the plays, she shows herself fully conscious of the dangerous ground she was treading. "One thing has. . . embarrassed me and often brought a blush to my cheek," she tells us. "It is that I have been compelled through the nature of this work to apply my mind and my pen to depicting the dreadful frenzy of those possessed by unlawful love and the insidious sweetness of passion—things which should not even be named among us. Yet if from modesty I had refrained from treating these subjects, I should not have been able to attain my object—to glorify the innocent to the best of my ability. For the more seductive the blandishments of lovers, the more wonderful the divine succor and the greater the merit of those who resist, especially when it is fragile woman who is victorious and strong man who is routed with confusion."

Safely ensconced behind this laudable and appropriate excuse, Hrotsvitha proceeded to write the first romance of modern literature, her third play, *Callimachus*. The curious external resemblances between *Callimachus* and *Romeo and Juliet* are no less striking than the atmosphere of passionate romanticism which emanates from the whole. The plot concerns the fatal love of Callimachus for Drusiana, wife of Prince Andronicus. Drusiana had dedicated herself to God, renouncing "even that which is lawful," her husband's bed, and, rather than break her vows of chastity, she prays for death to deliver her from the tempting importunities of her lover. She dies at once, and is buried, but Callimachus's passion follows her into the grave. The scene at the tomb of Drusiana, when Callimachus, aided by the faithless servant Fortunatus, finds himself in the presence of his dead love, strikingly prefigures the famous climax of Shakespeare's tragedy. The deaths are almost as numerous, too, for both Callimachus and Fortunatus are killed by miraculous intervention. The resurrection of all three, and the repentance and conversion of Callimachus is the religious dénouement needed to justify Hrotsvitha's bold attempt at romantic drama and is of less importance than her obvious preoccupation with her love story.

Hrotsvitha's characterizations, embryonic as they are, show her originality. Drusiana, unlike the strong-minded saints of the martyr plays, sure of their faith and of their ultimate victory, is conscious of her own weakness in the face of temptation. Touched by the ardor of Callimachus, she is afraid that she will be unable to resist him, and, determined neither to rouse the anger of her husband against him nor fall from the grace she has obtained, she prays for death. In the few lines that are allotted to her, from her first scene with Callimachus, where she attempts, rather pathetically, to put off his advances, to her final act after her resurrection, when she restores to life the villain who betrayed her dead body to her lover, the character of Drusiana is consistently gentle, loving, and tender—as far removed from the colorless heroines of the Latin theatre as it is from the heroic figures of Greek tragedy.

The distracted husband, Andronicus, is also, traditionally speaking, a creation of Hrotsvitha's own imagination. Certainly the husbands and fathers of Latin comedy established no precedent on which to model this forbearing and kindly gentleman. One wonders even more where among the barons and fighting lords of the Dark Ages, his prototype could have been found. His love for Drusiana never wavers, though she has left his bed, and though he knows she has died in order to escape the importunities of another man. His devotion and faith are so great that it is he, rather than the Apostle John, who is made the mouthpiece for the moral of the tale. Standing over the dead bodies of Callimachus and the servant, he meditates on the heavenly revelation which he had just received: "What astonishes me most," he says, "is that the Divine Voice should have promised the resurrection of [Callimachus] who planned the crime and not of him who was only an accomplice. Maybe it is because the one, blinded by passion of the flesh, knew not what he did, while the other sinned of deliberate malice." Hrotsvitha had not forgotten the words of One whose understanding was so great that He could say of a certain sinner, "Her sins, which are many, are forgiven, for she loved much."

In the character of Callimachus, Hrotsvitha gives a vivid outline sketch of an experienced worldling, not unlike the dashing Romeo. In the first scenes of the play he talks to his friends, in the tenth-century equivalent of Euphuism, a scholastic splitting of phrases that only half veils the intensity of his ill-advised passion. His relations with Drusiana show him to be as thoughtless of her happiness and safety as Romeo himself. He pursues her even into the grave, and here we see the Benedictine nun handling with extraordinary delicacy and understanding a situation as bold, one might almost say as lurid, as anything the Elizabethans could have invented. Hrotsvitha was evidently so moved by a strong sympathy for the miseries of frustrated love that she did not hesitate to present it in all its intensity. Callimachus's outburst over the dead body of Drusiana has an authentic ring of passion: "O Drusiana, Drusiana, I worshiped you with my whole soul! I yearned from my very bowels to embrace you! And you repulsed me, and thwarted my desire. Now you are in my power, now I can wound you with my kisses, and pour out my love upon you."

Strange words to echo in a convent hall, bringing suddenly to the surface the troubled and violent stream of imprisoned feeling. Hrotsvitha's intense and passionate nature is revealed for a moment only, to be quickly covered by the accustomed mantle of sober piety. But Callimachus's conversion and frenzied repentance is merely another phrase of an intense emotional experience.

"I came here for an evil purpose," he exclaims after his resurrection, "but the pangs of love consumed me. I was beside myself." And John answers him. "What mad folly possessed you, that you should dare think of such a shameful outrage to the chaste dead!" Callimachus can only repeat: "I was mad! . . . I am overwhelmed by the thought of my abominable crime. I repent with my whole heart and bewail my sin. . . . Oh, hasten then to help a man in dire need—give me some comfort! Help me throw off the grief that crushes me! Show me how a pagan may change into a Christian, a fornicator into a chaste man! Oh, set my feet in the way of truth! Teach me to live mindful of the divine promises."

His plea is not in vain. For all his black sin, Callimachus is forgiven. The note of peace after the storm rings like the quiet tolling of the Angelus, reminding the nuns of Gandersheim that they have found a refuge from the "dreadful frenzy of passion." The Judge who could forgive Callimachus because he loved too greatly could be counted upon to "search the heart and reins and reward or punish fairly."

The plays of Hrotsvitha, after long years of neglect, have recently been studied with great interest and attention, and have even been acted in English both in London and New York with varying degrees of artistic success. The impossibility of recapturing an atmosphere as alien to us as that of medieval Christianity will always make their presentation peculiarly difficult. Few indeed are the playwrights who have actually survived their own day unless, in addition to possessing dramatic gifts, they have been poets of such high order that the hungry generations have listened in awe to their music. Hrotsvitha was not a great poet. She was an acute observer, an avid scholar, an adventurous and enterprising soul. To enjoy her style one must have a taste for the phrase that suggests rather than describes, for a simplicity which is at once naive and full of wisdom. Like the early painters, her work is stiff, clear-cut, often harsh, and occasionally crude, but none the less vital for all its shortcomings. Her plays are all brief, her characterizations often no more than outline sketches, yet in the quick strokes with which she defines an individual she shows a master's hand. Her comedies have a vivacity, a directness of approach, and, in spite of much that is incredible, an essential veracity which gives them permanent value.

If it is true, as the scholars tell us, that Hrotsvitha had no imitators or successors, she nevertheless foreshadowed a new dramatic dispensation, where love, human and divine, were to reign supreme, and where the romantic ideal of individual freedom was finally to replace the Greek conception of inescapable fatality. Working alone in her remote Saxon convent, where plays and players had never been seen, surrounded by a social order barely emerging from barbarism, this Benedictine nun cherished in secret the wavering flame of a great tradition, pouring into it the new oil of the Christian religion and handing it on, sweetened and strengthened by her care, to later generations of those who know and love the theatre.

Dance:
Earth Spirit Rising

Isadora Duncan

Martha Graham

Katherine Dunham

Isadora Duncan

[1878–1927]

AN INTRODUCTION

FOR ISADORA DUNCAN, dance was the animated soul, the spirit-force of life moving through woman's body. "She was *obliged* to dance, as we are obliged to breathe," wrote her friend Eva Le Gallienne in tribute at Isadora's death. "There was to her no difference between dancing and living. She felt that through the dance one became inseparably a part of the great rhythm of the Universe, and that this harmony between Self and Centre of Being resulted as a matter of course in harmonious living."[1]

To Isadora, ballet—pretending that the laws of gravity do not exist, removed from the continual ebb and flow of life—was artificial movement. She viewed social conventions, corsets, marriage, the church, and hypocrisies of all sorts as restrictions upon the human soul and felt that without the soul's perfect freedom there could be no dance. Ballet, she declared, was the dance form of the upper classes; her dance was for the people, and through her dance she meant to lift the common spirit higher, towards a dream of freedom.

"The Dance of the Future," the lecture-essay which follows, was completed in 1902 or 1903 with the help of her brother Raymond Duncan. It pulses with the joyous optimism that was Isadora's when, as a young woman, she took members of her family with her to live in the rocky hills of Greece while she created a modern dance that would be as spiritually exultant as the ancient dance of that ancient land. She had no doubt this new dance would be the work of women—and that in its making women would liberate themselves.

Liberation—personal, political, artistic—was the theme of her whole life, her work, her thought. This woman, who took so many lovers, was a virgin in the original sense of the word—a woman in possession of herself. She was also a woman of enormous capacity for feeling, shirking from neither joy nor sorrow, experiencing each to its fullest, making her art rich with experience.

Beginning a concert tour in Russia in 1905, she witnessed the early morning burial of the working men and women who had been shot down as they marched, unarmed, toward the Winter Palace to ask the Czar for bread. In her autobiography, *My Life*, completed the summer before her death in November 1927, she recalled the scene.

> If I had never seen it, all my life would have been different. There, before this seemingly endless procession, this tragedy, I vowed myself and my forces to the service of the people and the downtrodden. Ah, how small and useless now seemed all my personal love desires and sufferings! How useless even my Art, unless it could help this.[2]

Like many revolutionary American artists, Isadora had to go abroad to find the understanding necessary to her art. She had gone to Greece for inspiration and she went to the capitals of Europe for acclaim. "How strange it is," Le Gallienne wrote, "that a country born and cradled in Revolution should so consistently turn its austere back on its greatest and most typical children. The inevitable comparison of Walt Whitman and Isadora at once springs to mind."[3]

If America failed her, so also did Russia. She left Russia in 1921, after the promise of the Russian Revolution had dulled and hardened and the dance school for children she had established at the invitation of the revolutionary government had become impossible to maintain. She wrote to her friend, the anarchist Alexander Berkman, who was in exile in France, asking if she might come dance for him. "You see, I am always ready to believe in a new 'myth' since the bolshevik one didn't turn out."[4]

Perhaps the "myth"—or recurrent human possibility—she cherished most was that the children of all nations would learn to dance and, in this way, give enduring form to the pulse of freedom which restrictive societies harden and destroy.

Isadora felt a most wondrous love for her own children and found much artistic stimulation in their daily doings. If her births were long and painful, her pregnancies were ecstatic, and the sight of the new babe left her feeling "very near the edge, the mystery, perhaps the knowledge of Life." Ellen Terry's son, Gordon Craig, was the father of Isadora Duncan's daughter, Deirdre. During Isadora's pregnancy, the famous actress appeared twice in her dreams "and, in her marvelous voice, she called to me—Isadora, love. Love. . . love. . . ."[5] A boy, Patrick, was born to Isadora several years after Deirdre. She was teaching them both to dance and would, most likely, have worked with them when they were grown, as Terry sometimes did with her children, had they lived.

The deaths of her two small children in an automobile accident caused a nearly unendurable grief which gave to her character a tragic wholeness, making her kin to the earth mother, Demeter, and completing, through the most terrible of sorrows, her understanding of a woman's ethic and esthetic:

Only twice comes that cry of the mother which one hears as without one's self—at Birth and at Death—for when I felt in mine those little cold hands that would never again press mine in return I heard my cries—the same cries as I had heard at their births. Why the same—since one is the cry of supreme Joy and the other of Sorrow? I do not know why but I know they are the same. Is it that in all the Universe there is but one Great Cry containing Sorrow, Joy, Ecstasy, Agony, the Mother Cry of Creation?[6]

—K.M.

Isadora Duncan
[1878–1927]

SELECTION

From *The Art of the Dance*

The Dance of the Future

A woman once asked me why I dance with bare feet and I replied, "Madam, I believe in the religion of the beauty of the human foot." The lady replied, "But I do not," and I said, "Yet you must, Madam, for the expression and intelligence of the human foot is one of the greatest triumphs of the evolution of man." "But," said the lady, "I do not believe in the evolution of man"; at this said I, "My task is at an end. I refer you to my most revered teachers, Mr. Charles Darwin and Mr. Ernst Haeckel." "But," said the lady, "I do not believe in Darwin and Haeckel." At this point I could think of nothing more to say. So you see that to convince people, I am of little value and ought not to speak. But I am brought from the seclusion of my study, trembling and stammering before a public and told to lecture on the dance of the future.

If we seek the real source of the dance, if we go to nature, we find that the dance of the future is the dance of the past, the dance of eternity, and has been and will always be the same.

The movement of waves, of winds, of the earth is ever in the same lasting harmony. We do not stand on the beach and inquire of the ocean what was its movement in the past and what will be its movements in the future. We realize that the movement peculiar to its nature is eternal to its nature. The movement of the free animals and birds remains always in correspondence to their nature, the necessities and wants of that nature, and its correspondence to the earth nature. It is only when you put free animals under false restrictions that they lose the power of moving in harmony with nature, and adopt a movement expressive of the restrictions placed about them.

So it has been with civilized man. The movements of the savage, who lived in freedom in constant touch with Nature, were unrestricted, natural and beautiful. Only the movements of the naked body can be perfectly natural. Man, arrived at the end of civilization, will have to return to nakedness, not to the unconscious nakedness of the savage, but to the conscious and acknowledged nakedness of the mature Man, whose body will be the harmonious expression of his spiritual being.

And the movements of this Man will be natural and beautiful like those of the free animals.

The movement of the universe concentrating in an individual becomes what is termed the will; for example, the movement of the earth, being the concentration of surrounding forces, gives to the earth its individuality, its will of movement. So creatures of the earth, receiving in turn these concentrating forces in their different relations, as transmitted to them through their ancestors and to those by the earth, in themselves evolve the movement of individuals which is termed the will.

The dance should simply be, then, the natural gravitation of this will of the individual, which in the end is no more nor less than a human translation of the gravitation of the universe.

The school of the ballet of today, vainly striving against the natural laws of gravitation or the natural will of the individual, and working in discord in its form and movement with the form and movement of nature, produces a sterile movement which gives no birth to future movements, but dies as it is made.

The expression of the modern school of ballet, wherein each action is an end, and no movement, pose or rhythm is successive or can be made to evolve succeeding action, is an expression of degeneration, of living death. All the movements of our modern ballet school are sterile movements because they are unnatural: their purpose is to create the delusion that the law of gravitation does not exist for them.

The primary or fundamental movements of the new school of the dance must have within them the seeds from which will evolve all other movements, each in turn to give birth to others in unending sequence of still higher and greater expression, thoughts and ideas.

To those who nevertheless still enjoy the movements, for historical or choreographic or whatever other reasons, to those I answer: They see no farther than the skirts and tricots. But look—under the skirts, under the tricots are dancing deformed muscles. Look still farther—underneath the muscles are deformed bones. A deformed skeleton is dancing before you.

This deformation through incorrect dress and incorrect movement is the result of the training necessary to the ballet.

The ballet condemns itself by enforcing the deformation of the beautiful woman's body! No historical, no choreographic reasons can prevail against that!

It is the mission of all art to express the highest and most beautiful ideals of man. What ideal does the ballet express?

No, the dance was once the most noble of all arts; and it shall be again. From the great depth to which it has fallen, it shall be raised. The dancer of the future shall attain so great a height that all other arts shall be helped thereby.

To express what is the most moral, healthful and beautiful in art—this is the mission of the dancer, and to this I dedicate my life.

These flowers before me contain the dream of a dance; it could be named "The light falling on white flowers." A dance that would be a subtle translation of the light and the whiteness. So pure, so strong that people would say: it is a soul we see moving, a soul that has reached the light and found the whiteness. We are glad it should move so. Through its human medium we have a satisfying sense of movement, of light and glad things. Through this human medium, the movement of all nature runs also through us, is transmitted to us from the dancer. We feel the movement of light intermingled with the thought of whiteness. It is a prayer, this dance; each movement reaches in long undulations to the heavens and becomes a part of the eternal rhythm of the spheres.

To find those primary movements for the human body from which shall evolve the movements of the future dance in ever-varying, natural, unending sequences, that is the duty of the new dancer of today.

As an example of this, we might take the pose of the Hermes of the Greeks. He is represented as flying on the wind. If the artist had pleased to pose his foot in a vertical position, he might have done so, as the God, flying on the wind, is not touching the earth; but realizing that no movement is true unless suggesting sequence of movements, the sculptor placed the Hermes with the ball of his foot resting on the wind, giving the movement an eternal quality.

In the same way I might make an example of each pose and gesture in the thousands of figures we have left to us on the Greek vases and bas-reliefs; there is not one which in its movement does not presuppose another movement.

This is because the Greeks were the greatest students of the laws of nature, wherein all is the expression of unending, ever-increasing evolution, wherein are no ends and no stops.

Such movements will always have to depend on and correspond to the form that is moving. The movements of a beetle correspond to its form. So do those of the horse. Even so the movements of the human body must correspond to its form. The dances of no two persons should be alike.

People have thought that so long as one danced in rhythm, the form and design did not matter; but no, one must perfectly correspond to the other. The Greeks understood this very well. There is a statuette that shows a dancing cupid. It is a child's dance. The movements of the plump little feet and arms are perfectly suited to its form. The sole of the foot rests flat on the ground, a position which might be ugly in a more developed person, but is natural in a child trying to keep its balance. One of the legs is half raised; if it were outstretched it would irritate us, because the movement would be unnatural. There is also a statue of a satyr in a dance that is quite different from that of the cupid. His movements are those of a ripe and muscular man. They are in perfect harmony with the structure of his body.

The Greeks in all their painting, sculpture, architecture, literature, dance, and tragedy evolved their movements from the movement of nature, as we plainly see expressed in all representations of the Greek gods, who, being no other than the representatives of natural forces, are always designed in a pose expressing the concentration and evolution of these forces. This is why the art of the Greeks is not a national or characteristic art but has been and will be the art of all humanity for all time.

Therefore dancing naked upon the earth I naturally fall into Greek positions, for Greek positions are only earth positions.

The noblest in art is the nude. This truth is recognized by all, and followed by painters, sculptors and poets; only the dancer has forgotten it, who should most remember it, as the instrument of her art is the human body itself.

Man's first conception of beauty is gained from the form and symmetry of the human body. The new school of the dance should begin with that movement which is in harmony with and will develop the highest form of the human body.

I intend to work for this dance of the future. I do not know whether I have the necessary qualities: I may have neither genius nor talent nor temperament. But I know that I have a Will; and will and energy sometimes prove greater than either genius or talent or temperament.

Let me anticipate all that can be said against my qualification for my work, in the following little fable:

The Gods looked down through the glass roof of my studio and Athene said, "She is not wise, she is not wise, in fact, she is remarkably stupid."

And Demeter looked and said, "She is a weakling; a little thing—not like my deep-breasted daughters who play in the fields of Eleusis; one can see each rib; she is not worthy to dance on my broad-wayed Earth." And Iris looked down and said, "See how heavily she moves—does she guess nothing of the swift and gracious movement of a winged being?" And Pan looked and said, "What? Does she think she knows aught of the movements of my satyrs, splendid ivy-horned fellows who have within them all the fragrant life of the woods and waters?" And then Terpsichore gave one scornful glance; "And she calls that dancing! Why, her feet move more like the lazy steps of a deranged turtle."

And all the Gods laughed; but I looked bravely up through the glass roof and said: "O ye immortal Gods, who dwell in high Olympus and live on Ambrosia and Honey-cakes, and pay no studio rent nor bakers' bills therof, do not judge me so scornfully. It is ture, O Athene, that I am not wise, and my head is a rattled institution; but I do occasionally read the word of those who have gazed into the infinite blue of thine eyes, and I bow my empty gourd head very humbly before thine altars. And, O Demeter of the Holy Garland," I continued, "it is true that the beautiful maidens of your broad-wayed earth would not admit me of their company; still I have thrown aside my sandals that my feet may touch your life-giving earth more reverently, and I have had your sacred Hymn sung before the present day Barbarians, and I have made them listen and to find it good.

"And, O Iris of the golden wings, it is true that mine is but a sluggish movement; others of my profession have luted more violently against the laws of gravitation, from which laws, O glorious one, you are alone exempt. Yet the wind from your wings has swept through my poor earthly spirit, and I have often brought prayers to your courage-inspiring image.

"And, O Pan, you who were pitiful and gentle to simple Psyche in her wanderings, think more kindly of my little attempts to dance in your woody places.

"And you most exquisite one, Terpsichore, send to me a little comfort and strength that I may proclaim your power on Earth during my life; and afterwards, in the shadowy Hades, my wistful spirit shall dance dances better yet in thine honour."

Then came the voice of Zeus, the Thunderer:

"Continue your way and rely upon the eternal justice of the immortal Gods; if you work well they shall know of it and be pleased thereof."

In this sense, then, I intend to work, and if I could find in my dance a few or even one single position that the sculptor could transfer into marble so that it might be preserved, my work would not have been in vain; this one form would be a gain; it would be a first step for the future. My intention is, in due time, to found a school, to build a theatre where a hundred little girls shall be trained in my art, which they, in turn, will better. In this school I shall not teach the children to imitate my movements, but to make their own. I shall not force them to study certain definite movements; I shall help them to develop those movements which are natural to them. Whosoever sees the movements of an untaught little child cannot deny that its movements are beautiful. They are beautiful because they are natural to the child. Even so the movements of the human body may be beautiful in every stage of development so long as they are in harmony with that stage and degree of maturity which the body has attained. There will always be movements which are the perfect expression of that individual body and that individual soul; so we must not force it to make movements which are not natural to it but which belong to a school. An intelligent child must be astonished to find that in the ballet school it is taught movements contrary to all those movements which it would make of its own accord.

This may seem a question of little importance, a question of differing opinions on the ballet and the new dance. But it is a great question. It is not only a question of true art, it is a question of race, of the development of the female sex to beauty and health, of the return to the original strength and to natural movements of woman's body. It is a question of the development of perfect mothers and the birth of healthy and beautiful children. The dancing school of the future is to develop and to show the ideal form of woman. It will be, as it were, a museum of the living beauty of the period.

Travelers coming into a country and seeing the dancers should find in them that country's ideal of the beauty of form and movement. But strangers who today come to any country, and there see the dancers of the ballet school, would get a strange notion indeed of the ideal of beauty in that country. More than this, dancing like any art of anytime should reflect the highest point the spirit of mankind has reached in that special period. Does anybody think that the present day ballet school expresses this?

Why are its positions in such contrast to the beautiful positions of the antique sculptures which we preserve in our museums and which are constantly presented to us as perfect models of ideal beauty? Or have our museums been founded only out of historical and archaeological interest, and not for the sake of the beauty of the objects which they contain?

The ideal of beauty of the human body cannot change with fashion but only with evolution. Remember the story of the beautiful sculpture of a Roman girl which was discovered under the reign of Pope Innocent VIII, and which by its beauty created such a sensation that the men thronged to see it and made pilgrimages to it as to a holy shrine, so that the Pope, troubled by the movement which it originated, finally had it buried again.

And here I want to avoid a misunderstanding that might easily arise. From what I have said you might conclude that my intention is to return to the dances of the old Greeks, or that I think that the dance of the future will be a revival of the antique dances or even of those of the primitive tribes. No, the dance of the future will be a new movement, a consequence of the entire evolution which mankind has passed through. To return to the dances of the Greeks would be as impossible as it is unnecessary. We are not Greeks and therefore cannot dance Greek dances.

But the dance of the future will have to become again a high religious art as it was with the Greeks. For art which is not religious is not art, is mere merchandise.

The dancer of the future will be one whose body and soul have grown so harmoniously together that the natural language of that soul will have become the movement of the body. The dancer will not belong to a nation but to all humanity. She will dance not in the form of nymph, nor fairy, nor coquette, but in the form of woman in her greatest and purest expression. She will realize the mission of woman's body and the holiness of all its parts. She will dance the changing life of nature, showing how each part is transformed into the other. From all parts of her body shall shine radiant intelligence, bringing to the world the message of the thoughts and aspirations of thousands of women. She shall dance the freedom of woman.

Oh, what a field is here awaiting her! Do you not feel that she is near, that she is coming, this dancer of the future! She will help womankind to a new knowledge of the possible strength and beauty of their bodies, and the relation of their bodies to the earth nature and to the children of the future. She will dance the body emerging again from centuries of civilized forgetfulness, emerging not in the nudity of primitive man, but in a new nakedness, no longer at war with spirituality and intelligence, but joining with them in a glorious harmony.

This is the mission of the dancer of the future. Oh, do you not feel that she is near, do you not long for her coming as I do? Let us prepare the place for her. I would build for her a temple to await her. Perhaps she is yet unborn, perhaps she is now a little child. Perhaps, oh blissful! it may be my holy mission to guide her first steps, to watch the progress of her movements day by day until, far outgrowing my poor teaching, her movements will become godlike, mirroring in themselves the waves, the winds, the movements of growing things, the flight of birds, the passing of clouds, and finally the thought of man in his relation to the universe.

Oh, she is coming, the dancer of the future: the free spirit, who will inhabit the body of new woman; more glorious than any woman that has yet been; more beautiful than the Egyptian, than the Greek, the early Italian, than all women of past centuries—the highest intelligence in the freest body!

Martha Graham

[1894–   ]

AN INTRODUCTION

THE NOTEBOOKS OF MARTHA GRAHAM are a series of intellectual, spiritual, and psychological questions, often in the form of images or quotations, which become the "scripts," or what can be said in words, about the dance-dramas which finally exist only in the moment of their actual experience. As fragmentary as the *Notebooks* may seem at first, they present, nevertheless, a map of the creation, a journey into the "landscape of the mind" of the woman-creator and out again to descriptions of the actual choreographic realization of the dance.

Nothing in her background seemed to prepare Martha Graham for the position she now occupies in the history of modern dance. She was born into a rather proper home in Philadelphia, one of three daughters. Her father was a physician. When she was a teenager she moved to California with her mother and sisters. Her father remained at work in the East, but on one of his frequent trips to visit the family, he took her to see Ruth St. Denis dance. Graham was captivated. Never before had she seen anything like the freedom and passion expressed in St. Denis's "exotic" dances. In 1916, when Graham was twenty-two, she entered the newly formed Denishawn dance school in Los Angeles, founded by St. Denis and her husband, Ted Shawn. Graham was older than most of the other students and without previous dance training. She seemed an unlikely student, yet it was not long before her determination gave way to a fierce stage energy. She had a *presence,* and soon began to dance professionally with the Denishawn company.

Graham began her own dance company in 1929. For a decade she worked only with women dancers, looking for a movement vocabulary shorn of all that was not hers. Then she added male students to the ensemble, Erick Hawkins and Merce Cunningham, and began delving into the tensions between male and female, a recurring concern in all her subsequent work.

Men were added to deepen, not detract from, the complexities of her central quest: revelation through the dance of a woman's inner life. The great heroines and female archetypes have been her most persistent subject matter—the tripartite goddess, Medea, Clytemnestra, Phaedra, Jocasta, Judith, the Witch of Endor, Mary Queen of Scots, Heloise, Joan of Arc. The Brontë sisters and Emily Dickinson have also inspired Graham dances.

The *Notebooks* show her borrowing from world literature, from Celtic, Greek, and Oriental myth and epic. Paragraph by paragraph she moves from thinker to thinker, from culture to culture, from past to present as quickly as her mind associates image with image, idea with idea. What she takes becomes uniquely hers. She is not a scholar, painstakingly building fact on fact to prove a single theory, but an alchemist who magically transmutes the gathered raw materials into an imagined world which is itself a new and shining whole.

Her dances are essentially dramatic. They tell a story, but, more than that, they reveal characters' inner psychic quests. Her images are breathtaking, not because they are technically difficult, but because they are so rooted in human emotion, human passion. Graham's work reminds us that dance is a vehicle for fierce dramas of the inner life. The women who pioneered modern dance once used it to exalt all women's highest aspirations, our most profound despairs. From the *Notebook* excerpts that follow, Graham's need to reenter, reimagine, and reinvent women's mythic origins emerges startling and clear.

—K.M.

Martha Graham
[1894–   ]

SELECTIONS

From *The Notebooks of Martha Graham*

Deaths & Entrances

Feb 18—1950
Tonight in Deaths & Entrances while standing I suddenly knew what witchcraft is—in microcosm—It is the being within each of us—sometimes the witch, sometimes the real being of good—of creative energy—no matter in what area or direction of activity. The witches' sabbath is the anger we know at times. The sacrament is taken but the wine of life is the blood of death—It is the abomination which is partaken of rather than the essence of life—when I lose my temper it is like a witches' sabbath—the Black Mass—the world is given over to the powers of darkness & the rule of the blood—It is Kali in her terrible aspect—It is Shiva the destroyer—It is Lucifer—"as proud as Lucifer"—the obverse of God—
This, too, is what D & E is about—only I did not know enough to quite see it through—

All the repentence is of no avail. It is "giving for" one mood the other state of consciousness—doing it quite consciously—in face of all temptation to do otherwise & to "ride the broom-stick." Strength comes from a use of the muscles—The athletes of God wrestled & grew strong. They chose, & they acted.
What I do must be done in full sunlight of awareness—I must learn a means of changing the mood—the state of consciousness—without double-mindedness or tho't of gain.

Center of the Hurricane
People say—
How did you begin?
Well—that is the question
And who knows—
Not I—

How does it all begin?
I suppose it never begins, it just continues—
Life—
generations
Dancing—

One takes it up when one arrives with all the richness of blood as one
takes up one's ancestral physical heritage—
Of course, there must be strength of bone & muscle & heart & faith—
but one takes up at the time the necessity of one's heritage & in time it
may become one's "calling," one's "destiny," one's "fame"—
one's "immortality"—

I am a thief—and I am not ashamed. I steal from the best wherever
it happens to me—Plato—Picasso—Bertram Ross—the members
of my company never show me anything—except you expect me to
steal it—

I am a thief—
and I glory in it—
I steal from the present and from the glorious past—and I stand in the
dark of the future as a glorying & joyous thief—There are so many
wonderful things of the imagination to pilfer—so I stand accused—
I am a thief—but with this reservation—I think I know the value of
that I steal & I treasure it for all time—not as a possession but as a
heritage & a legacy—

Shelter Island—
a pirate's lair—(place)
a recluse from the traditional puritan—
It is strange it should begin to be written here—in a pirate's
sanctuary—because I, too, am a thief

Voyage
The passage of a night into dawn—a new day—
another time—
an incident of re-birth—

> Voyage was the decision
> to make the journey—
> This follows voyage—

The passage of any night is ended by an emergence into Dawn—
a fresh beginning—

A woman's storm at sunset—anyone's storm at the end of a day—
   The rituals necessary for re-birth of day
     The new moon—

         tender youngness
The young queen   fresh, shy,
         propitiation rites to this goddess who rules our
         lives—the acceptance of her domination—

The storm of memories—
The fear of the dark—

The battle cry of the full moon—
    love, lust, passion,
the emergence of the whole being—

The waning moon—
    The flight—the desperation—the ravenings—   *fear of the complete*
    the prophecies—destruction—   *anonymous dark*

The dark—
    a softness to the despair—
    a round dance?

Prayer at Sunset

Storm at sunset

Rituals necessary for the birth of Day —

Sunset —
    Return   togetherness
    Departure   separateness —
The emergence of the warrior in the woman —

House at Night —

Ghost in the House

The storm of memories   sunset
The battle cry   full moon
The prophecy   waning moon
The Love Song   Dawn
    (Eos)

The facing of the inner being —
    Sunset
    waxing moon —
    Full moon — Battle cry of one's
                 powers of love & lust.
    waning moon —

Sunset is departure — leave-taking — farewell —
It can be an end, or a beginning of a new time —
It can be the herald of dawn — if night is the cradle of the new,
rather than the death of the past —

There are many sunsets in our lives —

It is a time of rich color, of remembrance,   unease
unbearable beauty and inescapable anguish — longing —
                   fear of the approaching night —
                          dark
It lasts a short space of time — like the voluptuous sunset near
Boulder Dam — all rose, all hushed, even the water in which one swam
rose, heavy in texture, slow-moving —
an instant of intense awareness, an hiatus in activity, an arrest, before
the plunge of the grey and the final dark —
                   anonymity of the dark

The ghosts who come during the strange hours we call night are the age-old memories — the race remembrances — those moments of residence in the anonymity of night when we re-assemble to be born again. "You have so little time to be born to this instant" — The ritual of the Goddess of Renewal — the crescent Moon — implicit with promise of fulfillment —

Night is the Time of the Goddess —
Day is the Time of the God —

Night is the Time one enters the regions
    of Demeter
        Persephone
        Isis
        Mary the Mother of God
        Hecate — the prostitute —

        Death
        change —
        Renewal

The World of the Woman —
    where continuity is the dynamic

The Gods of the Greeks — Kerenyi.
. . . "Zeus stood in sacred awe of the goddess — Night"
. . . Three great goddesses play the part of Mother of the World: the sea-goddess Tethys, the goddess Night, & Mother Earth. They constitute a Trinity . . . . All thru mythology one comes across 3 goddesses. Real Trinities, sometimes almost forming a single Threefold Goddess."

"Our lunar month was divided into 3 parts, & our moon had
3 aspects: as the waxing
           "   full
           "   waning
sign of a divine presence in the sky"

Three Fates
    Spinner —   Klotho
    apportioner —   Lachesis   — oldest —
    Inevitable —   Atropos (smallest — most powerful)

"When the moon shone, Artemis was present, & beasts & plants would dance"

Voyage —
The Sphinx —   The Challenger —
demanding an answer
to the riddle —

The answer is the
wholeness of Experience —
(man as manifestation)

a woman stands at the threshold of night
a woman stands at the threshold of recognition
night is the cradle of the day —

muezzin —
    woman flat on floor — as in prayer
                        despair
                        wonder
rises —
        coat of fur   Perhaps shrouded as
        dagger —   in burnoose as she rises.

        dance of half beast
                half woman
                    contrasts
gentleness   violence
elegance   beastliness —
wonder   stupidity —

Dancer in a night cafe?

Night of Vision
        Illumination —
                        Luminaries
                            they burn at Fiesta time —
                    Dawn —
"Stella Maria Maris, hodie processit ad ortum"
Mary Star of the Sea is risen today —

Bugle of the watch announced the Dawn
                        (Suso)

"One day . . . whilst the Servitor was still at rest, he heard within
himself a gracious melody by which his heart was greatly moved. And at
the moment of the rising of the morning star, a deep sweet voice sang
within him these words: Stella Maria Maris, hodie processit ad ortum.
That is to say, Mary Star of the Sea is risen today. And this song which
he heard was so spiritual & so sweet, that his soul was transported by it,
and he too began to sing joyously . . . and one day — it was in carnival
time — the Servitor had continued his prayers until the moment when the
bugle of the watch announced the dawn. Therefore, he said to
himself, Rest for an instant before you salute the shining Morning Star.
And whilst his senses were at rest, behold! angelic spirits began to sing
the fair Respond: Illuminare, illuminare, Jerusalem! . . . "

The Traveler's journey to god is complete when he retains knowledge of
Him — "Illumination," in the language of European mystics. The point at
which this is reached is called The Tavern, the resting place along
the road . . .

Image —
    woman seated —   *Voyage Bob?*
        wide skirt making cavern of legs —
        man kneeling between her wide knees —
        Her feet clasp about him & he falls backward — down steps as
        she rises —

                Voyage Stuart —
Image —
        man & woman with crossed daggers —

Image —
        white silk curtain — as at window —
        lights of sunset thrown on it —
        occasionally it blows out as in a breeze —
        perhaps at the end when it is apparent sun has set — color gone —
           woman in silhouette as watching — waiting —
  —   or
        pieces of curtain come in slowly as in Picasso painting — to fit
        into design behind woman during muezzin —
        Then she dances dramatically tragically, beautifully to end of Day —
        colors fly out & night begins —
        (people could walk colors in — especially if it is carnival time)

Image —
    Woman   &man   seated
     ↑   hands joined   ↑
   carries a dagger   sword between legs
                        rapier
    Valley of the Sphinx —
each section a vision of the race memory —

a participation in a state of "blessed madness" in the ritual of
anonymity, the race memory of ritualistic things.
    The Young Moon —

The drama is in the strangeness of meetings in the midst of the
rituals — the "shock of recognition —"

How one arrives at the dominion ruled by the "White Goddess" —
    she of inspiration —
    she the exciter of the Muse —
    She the Muse herself,
        who rules all expression —

The passage of sunset into night — with its moon-rise, moon high,
moon set, deep dark, dawn, — as the souls rite of passage from the
death of color into birth of new color — as self-examination —

Sunset
Night   Moon
    new moon   at waxing
    full moon   " full
    old moon   " waning
    Divine Dark
Dawn —

new moon —   "moons of wonder"
a fantasy —   time of ritual to woman —
    young girls
    The Goddess
    Young bulls
full moon —   time of love
                   of battle

                                        of wildness

old moon   "Walls of Tragedy"

"O thou desire" —

This is a woman's experience as a woman not as a symbol as in
Voyage —

This is her drama of return — in which she is a woman besieged by
strange and terrifying powers & visions —

It is a telling of how she meets them — emerges into song again —

Katherine Dunham
[1910–   ]

AN INTRODUCTION

KATHERINE DUNHAM was a student at the University of Chicago when she received a fellowship to study anthropology and dance in the West Indies. The resulting book, *Journey to Accompong*, first published in 1946, is a personal account of her search for the African forms of dance still existing among the Maroons, descendants of a tribe of fugitive slaves who lived isolated but free in the mountains of Jamaica.

References to the Maroons in various anthropological studies had brought the young student to their village. She was hoping they would show her the African dance forms she sought as a key to her own creative work. Publicly, the Maroons danced the stiff Scottish reels of the ruling class; privately, she thought, they remembered the sacred drums and dances leading to possession by the ancient deities. One night toward the end of her stay, just as she had given up hope of proving her theory, Dunham heard the forbidden sounds of the sacred drum beats—some of the villagers were initiating the new goombay drum she had asked them to make for her. Dunham followed the sound to a clearing. There she saw and took part in the ritual dances. The next night she was initiated into the old religion as a priestess, and she received the spirit of an ancestor as her spiritual guide.

In the years that followed her trip to Accompong, Katherine Dunham was to become the high priestess of black dance in America. Her interest in primitive dance and her pioneering studies of its forms created a resurgence of the African rythmns and ritual dances slavery and assimilation had threatened to obliterate from Afro-American consciousness. Thus, with her choreography she restored to us a vital, life-giving part of our cultural heritage.

Katherine Dunham Dancers dance her choreographic intepretations of ancient fertility rites and mourning and marriage ceremonies, blending modern and primitive dance forms into a style that has influenced the succeeding three generations of major black dancers and choreographers, many of whom received their training at the old Dunham School on Broadway and Forty-third Street in New York City. Dunham dancers move to the sound of the sacred drums, in which the spirits of the ancient deities reside. That galvanizing beat calls the living into contact with their own sacred spirit and releases in them the sense of oneness with the natural world which is the essence of all primitive cultures (and an essential part of any planet-saving culture we now build).

When Dr. Martin Luther King was shot down from the balcony where he stood leading the nonviolent civil rights movement, Katherine Dunham walked through East St. Louis, Illinois, where she was then teaching, and gave her drums to the crowds of young men who gathered in the streets. They played all through the night in that crumbling city, and who knows what old spirits came to comfort them and give them the strength to create music from their anger and their grief. Dunham founded, and for twenty years has been the director of, the Performing Arts Training Center at Southern Illinois University in East St. Louis.

Her long career in dance and theatre began in 1931 when she appeared in *A Negro Rhapsody* with the Chicago Opera Company. She has danced on Broadway, in film, and has choreographed many Broadway musicals, ballets, and operas (Scott Joplin's *Treemonisha* among them), as well as many Broadway seasons for her own company. With her company, and alone, she has toured in over sixty foreign countries since 1947.

Katherine Dunham holds a Ph.D. degree in anthropology from the University of Chicago and is a member of the Royal Society of Anthropology, London. Her studies of black dance forms are a perfect example of the practical application of anthropological knowledge. Through them she has brought a pride, a purpose, and energy to black dance in America that continues to determine its history and course.

—K.M.

Katherine Dunham

[1910–   ]

SELECTION

From *Journey to Accompong*

Twenty-seventh Day

This afternoon I was very despondent. Mai was away on private business of her own, Ba' Teddy and Ba' Weeyums were at work in the fields, Rachel and Hannah and Sweetie were in Maggotty, and all of my old friends seemed to have deserted me. I would even have welcomed the Colonel, but he was in Balaclava visiting his sick daughter. Any other afternoon I would have been much relieved to have a few moments to myself, but today I must begin to think about leaving this country, and being alone, the thing that had been secretly troubling me for some days again confronted me. What a failure to come so far to see the dances of the Koromantee, and to have them always elude me! To find the quadrille and the shay-shay the sole expressions of the dance among these isolated people. Where, then, my theory on the survival of this particular art form which is among all primitive peoples so closely bound up with their superstitions and joys and sorrows and religion and cosmology? The one fleeting moment at Mis' Ma'y Cross's gravediggin' when Ba' Weeyums and his friends, well under the influence of rum, had entered the hut was the only indication that it existed here, aside from the Colonel's promises. And if I met with such failure on this first stop, would further wanderings through the islands of the West Indies be more fruitful?

For long I had doubted my own ability to gain the confidence of the people. Then I began to feel the hypocrisy of the Colonel and his promises. Then I was certain that such dances did not exist here, had been long ago forgotten, and were buried in the dust of the old goombay. Then a little demon would hop up and ask me what dances the Colonel *would* have taken

to Kingston, whether he could or not; how could he have planned on and
promised these dances if they really were forgotten, as some said, or if he
forbade them, as others said, or if there was no goombay and no one to play
it if there were one? It all seemed very complicated, and the more I thought
about it the more depressed I became; so I decided to begin to pack, because
early tomorrow I would have to go to Maggotty on business, and the remaining days would be crowded with last-minute preparations for departure. But first I read a little from my notes on these dances, more to torment
myself than for consolation. According to Edward Long, *History of Jamaica*
(London, 1774, Vol. II):

> The "goombah," another of their musical instruments, is a hollow block of
> wood covered with a sheepskin stripped of its hair. . . . Their tunes for dancing
> are usually brisk and have an agreeable compound of the *vivace* and *larghetto*,
> gay and grave. They seem also well adapted to keep their dancers in just time
> and regular movements. The female dancer is all languishing and easy in her
> motions; the man is all action, fire, and gesture; his whole person is variously
> turned and writhed every moment, and his limbs agitated with such lively
> exertions as serve to display before his partner the vigor and elasticity of his
> muscles. The lady keeps her face toward him and puts on a modest and de-
> mure look, which she counterfeits with great difficulty. In her paces she
> exhibits a wonderful address, particularly in the motion of her hips, and
> steady position of the upper part of her person: the right execution of this
> wriggle, keeping the exact time with the music is esteemed among them a
> particular excellence and on this account they begin to practice it early in life. . .

Then notes from James Phillip's *Jamaica* (London, Snow, 1843), wherein
he discusses the myal dances, of which the Maroons denied all knowledge:

> Myalism, as well as fetishism, were constituent parts of obeism and in-
> cluded a mystery of iniquity which perhaps was never revealed to the unini-
> tiated. The votaries of this art existed as a fraternity composed of individuals
> from the surrounding neighborhood who were regularly inducted into it in a
> dance with certain demoniacal forms. . . . The master of ceremonies, who was
> usually a denominated doctor, by violent and excessive dancing, as well as
> use of poisonous drugs deprived his victims of sensibility and apparently of
> life. . .

So apparently, at one time, the Maroons danced something quite different from the set dances at the parade. And that was not so long ago that they
should profess this state of amnesia.

I began to gather odds and ends which I must pack: the woven hammock and the rice sifter and the tambourine and the flute and my bowl of cedar-wood and the table scarf Hannah had embroidered and presented as a gift to me and the river reed basket Mis' Holiday had sent me and numerous other trinkets. Suddenly I rememberd that I must leave room for the goombay. And after all, why wasn't the goombay here by now? Ba' Foster had promised it for yesterday. It was growing dusk, and glad for an excuse to leave the house, which seemed a little dreary in the half-light, I decided to walk down the mountain to Ba' Foster's yard and find out what was delaying it.

The two weird little mouse-bats whirled past my head as I stepped out into the yard, and settled under the rustling straw roof with a great flapping of wings and a contented squeaking. I had never liked them, and tonight they were especially repulsive with their flash of sharp white mouse teeth and webbed furry wings.

Nearing Ba' Foster's house, I began to feel an excitement in the air, and almost involuntarily my step quickened and I was breathing faster without knowing why. Then I became aware of a *drum*. Not the deep booming of the revivalist Salvation Army drum, but the sharp staccato of a goatskin drawn tightly over a small hollowed trunk and beaten expertly by gnarled black palms. . .

I skidded down the last rocky decline and directly into Ba' Foster's yard. This was deserted. But farther down in the hollow, well hidden from the road behind a tangle of pimientó and breadfruit and coconut trees, I could see the smoky glow of kerosene torches and a circle of tense eager bodies, faces ecstatic in the flickering half-light; and in the middle of the circle, Mis' Mary and on old man whom I did not know performing a strange ritual, more pantomime than dance. And to one side Ba' Weeyums, squatted over the goombay, *my* goombay, his face streaked with perspiration, his eyes brilliant, and his hard palms beating the goatskin, the tone changing from sharp to sullen, from a command to a coaxing by a deft sliding of the side of the palm along the face of the drum.

Ba' Teddy saw me first. Yes, even he was there. I felt suddenly in the midst of traitors to find here these, my bosom friends.

"Evenin', evenin', Missus," said Ba' Teddy softly.

"Evenin'," I replied, winking back a tear. Ba' Foster stepped quickly forward with the goombay under one arm.

"Me *jus* gwi bring eem you, Missus!" he said, with too much emphasis. "Me on de way now we'n we meet up wid' Ba' Weeyums en eem ax er play eem jus' dis' once."

I looked at Ba' Weeyums. He was first on one foot and then on the other, twisting his little felt hat around his forefinger and looking anxiously at me

the while. Then suddenly I realized that this was the long hoped-for opportunity—that here were the dances I had waited so many weeks to see, and
that it was not for fieldworker to bear personal grudges and carry personal
grievances, but to get what the field has to offer in as graceful a manner as
possible. Now it was my turn to look anxiously at Ba' Weeyums.

"But everyone's going!" I said. And to be sure, of the score of old and
young who had circled the dancers when I arrived, there were now less than
half.

"De goombay eem good 'nuf," said Ba' Weeyums slowly, "but eem need
rum. Don't no goombay talk like eem should talk eef eem no had de *rum*."

The rum! The rum! Of course. I loudly asked Ral if he would go up to my
cottage and bring down the jug of rum from under Mai's bunk in the
kitchen. He was off with unusual alacrity, whether because of the rum or
because of the chance that Mai might by this hour have retired to the bunk,
I do not know.

While we waited Ba' Weeyums explained that of course he could have
beat the drum for me any day, but that there had been no drum to beat. Ba'
Teddy explained further that all this was strictly forbidden by the Colonel,
that he had cautioned them against doing these dances while I was there (my
suspicions of hypocrisy were well founded), that Ba' Foster's story was true
that nothing had been planned but only by the accident of Ba' Weeyums
drum beating had these passers-by gathered, and that were the Colonel not
at Balaclava even this would have been out of the question. Of course I must
not mention these dances to anyone, and tomorrow it would be best if I
would have forgotten all about them. Further, we must be very brief tonight, because while the thicket and the seclusion of the spot and the direction of the wind prevented the sound of the drum from traveling far, it
wouldn't be long before all Accompong would be aroused by these almost-
forgotten drum rhythms which stripped them of the veneer of the Scotch
minister and cricket games at the parade and set dances, and the sleeping
Koromantee and Eboe and Nago would come to the fore and things would
happen that the Colonel would be certain to hear about, even at Balaclava.
Just a little while, I pleaded, to break in the goombay and so that I might
partake once of the things that belonged to the Maroons in the old days.

Ral returned, and Ba' Weeyums took drum and bottle off to one side.
There he poured rum on the goatskin head, rubbed it in, took a long drink
himself, then spat a mouthful at the drum again. Between times he mum-
bled in a tongue which I gathered was Koromantee. Then he poured a few
drops on the ground, and the baptism was over. This was for the spirit of the
drum, he explained. Then he squatted over the drum again, and indeed it

seemed to me that it was suddenly alive. Though the body of the drum was shallow, and it more resembled a square stool than any drum I had previously seen, the tone was full and less staccato than before, and I was almost inclined to believe that it was alive, and that it was the spirit of some Gold Coast god come to life to grumble a protest against the long silence.

Gradually they returned, slipping from behind the coconut palms and up from the ravines and down from the mountains. I don't know how many, because I was in the midst, and there was now only one kerosene torch, and the rum was going the rounds and it all became unreal, though it all happened because the dances are still very clear to me.

I might not have come at all, for the difference that it has made. I was accepted and one of them.

The dance I had interrupted was a myal dance. Ba' Teddy explained it, as, fascinated, I watched Mis' Mary and the old man. They were facing each other. The old man took the part of the myal "doctor" and the dance was to entice into his power an evil spirit, the "duppy" of some dead worker of black magic. Ba' Weeyums led a chant in Koromantee, and the women answered. The dance interested me too much for me to try and remember the sound of the words. The evil spirit circles around the doctor hesitant, advancing and retreating, her eyes fixed, mouth clamped shut tightly, body rigid. The doctor squatted in front of her, arms wide as though to embrace her, fingers wide open and hands trembling violently. As he advanced slowly toward her, his pelvis began to move with an unmistakable sexual purpose, and the duppy responded in like manner. They hesitated in front of each other, swaying. Then she eluded his embrace with a sharp convulsive bend, and was on the other side of the circle, taunting, enticing features still hard and set but body liquid and so full of desire that I could scarcely believe that it was old Mis' Mary, grandmother of goodness knows how many.

The doctor reached out for her, gesticulating, grimacing, insinuating. Then she came to life suddenly and the pursuit was reversed. The doctor was afraid of this thing which he had done, of this woman whom he had raised from the dead with these fleshly promises. They were face to face, bodies touching, both of them squatting now with arms pressed close to their sides, elbows bent, and widespread fingers quivering violently. Ba' Teddy had stopped explaining and among the onlookers there was no sound except heavy breathing, but the chant continued and the drum, and it seemed that the air was heavy with some other heat and sound. The duppy leaned over the man, who cowered in fear from her, though their bodies were pressed tightly together. As I decided that I must close my eyes for a moment, Ba'

Teddy raised his hand, and the drum and chant stopped on a single note: there was a blank silence that left both dancers and spectators dangling helplessly in mid-air.

"Dat dance bad dance," Ba' Teddy muttered, trying to calm his voice and appear merely annoyed in spite of his quick breathing. I opened my mouth to speak, but he anticipated my question and answered sharply. "Bes don' ax no furder questions, missus. Me don' see dat fer long time, en hit bad. Dat mix up wid bad biznuss. Better fer missus ef she fergit."

I was almost relieved to be thus reprimanded. But the mood of the dance had already changed, and to a far livelier rhythm. Two men were hopping about in the circle mimicking two cocks in the thick of a fight. They switched their middles, bobbed their heads, wrinkled their faces, and stuck their necks far out crowing a challenge. The audience, tense a moment before, was now in a hysteria of laughter. One of the dancers picked up his foot high and hopped around in a circle, the other following at a gallop, hand thrust in coat pocket and flapping widely for wings. Finally one was vanquished and with a feeble squawk rolled over sadly, feet in the air. The other strutted over to him, looked disdainfully around, and flapped his wings in victory as he trotted around the circle.

I plead with Ba' Weeyums for a Koromantee war dance, and find that it is no other than the wild dance which I saw only a suggestion of at Ol' Mis' Cross's gravedigging. In this I join, along with Simon Rowe and others who have only watched so far. The few young people who are here, however, do not join in these traditional dances. They are ashamed, and I am sure that I shock them greatly; on the other hand, I feel that they watch us rather wistfully, wishing that they had the courage to give themselves up for a moment to their traditions and forget that there is a market at Maggotty and cricket games on the outside, and store-bought shoes.

The war dances are danced by both men and women. The introduction seemed to be a disjointed walking around in a loose circle, much like the warming up of an athlete. Then Henry Rowe and I are facing each other doing a step which could easily be compared to an Irish reel. Hands on hips, we hop from one foot to the other, feet turned out at right angles to the body or well "turned out," in ballet vernacular. This hopping brought us closer together, and I had to watch the others closely to keep up with Henry. We turned our backs and walked away, then turned suddenly again and hopped together. The songs are in lusty Koromantee, and from somewhere a woman procured a rattle and is shaking it in accompaniment to Ba' Weeyums. Some of the men wave sticks in the air, and the women tear off their handkerchiefs and wave them on high as they dance. Henry and I grabbed each other around the waist and ran circles around each other, first one way, then the other. A few of these turns and we separate in a melee of leaping, shouting warriors; a moment later we are "bush fightin'," crouching down and advancing in line to attack an imaginary enemy with many feints, swerves, and much pantomime. At one stage of the dance Mis' Mary and I are face to face, she no longer a duppy but a Maroon woman of the old days working the men up to a pitch where they will descend into the cockpit and exterminate one of his Majesty's red-coated platoons. She grabbed me by the shoulders and shook me violently, then we were again hopping around each other with knees high in the air, handkerchiefs and skirts flying.

When this was over we were all exhausted. The Maroons have not been accustomed to this sort of thing for a long time; nor am I who until now have known only the conventional techniques, and the far less strenuous set dances. We dispersed and I was in possession of the goombay. Ba' Teddy and Ba' Weeyums and I labored up the mountainside, and behind us shutters closed and candles were extinguished and I knew that they were all talking about the escapade of the evening, and how angry the Colonel would be if he knew, and that the "missus" must have known things that she hadn't so far divulged, about myal and obi and the old Koromantee traditions, maybe even the language. . .

At my cottage, I could hear Mai snoring peacefully within, and this was very comforting after the orgy in the ravine. I remembered vaguely that Ral had left the dancing soon after he returned with the rum, and was certain that he was responsible for Mai's not having come to the dance, and perhaps for her peaceful snoring.

I pulled off my muddy shoes and crawled on top of the marosh, ignoring the bowl of rice and gourd of fresh coconut water that Mai had thoughtfully left on the kitchen table for me. I felt extremely tired and extremely comfortable. My notebook still lay open on the table. Earlier in the day I had harbored a strong resentment against the Maroons and a strong disappointment in myself. Now I had the delicious thrill of accomplishment, of having conquered an unseen enemy (the Colonel, no doubt), and of belonging completely. I only regretted as I pulled the sheet up around my chin that it had all happened so late. Well, if I ever return—and I sincerely hope that I shall—at least I shall know where to begin.

Playwriting:
The Voice Within

Augusta Gregory

Susan Glaspell

Gertrude Stein

Lorraine Hansberry

Augusta Gregory

[1852–1932]

AN INTRODUCTION

WITH THE ADDED TALENT of John Millington Synge and, later, Sean O'Casey, and with the help and hindrance of many others, Lady Augusta Gregory and William Butler Yeats made a theatre for Ireland unsurpassed in poetry and force of vision by any other in the world. A theatre "with a base of reality and an apex of beauty," she used to say.

Together Gregory and Yeats set out to destroy the myth of the stage Irishman or Irishwoman (as drunken buffoon or charlady) and to create remembrance of the lofty aspirations and mystic wills of this proud people who have been oppressed so long. They were "not fighting" the British "for Home Rule," Lady Gregory would say, they were "preparing for it." Though Anglo-Irish, she held the "true Celtic notion" of the "importance" of art and put "politics far below, as do all the races to whom Nature allots the artist's temperament."[1] She intended to use the words and visions, legends and beliefs of the Irish people to forge for them a new, free notion of themselves.

Augusta Gregory did not write a play till she was fifty, then wrote nearly fifty plays before she died. She has told the story of the Abbey Theatre in *Our Irish Theatre*, saying its existence "called up the need for playwriting among us," then related how she began writing comedies because some relief was needed after the intensity of Yeats's verse dramas.

But I have always been drawn to her tragedies and tragicomedies because they seem to have more of the woman in them, more of the woman whose life was given in chaste service to male artists, to the Abbey Theatre, to the needs of the grounds and tenants at Coole Park, to Ireland, yet who burned with a passionate intensity she let loose only in her plays.

She was a devoted folklorist. Her arrangements of the ancient Irish myths into rhythmic English prose provided the seeds and scenarios for many of Yeats's plays as well as for many of her own. *Of Gods and Fighting Men, Cuchulain of Muirthemne, Visions and Beliefs in the West of Ireland* are still a

133

source of inspiration for writers who would speak of that region of the heart where seen and unseen worlds meet.

Besides presenting Yeats with the research that inspired many of his plays (as he, in fact, had inspired her research of the Galway legends with his book on Sligo, *The Celtic Twilight*), she worked with him to complete many of his manuscripts. In *Our Irish Theatre*, she explains the nature of her early collaboration with Yeats:

> I began by writing bits of dialogue, when wanted. Mr. Yeats used to dictate parts of *Diarmuid and Grania* to me, and I would suggest a sentence here and there. Then I, as well as another, helped fill in spaces in *Where There is Nothing* [which they later rewrote as *The Unicorn from the Stars*—ED.]. Mr. Yeats says in dedicating it to me: "I offer you a book which is in part your own. . . for my eyes were troubling me. . . you said I might dictate to you, and we worked in the mornings at Coole, and I never did anything that went so easily and quickly; for when I hesitated you had the right thought ready and it was almost always you who gave the right turn to the phrase and gave it the ring of daily life. We finished several plays, of which this is the longest, in so few weeks that if I were to say how few, I do not think anybody would believe me.[2]

Aside from the prose plays they wrote together, Lady Gregory worked with Yeats on the "plot and construction of some of the poetic plays, especially *The King's Threshold* and *Dierdre*."[3] Among her major contributions to Yeats's work are, I would guess, a stronger narrative line and finer character development. She lived among the people and knew how people talked to one another, how they felt when they interacted, how complexly less than perfect social arrangements always are. She shared her gift for dialogue and tale telling, her sense of human interaction, with the withdrawn, lyric poet Yeats. Still her help in the making of his plays was mainly unreciprocated by him. She says of her efforts to write the first of the Abbey's historical plays: "I made many bad beginnings, and if I had listened to Mr. Yeats's advice I should have given it up. . . ."[4]

The unspoken sorrow of her ultimate isolation is suddenly so clear. While she could give her plots, scenarios, and cadences to Yeats, Douglas Hyde, and the other men who gathered at her estate to make the Irish Literary Revival, her own creative agonies took place alone, and all the plays that bear her name were mined in private from her soul.

Partly because few of her plays, except the comedy *The Workhouse Ward*, are readily available, at least in the U.S., and partly because she was surrounded by famous men, it is easy to see her as the helpmate of the Abbey

Theatre and to forget she is one of the most prolific and finest of women playwrights.

What held her back from achieving the full measure of greatness that was in her, aside from the late start at writing that is also, too often, a condition of our sex, was her unstated reluctance to express the sorrows and joys of a woman's life as fully as she might. Reading her, one is always dimly aware of that which remains unsaid, of the road not taken, the vision unexplored. There is nothing like this veil in Yeats's plays. In *The King's Threshold*, which she helped him write, every nuance of the aged male poet-character's mind, each shade of the relationships of his students and his lovers to him are fully explored. Lady Gregory's isolation from her sex told on her. The male mind, men's actions in the world, men's images of women are sanctioned subjects for the drama. Augusta Gregory's own life was noble and heroic, including the birth and death of a beloved son, a turning away from her Anglo-Irish upper class, the cocreation of a major theatre, careful management of a large piece of land. Yet because she was without the same fine companionship with an artist in full sympathy with her point of view, which she had offered freely to Yeats, she could not quite bring herself to write of the world as women live in it, could not quite challenge herself to see women as a major force for change or as fit heroic centers of the dramas.

When she did get close to the truths of women's souls she created her finest work. *The Gaol Gate*, a near-perfect one-act play, is a wonderful example of what Eleonora Duse called "the communal lamentation among women"; *Grania*, which was never staged at the Abbey, probably, as critic Elizabeth Coxhead has pointed out, because of its woman-centered content, is the story of a willful woman desperately struggling for control of her fate.[5] Coxhead speculates that Gregory may have turned against the play, since it was never even brought forward by her as a possible production although, as the notes to the play indicate, its theme had long compelled her. *McDonough's Wife* tells of the power a strong woman exerts over the imaginations of the Irish folk.

The power of the people's imagination was her favorite theme. Rewoven visions, tales, and dreams provide what she called the "machine," or structure, of her plays; and her compassion for the lives of the "folk," her understanding of their ageless dignity, provide the emotional commitment that was her "driving force."

She came late to her craft, after marriage and widowhood released her from certain of the restraints upon her sex. At Coole Park, she kept open house, creating there the literary community she was born to inhabit. For she had always had an artist's soul.

I know that even as a child my heart would feel oppressed at some rare moments with emotion, as I saw the snipe rise sidelong from the rushy marsh, sunset reflected in its pools, or the wild deer among the purple heather of the hills from which I looked on the distant mountain and sea. That feeling came again and again in later years, when some olive-belted hill, or lovely southern plain that well satisfied the eye, filled the heart with a hunger, a pain of longing, I knew not for what. I know now it was the artist's desire to capture, to express the perfect. And although fulfillment has fallen far, far short of vision, I know how barren one side of my life would have been without that poetry of the soil, those words and dreams and cadences of the people that helped me to give some echoed expression to that dragging driving force.[6]

Perhaps because she came late to her craft, as so many women have had to, she became used to investing each of her daily acts with something of the poetry she loved and sought. There is scant separation between her life and her work; she filled each with the same nobility, compassion, gentle humor, and fine imagination.

—K.M.

Augusta Gregory

[1852–1932]

SELECTIONS

From "Making a Play"

First Version

A dozen years ago I thought as little I should ever write a play as that I should ever cross the ocean to Boston. Yet I have done both, indeed I may almost say the greater is contained within the less, the great pleasure of my visit here in the drudgery of creating and writing. My excuse for this talk must be that we who are on the brink of old age must hold our own. We must not give up all to the youngsters who have the benefit we never had for an education on writing drama. I have been a pioneer for I don't think anyone ever began playwriting both at so ripe an age and with such profound ignorance as I did, and if I have not got as far as I wish to those heights of which in enthusiasm or beginning a new play I have sometimes dreamed, anyhow I am a pioneer, a discoverer that the weight of years ought not to put us off beginning anything.

I knew nothing about drama. I had been brought up in a house where the theatre was considered a very wicked place; I was not even allowed to read Shakespeare till the age of eighteen had freed me some extent from such trammels.* Then I began interest in Theatre and I began to read plays and to comment on them, to write in a bit of dialogue for one writer, to make a scenario for another, till at last I made my own venture.

From "Making a Play," an essay by Lady Augusta Gregory. Used with permission of the Henry W. and Albert A. Berg Collection, New York Public Library, Astor, Lenox and Tilden Foundation.

*She was married at eighteen to Sir William Gregory, who was many years her senior. It was not until he died that she began to write.

137

Second Version

There are certain principles I have worked out for myself on the Making of a Play, or have been taught by my fellow writers. I think to begin with that as in most other constructive arts there must be a machine and a driving force. We make the engine and it is driven by the power of steam, or by the rushing force of a river or a current of electricity. The machine is made by man, the power is the possession of nature, the creation of God. To create a force that can carry out a purpose, that is not accidental, wasted, Nature and man must collaborate, the machine and the driving force are necessary to one another.

Now in making a play it seems to me one must choose a fable, that is the machine; and before the actual writing of the play begins, before it comes into being one must be chosen by some idea, some strong emotion that is the driving force. When I say "chosen" by an idea, I am saying what Blake said in one of his poems "The Authors Are in Eternity." There are moments of insight that come to an individual, perhaps very seldom in a lifetime, that is one way of getting the flame, as by lightning, and there is a smouldering in the world about us, like latent fire in the sods under the ashes of the hearth, a great mass of what in Ireland we call the memory of the people, something that is part history, part belief, part myth, that comes from ages past men's memory, that dominates the thought of the race. . . .

Without the fable the play would be without form, without the strong and rich emotion it must be cold. One may sit down and write the fable by effort of will that one has control over, and that is one's own; but I believe the driving force is not one's own; it is part of the collaboration with the unseen which all art is an effort to express. . . .

Now having the fable, the machine, and the emotion, the driving force, you want the texture, the clothing, something that will cover the ribs of your framework as fur and feather cover squirrel or bird, something not necessarily beautiful, but at least fitting, flexible, and abundant. Speech in its highest expression is given in the verse plays of Mr. Yeats, and we are happy in having them to act in our Irish Theatre. We give them there, and though some visitors say they don't care for poetry, and find it an effort to listen to, we never have that complaint from the cheap places, from the people. Their ear is trained by love of oratory and by long use of rhythmical language to the cadence of verse. . . .

Language is a thing we must not be stinted in and we writers in Ireland are in no danger of that.

The Gaelic language is extraordinarily abundant, its poets pride themselves upon alliteration, they pour out cataracts compared to which any

English vocabulary is as Lodore to Niagara. Our country people try to rival this abundance in the English language. They have the Gaelic rhythm in their mind; as when Bartley Fallon says, "I'm thinking if I went to America it's long ago the day I'd be dead." Our people get by instinct the weighty word, the balanced phrase, and it may be a word that came into England at the time of Elizabeth or Cromwell and has lived here while death and burial has awaited it in England.

Our people also get the repetition of the one idea in a second phrase, that is the essence of Hebrew poetry. We know it in the Bible: "He maketh the barren woman to keep house and to be a joyful mother of children." "He maketh the solitary place to be glad for them, and the desert shall rejoice and blossom as the rose." "Then should I have lain still and quiet, I should have slept, then should I have been at rest." Our people say, "She is buried and gone to the grave." "He is dead and he is not living." They take joy in the very sound. I asked one of my workmen at what hour his sister had died and he said, "at seven o'clock and the bell ringing."

The repetition of idea may sometimes be carried a little too far. A basket maker at my door told me the other day in speaking of the war, "The Kaiser was preparing for it this long time; he must be a terrible man. That was the way in ancient Rome with an Emperor called Diocletian. Killing men all the day he was, and his valet catching flies for him to kill at night."

I have but to sit and listen to tramp or piper or beggar at my door, and it is a wonder if my store of speech is not enriched, by the abundance of the store poured forth. An old woman came to ask for something for Christmas the other day. She is perhaps not quite right in the head, but she is very right in her phraseology. She was talking about the war and she said: . . . "That building that was best out in the blessed land; three hundred years it was building and I don't know was it four or five. The best building out in France it was; they blew it and broke it down; there is many a sore heart through them; they are the terriblest swarm that ever came into the world." . . .

Dramatists can't complain of want of fur and feather for our skeletons having this abundance ready to hand.

All countries have not this abundant and flexible language. But all have a living language and a living language is essential for the expression of a play. Poetry has its own speech but the literary phrase will not go across the footlights.

We wanted to play Molière in our Theatre and we tried I think five trans-lations, reading them from the stage. But they did not go, they did not carry. I, who Mr. Bernard Shaw has described as the charwoman of the

Theatre, had to put my hand to that work, and I made versions that do carry. I do not take for myself more credit for this than that of industry, if indeed that is not the greatest credit we can take, for we make ourselves industrious, it is God gives us the rest. The credit goes to the living language that I took. Collaboration again, collaboration with the unseen as in the driving force, and as Synge said, collaboration with the people in the language.

The circumstances of our Theatre have forced me to write comedy. The strain of the attention necessary for listening to verse requires a relaxing afterwards, and our young writers are serious and have problems to think out before they can let themselves laugh. But I think tragedy is easier. Tragedy shows humanity in the grip of circumstance, of fate, of what our people call "the thing will happen, the woman in the stars that does all." . . .

Fate himself is the protagonist, and your actor cannot carry much character, it is out of place. You don't want to know the character of a wrestler you see trying his strength at a show. Take Hamlet out of his surroundings and set him in this city and unless it might be that his beautiful Elizabethan speech betrayed him, he would not be much noticed, it would be hard to prophesy the nature of his blameless days. But take Molière's Scapin, let him loose here and see if before the year is out he has not picked your pocket in some agreeable way and made himself indispensable to your affairs.

In writing a little tragedy, *The Gaol Gate,* I made the scenario in this way, in three lines "He is an informer. He is dead. He is hanged." Two women come to the gate of the Gaol. They have believed a rumour that the prisoner, the son of the one, the husband of the other, is an informer. They hear he has died in gaol, they make their lament, with the more bitterness, because none of the neighbors will mourn with them for one that was a traitor. Then the warden tells them he did not die by visitation of God, but he was hanged. He had not been an informer, he had refused to tell who had fired the shot. The young woman still laments, but the mother calls out to all the people to join in praises: "was there ever heard in Galway such a thing to be done, a man to die for his neighbor". . . My poor women were in the clutch of the woman in the stars, though the one of them broke from it at the last in exultation . . . .

In the whole course of our work at the Theatre we have, I may say, been drenched with advice by friendly people who for years gave us the reasons we did not succeed, but who have not yet begun to tell us the reason why we do. We ought to put on work that would appeal to the many. We should bring in the common mind with common work. We ought to appoint a representative body to choose our plays. We ought to put on every one that was sent us. All this advice or at least some of it might have been good if we had wanted to make money, to make a common place of amusement. The advisers did not see that we wanted to build up a theatre with a base of realism, an apex of beauty, but without any play in it we could not justify for vigour, honesty or art.

From *Collected Plays II*

Notes to the Plays

THE GAOL GATE

I was told a story someone had heard, of a man who had gone to welcome his brother coming out of gaol, and heard he had died there before the gates had been opened for him.

I was going to Galway, and at the Gort station I met two cloaked and shawled countrywomen from the slopes of Slieve Echtge, who were obliged to go and see some law official in Galway because of some money left them by a kinsman in Australia. They had never been in a train or to any place farther than a few miles from their own village, and they felt astray and terrified "like blind beasts in a bog" they said, and I took care of them through the day.

An agent was fired at on the road from Athenry, and some men were taken up on suspicion. One of them was a young carpenter from my old home, and in a little time a rumour was put about that he had informed against the others in the Galway gaol. When the prisoners were taken across the bridge to the court-house he was hooted by the crowd. But at the trial it was found that he had not informed, that no evidence had been given at all; and the bonfires were lighted for him as he went home.

These three incidents coming within a few months wove themselves into this little play, and within three days it had written itself, or been written. I like it better than any in the volume, and I have never changed a word of it.

GRANIA

I think I turned to Grania because so many have written about sad, lovely Deirdre, who when overtaken by sorrow made no good battle at the last. Grania had more power of will, and for good or evil twice took the shaping of her life into her own hands. The riddle she asks us through the ages is, "Why did I, having left great grey-haired Finn for comely Diarmuid, turn back to Finn in the end, when he had consented to Diarmuid's death?" And a question tempts one more than the beaten path of authorized history. If I

From *Collected Plays II* by Lady Augusta Gregory (Buckinghamshire, Great Britain: Colin Smythe Limited, Publishers, 1971). Used with permission of the publisher.

have held but lightly to the legend, it is not because I do not know it, for in *Gods and Fighting Men* I have put together and rejected many versions. For the present play I have taken but enough of the fable on which to set, as on a sod of grass, the three lovers, one of whom had to die. I suppose it is that "fascination of things difficult" that has tempted me to write a three-act play with only three characters. Yet where Love itself, with its shadow Jealousy, is the true protagonist I could not feel that more were needed. When I told Mr. Yeats I had but these three persons in the play, he said incredulously, "They must have a great deal to talk about." And so they have, for the talk of lovers is inexhaustible, being of themselves and one another.

As to the Fianna, the Fenians, I have heard their story many a time from my neighbours, old men who have drifted into workhouses, seaweed gatherers on the Burren Coast, turf-cutters on Slieve Echtge, and the like. For though the tales that have gathered around that mysterious race are thought by many to come from the earliest days, even before the coming of the Aryan Celt, the people of the West have a very long memory. And these tales are far better remembered than those of the Red Branch, and this, it is suggested, is part proof of their having belonged to the aboriginal race. Cuchulain's bravery, and Deirdre's beauty "that brought the Sons of Usnach to their death" find their way, indeed, into the folk-poetry of all the provinces; but the characters of the Fianna, Grania's fickleness, and Conan's bitter tongue, and Oisin's gentleness to his friends and his keen wit in the arguments with St. Patrick, and Goll's strength, and Osgar's high bravery, and Finn's wisdom, that was beyond that of earth, are as well known as the characteristics of any noticeable man of modern times.

An old man I talked with on the beach beyond Kinvara told me, "They were very strong in those days, and six or seven feet high. I was digging the potato garden one day about forty years ago, and down in the dyke the spade struck against something, and it was the bones of a man's foot, and it was three feet long. I brought away one bone of it myself, and the man that was along with me, but we buried it after. It was the foot of one of those men. They had every one six or seven dogs, and first they would set two of the dogs to fight, and then they'd fight themselves. And they'd go to all countries in curraghs that were as strong as steamers; to Spain they went in their curraghs. They went across from this hill of Burren to Connemara one time, and the sea opened to let them pass. There are no men like them now; the Connemara men are the best, but even with them, if there was a crowd of them together, and you to throw a stick over their heads, it would hardly hit one, they are mostly all the one height, and no one a few inches taller than another."

Another man says, "They were all strong men in those times; and one time Finn and his men went over to Granagh to fight the men there, and it was the time of the harvest, and what they fought with was sheaves, and every one that got a blow of a sheaf got his death. There is one of them buried now in Fardy Whelan's hill and there's two headstones, and my father often measured the grave, and he said it is seven yards long."

On Slieve Echtge I was told, "Oisin and Finn took the lead for strength, and Samson, too, he had great strength." "I would rather hear about the Irish strong men," said I. "Well, and Samson was of the Irish race, all the world was Irish in those times, and he killed the Philistines, and the eyes were picked out of him after. He was said to be the strongest, but I think myself Finn MacCumhail was stronger." And again, "It was before the flood those strong men lived here, Finn and Oisin and the others, and they lived longer than people do now, three or four hundred years.

"Giants they were; Conan was twelve feet high, and he was the smallest. But ever since, people are getting smaller and smaller, and will till they come to the end; but they are wittier and more crafty than they were in the old days, for the giants were innocent though they were so strong."

I hear sometimes of "a small race and dark, and that carried the bag," and that was probably the aboriginal one. "There was a low-sized race came, that worked the land of Ireland a long time; they had their time like the others." And, "Finn was the last of the giants, the tall strong men. It was after that the Lochlannachs came to the country. They were very small, but they were more crafty than the giants, and they used to be humbugging them. One time they got a sack and filled it with sand, and gave it to one of the Fianna to put on his back to try him. But he lifted it up, and all he said was, 'It is grain sowed in February it is.' " Another says, "An old man that was mending the wall of the house used to be telling stories about the strong men of the old time; very small they were, about three feet high, but they were very strong for all that."

Grania is often spoken of as belonging to that small race, as if her story had come from a very early time. "She was very small, only four feet. She was the heiress of the princes of Ireland, and that is why they were after her." "They say Diarmuid and Grania were very small. They made the big cromlechs, there's a slab on the one near Crusheen, sixteen men couldn't lift, but they had *their own way* of doing it." And again, "Diarmuid and Grania were very small and very thick." Another says, "Grania was low-sized; and people now are handsomer than the people of the old time, but they haven't such good talk."

I do not know if it is because of Grania's breach of faith, that I never hear her spoken of with sympathy, and her name does not come into the songs as Deirdre's does. A blind piper told me, "Some say Grania was handsome, and some say she was ugly, there's a saying in Irish for that." And an old basket-maker was scornful and said, "Many would tell you Grania slept under the cromlechs, but I don't believe that, and she a king's daughter. And I don't believe she was handsome either. If she was, why would she have run away?"

An old woman says, "Finn had more wisdom than all the men in the world, but he wasn't wise enough to put a bar on Grania. It was huts with big stones Grania made, that are called cromlechs now; they made them when they went away into the wilderness."

And again I was told at Moycullen, near Lough Corrib, "As they were passing a stream, the water splashed on Grania, and she said 'Diarmuid was never so near to me as that.' "

McDonough's Wife

In my childhood there was every year at my old home, Roxborough, or, as it is called in Irish, Cregroostha, a great sheep-shearing that lasted many days. On the last evening there was always a dance for the shearers and their helpers, and two pipers used to sit on chairs placed on a corn-bin to make music for the dance. One of them was always McDonough. He was the best of all the wandering pipers who went about from house to house. When, at my marriage, I moved from the barony of Dunkellin to the neighbouring barony of Kiltartan, he came and played at the dance given to the tenants in my honour, and he came and played also at my son's coming of age. Not long after that he died. The last time I saw him he came to ask for a loan of money to take the train to Ennis, where there was some fair or gathering of people going on, and I would not lend to so old a friend, but gave him a half-sovereign, and we parted with kindly words. He was so great a piper that in the few years since his death myths have already begun to gather around him. I have been told that his father was taken into a hill of the Danes, the Tuatha de Danaan, the ancient invisible race, and they had taught him all their tunes and so bewitched his pipes, that they would play of themselves if he threw them up on the rafters. McDonough's pipes, they say, had not that gift, but he himself could play those inspired tunes. Lately I was told the story I have used in this play about his taking away fifty sovereigns from the shearing at Cregroostha and spending them at a village near. "I said to him," said the old man who told me this, "that it would be better for him to have bought a good kitchen of bacon; but he said, 'Ah, when I want more, I have but to squeeze the pipes.' " The story of his wife's death and burial as I give it has been told to me here and there. That is my fable, and the emotion disclosed by the story is, I think, the lasting pride of the artist of all ages:

> *"We are the music makers*
> *And we are the dreamers of dreams. . . .*
> *We in the ages lying*
> *In the buried past of the earth*
> *Built Nineveh with our sighing,*
> *And Babel itself with our mirth."*

I wrote the little play while crossing the Atlantic in the *Cymric* last September. Since it was written I have been told at Kinvara that "McDonough was a proud man; he never would go to a wedding unasked, and he never would play through a town." So he had laid down pride for pride's sake, at that time of the burying of his wife.

In Galway this summer one who was with him at the end told me he had a happy death, "But he died poor; for what he would make in the long nights he would spend through the summer days." And then she said, "Himself and Reilly and three other fine pipers died within that year. There was surely a feast of music going on in some other place."

[When Lady Gregory gave the manuscript of this play to John Quinn, she attached a note which read: "I began to write this little play, *McDaragh's Wife*, on board the *Cymric*, first making my scenario on a Menu, and then writing in pencil as I lay down in my cabin, quiet and undisturbed. Then I added to it and typed it out in Boston, and then 'The Outlook' asked for it and printed it—so here it is in its several states; and being still new to me I think it worth offering to you, dear John Quinn, but you shall have a better one if a better one should come—tho' this will be all the more valuable if it should be my last. I don't suppose anyhow you will be able to read a word of it. Augusta Gregory." The title was later changed to *McDonough's Wife*.]

Susan Glaspell

[1882–1948]

AN INTRODUCTION

SUSAN GLASPELL'S HEROINES ARE among the most distinguished achievements in character creation in the entire range of American drama. They are rebels, every one of them—idealistic rebels," Eugen Solow wrote in *The World,* Sunday, February 9, 1930. Certainly, until the feminist movement began again in the 1960s, the American stage had few women characters as vibrant, strong, and rebellious as those Glaspell created in the teens and twenties for the Provincetown Players, which she and her husband, George Cram Cook, founded. Provincetown is generally best remembered as the theatre group that first produced the plays of Eugene O'Neill. Far less often is it said that the existence of the theatre turned the already well-known journalist and novelist Glaspell to the task of writing plays.

Trifles, the play whose creation she describes on the following pages, is one of the most widely anthologized and performed one-act plays in the American repertory. It is about a woman who murders her husband and is protected from the law by two other women, one of them the wife of the sheriff. The women know that the crime was committed because the hardened husband had first killed all that was beautiful and alive in his wife.

Equal to Glaspell's commitment to women was her commitment to all movements for social change and justice. But the high seriousness of her concerns did not still her frequently comic voice. *The People* is a one-act play about the quarrels on a radical newspaper, showing how the readers have been made fervent idealists by the same values the editors, in their constant struggle for survival, have become quite cynical about. *A Woman's Honor,* another one-act, shows many different women rushing to the defense of a young man determined to die on a murder charge rather than betray his whereabouts on the evening of the crime. The women, each for her own reason, are sick of the limits a false notion of honor (i.e., chastity) imposes on their sex. Each is eager to publicly abandon "virtue" in behalf of the accused.

Glaspell also wrote three-act plays: *Bernice*, about a woman's suicide; *The Verge*, which breaks with realism to enter the fantasy life of a woman seeking to transform herself; and *The Inheritors* and *Alison's House*, both produced by Eva Le Gallienne at the Civic Repertory. In the thirties Glaspell worked with Hallie Flanagan on the Federal Theatre Project as head of the Midwest Playreading Department.

Rachel France, editor of *A Century of Plays by American Women*, has commented perceptively on Glaspell: "Modern feminists cite her concern for "women's issues"; yet Glaspell's main preoccupation as a dramatist was to be the essential affinity between the enlightened individual and the creative forces of the universe." A feminist preoccupation of the profoundest sort, of course.

—K.M.

Susan Glaspell

[1882–1948]

SELECTION

From *The Road to the Temple*

The Old Wharf

Winters we went to New York. Our friends were living downtown in "The Village," so that is where we lived; it was cheaper, and arranged for people like us. Nice to have tea before your glowing coals in Milligan Place, and then go over to Polly's or Christine's for a good dinner with friends. Every once in a while, in the Sunday paper, I read of Greenwich Village. It is a wicked place, it seems, and worse than wicked, it is silly. Just what Greenwich Village is now, I do not know. Through the years I knew it, it was a neighborhood where people were working, where you knew just which street to take for good talk when you wanted it, or could bolt your door and work all day long. You had credit at the little store on the corner, and the coal man too would hang it up if the check hadn't come. I never knew simpler, kinder or more real people than I have known in Greenwich Village. I like in memory the flavor of those days when one could turn down Greenwich Avenue to the office of the Masses, argue with Max or Floyd or Jack Reed; then after an encounter with some fanatic at the Liberal Club, or (better luck) tea with Henrietta Rodman, on to the Working Girls' Home (it's a saloon, not a charitable organization) or if the check had come, to the Brevoort. Jig* loved to sit in the cellar of the Brevoort. He had his own corner, and the waiters smiled when he came in.

We went to the theatre, and for the most part we came away wishing we had gone somewhere else. Those were the days when Broadway flourished almost unchallenged. Plays, like magazine stories, were patterned. They might be pretty good within themselves, seldom did they open out to—

From *The Road to the Temple*, a biography of George Cram Cook by Susan Glaspell (New York: Frederic A. Stokes, 1941). Used by permission of Sirius C. Cook.

*George Cram Cook, her husband.

where it surprised or thrilled your spirit to follow. They didn't ask much of *you,* those plays. Having paid for your seat, the thing was all done for you, and your mind came out where it went in, only tireder. An audience, Jig said, had imagination. What was this "Broadway," which could make a thing as interesting as life into a thing as dull as a Broadway play?

There was a meeting at the Liberal Club—Eddie Goodman, Phil Moeller, Ida Rauh, the Boni brothers, exciting talk about starting a theatre.

Jig spoke the first word spoken by the Washington Square Players; amusing, in view of his feeling about the audience as collaborator, that he spoke it from the audience. "I've had enough of this!" he cried, and I said, "S—sh"; but he went into a violent outbreak about it being a quarter of nine, and the curtain not yet up. Whereupon Edward Goodman, hastening before that curtain, explained why it wasn't up, and he told what the Washington Square Players were about.

Two nights before Jig opened the season at the Bandbox, "we got off the car in the neighborhood of exuberant push-carts with flaring torches, black-eyed women in shawls, old men with patriarchal beards, and violent juvenile squadrons of roller-skaters. At No. 466 we located the Playhouse. It looked like the eighteenth century when it was new." He always loved the Neighborhood Playhouse, walls like the old parchment, letting you know just how bad the gilt rococo of the ordinary theatre is. That opening night, when we saw *Jephthah's Daughter,* we knew why the things we had been seeing uptown found no feeling in us. "Full of a strong inherited religious feeling beyond the command of any commercial manager, danced the Jewish youths and maidens of that neighborhood, their drama, much of it taken from the Hebrew ritual, full of feeling immeasurably old, the tribal religious feeling of the ancient Jews still a living thing to some of the Jews of Henry Street."

That night, before the glowing grate in Milligan Place, we talked of what the theatre might be. It is one of the mysterious and beautiful things of the world, if you are true to the thing you feel, across gulfs of experience you find in another the thing he feels.

That winter, while I was in Davenport, Jig saw the *Lysistrata* of Aristophanes. "I sat there in the darkness of the second balcony with the tears streaming. Something in the play (its beauty, its coming from so far away in time, its revelation of man and woman as they were two thousand years ago—and are—something in its great 'abstain from love' [as we are abstaining], 'I suffer—I suffer with need of you') struck something tremulous in me and made me very sad. I think maybe you were disappointed in not having a letter Monday, and I felt your sadness. Of course that may be only a fancy—that we can feel each other's emotion at a distance.

"I told Grace Potter of this sadness I felt at *Lysistrata* and tried to explain it as due to feeling through the Greek play something which was in Greek life and is not in ours—something we are terribly in need of. One thing we're in need of is the freedom to deal with life in literature as frankly as Aristophanes. We need a public like his, which itself has the habit of thinking and talking frankly of life. We need the sympathy of such a public, the fundamental oneness with the public, which Aristophanes had. We are hurt by the feeling of a great mass of people hostile to the work we want to do. We can write about taboos. If we do it just right, it will go. But that is not swinging free, like Aristophanes, with all the elements of life.

"I've been thinking how a people reflects itself in literature, regardless of what such-and-such writers want to write. It's interesting."

There was the great strike in the Paterson silk mills. John Reed brought the strikers over for a pageant at the big Madison Square Garden—"the first labor play," though not a written play, not even a designed pageant, but what he was able to do in suggesting them into showing some things from their experience. He put into it the energy of a great desire, and in their feeling of his oneness with them they forgot they were on a stage. That too was a night when we sat late and talked of what the theatre might be.

Those were the early years of psychoanalysis in the Village. You could not go out to buy a bun without hearing of some one's complex. We thought it would be amusing in a play, so we had a good time writing *Suppressed Desires*. Before the grate in Milligan Place we tossed the lines back and forth at one another, and wondered if any one else would ever have as much fun with it as we were having.

We wanted our play put on, as who doesn't, but even the little theatres thought *Suppressed Desires* "too special." Now it has been given by every little theatre, and almost every Methodist church; golf clubs in Honolulu, colleges in Constantinople; in Paris and China and every rural route in America. I wish I had the records of how many thousands of times Step-hen has been asked to be rooster. He has been far from special.

Well, if no one else was going to put on our play, we would put it on ourselves. Neith Boyce had a play—*Constancy*. We gave the two in her house one evening. Bobby Jones was there and helped us with the sets. He liked doing it, because we had no lighting equipment, but just put a candle here and a lamp there.

A few minutes before it was time to give our play, Jig and I took a walk up the shore. We held each other's cold hands and said, "Never mind, it will be over soon."

But when it was over we were sorry. People liked it, and we liked doing it.

Neighbors who had not been asked were hurt, so we gave the plays again. Margaret Steele had taken for studio the old fish house out at the end of the Mary Heaton Vorse wharf, across from our house. She let us have this, so more people could come. Jig became so interested he wrote another comedy, *Change Your Style,* having to do with Provincetown art schools, a jolly little play. Wilbur Steele had written *Contemporaries,* and those two we gave together. Thus ended the first season of the Provincetown Players, who closed without knowing they were the Provincetown Players.

It might have ended there—people giving plays in the summer, if it hadn't been—Do you remember Jig's dream city, how there was to be a theatre, and "why not write our own plays and put them on ourselves, giving writer, actor, designer, a chance to work together without the commercial thing imposed from without? A whole community working together, developing unsuspected talents. The city ought to furnish the kind of audience that will cause new plays to be written." "The Will to Form the Beloved Community of Life-Givers"—that is written through the papers of his years.

The summer people had gone. Jig would go out on the old wharf and "step" the fish-house. Weren't there two feet more than he had thought? He would open the sliding-door that was the back wall, through which fish, nets, oars, anchors, boats, used to be dragged, and stand looking across the harbor to the Truro hills, hearing the waves lap the piles below him. He would walk back slowly, head a little bent, twisting his forelock.

"To write alone will not content me. The blood of backwoods statesmen is in my veins. I must act, organize, accomplish, embody my ideal in stubborn material things which must be shaped to it with energy, toil."

We were back early in the spring, after seeing more Broadway plays. Jack Reed came home from Mexico, where he saw a medieval miracle play which has survived in unbroken tradition among the natives of a certain village, as the poems of Homer existed for some centuries in the Ionian villages of Asia Minor.

Students of dreams tell us our dreams use the things of the moment as vehicle, pattern, symbol, for the deeply-lying thing. In our activities, as in our dreams, the accidental is seized to be shaped by our deep necessities.

"One man cannot produce drama. True drama is born only of one feeling animating all the members of a clan—a spirit shared by all and expressed by the few for the all. If there is nothing to take the place of the common religious purpose and passion of the primitive group, out of which the Dionysian dance was born, no new vital drama can arise in any people."

He and Neith Boyce said it together. He came home and wrote it down as an affirmation of faith.

The people who came back that next summer had little chance of escaping. Purpose had grown in him, he was going to take whom he wanted and use them for the creation of his Beloved Community.

We hauled out the old boat, took oars and nets and anchors to various owners, bought lumber at the second wharf "up-along," and Jig, Nordfeldt, Ballantine, Joe O'Brien, others helping, converted the fish-house into the Wharf Theatre, a place where ninety people could see a play, if they didn't mind sitting close together on wooden benches with no backs. The stage, ten feet by twelve, was in four sections, so we could have different levels, could run it through the big sliding-door at the back, a variety of set surprising in quarters so small.

We gave a first bill, then met at our house to read plays for a second. Two Irishmen, one old and one young, had arrived and taken a shack just up the street. "Terry," I said to the one not young, "haven't you a play to read to us?"

"No," said Terry Carlin, "I don't write, I just think, and sometimes talk. But Mr. O'Neill has got a whole trunk full of plays," he smiled.

That didn't sound too promising, but I said: "Well, tell Mr. O'Neill to come to our house at eight o'clock to-night, and bring some of his plays."

So Gene took *Bound East for Cardiff* from his trunk, and Freddie Burt read it to us, Gene staying out in the dining-room while the reading went on.

He was not left alone in the dining-room when the reading had finished.

Then we knew what we were for. We began in faith, and perhaps it is true when you do that "all these things shall be added unto you."

I may see it through memories too emotional, but it seems to me I have never sat before a more moving production than our *Bound East for Cardiff*, when Eugene O'Neill was produced for the first time on any stage. Jig was Yank. As he lay in his bunk dying, he talked of life as one who knew he must leave it.

The sea has been good to Eugene O'Neill. It was there for his opening. There was a fog, just as the script demanded, fog bell in the harbor. The tide was in, and it washed under us and around, spraying through the holes in the floor, giving us the rhythm and the flavor of the sea while the big dying sailor talked to his friend Drisc of the life he had always wanted deep in the land, where you'd never see a ship or smell the sea.

It is not merely figurative language to say the old wharf shook with applause.

The people who had seen the plays, and the people who gave them, were adventurers together. The spectators were part of the Players, for how could it have been done without the feeling that came from them, without that sense of them there, waiting, ready to share, giving—finding the deep level where audience and writer and player are one. The last month of his life he wrote:

> *I who am audience insofar as the author is*
> *one with me,*
> *And author insofar as the audience is one*
> *with me,*
> *More than any person's name and fame*
> *I will to hear*
> *The music of the identity of men.*

People sometimes said, "Jig is not a business man," when it seemed opportunities were passed by. But those opportunities were not things wanted from deep. He had a unique power to see just how the thing he wanted done could be done. He could finance the spirit, and seldom confused, or betrayed, by extending the financing beyond the span he saw ahead, not weighing his adventure down with schemes that would become things in themselves.

He wrote a letter to the people who had seen the plays, asking if they cared to become associate members of the Provincetown Players. The purpose was to give American playwrights of sincere purpose a chance to work out their ideas in freedom, to give all who worked with the plays their opportunity as artists. Were they interested in this? One dollar for the three remaining bills.

The response paid for seats and stage, and for sets. A production need not cost a lot of money, Jig would say. The most expensive set at the Wharf Theater cost thirteen dollars. There were sets at the Provincetown Playhouse which cost little more. He liked to remember *The Knight of the Burning Pestle* they gave by Leland Stanford, where a book could indicate one house and a bottle another. Sometimes the audience liked to make its own set.

"Now, Susan," he said to me, briskly, "I have announced a play of yours for the next bill."

"But I have no play!"

"Then you will have to sit down to-morrow and begin one."

I protested. I did not know how to write a play. I had never "studied it."

"Nonsense," said Jig. "You've got a stage, haven't you?"

So I went out on the wharf, sat alone on one of our wooden benches without a back, and looked a long time at that bare little stage. After a time the stage became a kitchen—a kitchen there all by itself. I saw just where the stove was, the table, and the steps going upstairs. Then the door at the back opened, and people all bundled up came in—two or three men, I wasn't sure which, but sure enough about the two women, who hung back, reluctant to enter that kitchen. When I was a newspaper reporter out in Iowa, I was sent down-state to do a murder trial, and I never forgot going into the kitchen of a woman locked up in town. I had meant to do it as a short story, but the stage took it for its own, so I hurried in from the wharf to write down what I had seen. Whenever I got stuck, I would run across the street to the old wharf, sit in that leaning little theatre under which the sea sounded, until the play was ready to continue. Sometimes things written in my room would not form on the stage, and I must go home and cross them out. "What playwrights need is a stage," said Jig, "their own stage."

Ten days after the director said he had announced my play, there was a reading at Mary Heaton Vorse's. I was late to the meeting, home revising the play. But when I got there the crowd liked *Trifles*, and voted to put it in rehearsal next day.

It was a great summer; we swam from the wharf as well as rehearsed there; we would lie on the beach and talk about plays—every one writing, or acting, or producing. Life was all of a piece, work not separated from play.

I like to remember certain times late at night. The audience had gone home, the big door had been drawn shut; the last actor who wanted a drink had the last drop there was at our house, and Jig and I might stroll out on the wharf before going to bed. The sea had taken it all again—the wharf was the old wharf and the theatre the fish-house that had been there while so many tides came and went. Fishermen, people from deep in the land who wanted to write plays about both sea and land that—Why? At such times one wondered. It seemed now, on the wharf that jutted out from a sleeping town, as if we had not been at all; and before many more tides came in, it would indeed be as if we had not been at all. And yet, would it? Perhaps we wanted to write plays and put them on just because we knew, more intensely than the fishermen, that the tide comes, the tide goes. You cannot know that and leave things just as they were before.

Gertrude Stein

[1874–1946]

AN INTRODUCTION

G ERTRUDE STEIN WROTE her lecture on plays in the early thirties as part of her *Lectures in America*. At that time only one of her numerous plays, the opera *Four Saints in Three Acts*, with music by Virgil Thompson, had ever been performed. Stein was still in her formative stage as playwright. In a way, this theoretical essay marks the transition from the early work, which was often abstract in meaning as well as form, and the *Last Plays and Operas*, all of which are endowed with resonance and sense.

Currently, as women reclaim our heritage, a Stein revival is underway. In the fifties Judith Malina and Julian Beck staged *Ladies Voices* and *Dr. Faustus Lights the Lights*. Today, Nancy Rhodes's Encompass Theatre, Linda Mussman's Time and Space Limited Theatre and Al Carmines's Judson Poets Theatre are among the companies that periodically bring Stein's work to the stage. Not only the plays but adaptations of her prose are being staged with increasing frequency, and Pat Carroll's one-woman show about her was a hit of the 1980 season. Stein attracts theatre workers in growing numbers since the problems of production and interpretation in her plays provide endless reason to invent.

It's as if time has caught up with Stein while it has already passed by many of the other modernists, establishing them either as creators of classics in their fields or as makers of curiosities. Like her male contemporaries, (Braque and Picasso, Pound and Joyce), in the first part of this century, Stein was engaged in a search for essentials. She was opposed to storytelling, thinking it obscured what writing really is, just as composers sought to do away with melody and painters with representational form. She wanted an immediate experience, a happening, a direct connection between the emotion in the phrase or paragraph and the reader's own emotion.

The avant-garde was a response to the First World War, which had devastated the dream of Western civilization. The Renaissance was over; capitalism had arrived and, with it, the machine age and massive military destruction. Preparations for a second world war were already underway. Civil war in Spain foreshadowed the worldwide despair. Intellectuals, artists, and radicals sensed the coming holocaust and were seeking ways, as we must today, to call attention to the imminent disaster, as well as ways to continue to believe in life despite their powerlessness to reach the many who together might create the needed change.

Alienation, dissonance, the cube, the box, the line, pure form, biomechanics, surrealist emblems of disembodied consciousness, and expressionist dreams and nightmares became the signals uttered through the flames. But unlike the men who, with the prophetic vision of the artist, had foreseen the end of the world and made their art an angry out-cry of despair, Stein foresaw the end of one world—their world, the patriarchal world—and sensed beyond it something new, hopeful, healing, and creative, a world in formation, based upon deep bonds between women. Her plays betray this inner hope in all their outer buoyancy and humor. Stein reveled in reunion, not destruction. She sought that moment "when the excitement and action are abreast." And far from denying the uniqueness of each person caught up in the mechanized world, she wanted, by eliminating narrative storytelling, to find out what "made each one that one."

We live now with the very real threat of nuclear annihilation. Daily we see the planet suffering destruction and human life becoming less sacred. Yet we harbor the hope—which manifests itself in intimate relationships and in women's art—that there is an end to violence and that the end is not destruction. Stein hoped so too. Among the works of her contemporaries in the avant-garde, hers is the prophetic work.

—K.M.

Gertrude Stein
[1874–1946]

SELECTION

From *Lectures in America*

From *Plays*

In a book I wrote called *How to Write* I made a discovery which I considered fundamental, that sentences are not emotional and that paragraphs are. I found out about language that paragraphs are emotional and sentences are not and I found out something else about it. I found out that this difference was not a contradiction but a combination and that this combination causes one to think endlessly about sentences and paragraphs because the emotional paragraphs are made up of unemotional sentences.

I found out a fundamental thing about plays. The thing I found out about plays was too a combination and not a contradiction and it was something that makes one think endlessly about plays.

That something is this.

The thing that is fundamental about plays is that the scene as depicted on the stage is more often than not one might say it is almost always in syncopated time in relation to the emotion of anybody in the audience.

What this says is this.

Your sensation as one in the audience in relation to the play played before you your sensation I say your emotion concerning that play is always either behind or ahead of the play at which you are looking and to which you are listening. So your emotion as a member of the audience is never going on at the same time as the action of the play.

This thing the fact that your emotional time as an audience is not the same as the emotional time of the play is what makes one endlessly troubled about a play, because not only is there a thing to know as to why this is so but also there is a thing to know why perhaps it does not need to be so.

This is a thing to know and knowledge as anybody can know is a thing to get by getting.

And so I will try to tell you what I had to get and what perhaps I have gotten in plays and to do so I will tell you all that I have ever felt about plays or about any play.

Plays are either read or heard or seen.

And there then comes the question which comes first and which is first, reading or hearing or seeing a play.

I ask you.

What is knowledge. Of course knowledge is what you know and what you know is what you do know.

What do I know about plays.

In order to know one must always go back.

What was the first play I saw and was I then already bothered bothered about the different tempo there is in the play and in yourself and your emotion in having the play go on in front of you. I think I may say I may say I know that I was already troubled by this in that my first experience at a play. The thing seen and the emotion did not go on together.

This that the thing seen and the thing felt about the thing seen not going on at the same tempo is what makes the being at the theatre something that makes anybody nervous.

The jazz bands made of this thing, the thing that makes you nervous at the theatre, they made of this thing an end in itself. They made of this different tempo a something that was nothing but a difference in tempo between anybody and everybody including all those doing it and all those hearing and seeing it. In the theatre of course this difference in tempo is less violent but still it is there and it does make anybody nervous.

In the first place at the theatre there is the curtain and the curtain already makes one feel that one is not going to have the same tempo as the thing that is there behind the curtain. The emotion of you on one side of the curtain and what is on the other side of the curtain are not going to be going on together. One will always be behind or in front of the other.

Then also beside the curtain there is the audience and the fact that they are or will be or will not be in the way when the curtain goes up that too makes for nervousness and nervousness is the certain proof that the emotion of the one seeing and the emotion of the thing seen do not progress together.

Nervousness consists in needing to go faster or to go slower so as to get together. It is that that makes anybody feel nervous.

And is it a mistake that that is what the theatre is or is it not.

There are things that are exciting as the theatre is exciting but do they make you nervous or do they not, and if they do and if they do not why do they and why do they not.

Let us think of three different kinds of things that are exciting and that make or do not make one nervous. First any scene which is a real scene something real that is happening in which one takes part as an actor in that scene. Second any book that is exciting, third the theatre at which one sees an exciting action in which one does not take part.

Now in a real scene in which one takes part at which one is an actor what does one feel as to time and what is it that does or does not make one nervous.

And is your feeling at such a time ahead and behind the action the way it is when you are at the theatre. It is the same and it is not. But more not.

If you are taking part in an actual violent scene, and you talk and they or he or she talk and it goes on and it gets more exciting and finally then it happens, whatever it is that does happen then when it happens then at that moment of happening is it a relief from the excitement or is it a completion of the excitement. In the real thing it is a completion of the excitement, in the theatre it is a relief from the excitement, and in that difference the difference between completion and relief is the difference between emotion concerning a thing seen on the stage and the emotion concerning a real presentation that is really something happening. . . .

I have of course always been struggling with this thing, to say what you nor I nor nobody knows, but what is really what you and I and everybody knows, and as I say everybody hears stories but the thing that makes each one what he is is not that. Everybody hears stories and knows stories. How can they not because that is what anybody does and what everybody tells. But in my portraits I had tried to tell what each one is without telling stories and now in my early plays I tried to tell what happened without telling stories so that the essence of what happened would be like the essence of the portraits, what made what happened be what it was. And then I had for the moment gone as far as I could then go in plays and I went back to poetry and portraits and description.

Then I began to spend my summers in Bilignin in the department of the Ain and there I lived in a landscape that made itself its own landscape. I slowly came to feel that since the landscape was the thing, I had tried to write it down in Lucy Church Amiably and I did but I wanted it even more really, in short I found that since the landscape was the thing, a play was a thing and I went on writing plays a great many plays. The landscape at Bilignin so completely made a play that I wrote quantities of plays.

I felt that if a play was exactly like a landscape then there would be no dif-

ficulty about the emotion of the person looking on at the play being behind
or ahead of the play because the landscape does not have to make acquaintance. You may have to make acquaintance with it, but it does not with
you, it is there and so the play being written the relation between you at any
time is so exactly that that it is of no importance unless you look at it. Well I
did look at it and the result is in all the plays that I have printed as *Operas and
Plays*.

I had before I began writing plays written many portraits. I had been
enormously interested all my life in finding out what made each one that
one and so I had written a great many portraits.

I came to think that since each one is that one and that there are a number
of them each one being that one, the only way to express this thing each one
being that one and there being a number of them knowing each other was in
a play. And so I began to write these plays. And the idea in *What Happened,
A Play* was to express this without telling what happened, in short to make
a play the essence of what happened. I tried to do this with the first series of
plays that I wrote. . . .

The landscape has its formation and as after all a play has to have formation and be in relation one thing to the other thing and as the story is not the
thing as any one is always telling something then the landscape not moving
but being always in relation, the trees to the hills the hills to the fields the
trees to each other any piece of it to any sky and then any detail to any other
detail, the story is only of importance if you like to tell or like to hear a story
but the relation is there anyway. And of that relation I wanted to make a
play and I did, a great number of plays. . . .

The only one of course that has been played is *Four Saints*. In *Four Saints* I
made the Saints the landscape. All the saints that I made and I made a
number of them because after all a great many pieces of things are in a landscape all these saints together made my landscape. These attendant saints
were the landscape and it the play really is a landscape.

A landscape does not move nothing really moves in a landscape but
things are there, and I put into the play the things that were there.

Magpies are in the landscape that is they are in the sky of a landscape,
they are black and white and they are in the sky of the landscape in Bilignin
and in Spain, especially in Avila. When they are in the sky they do something that I have never seen any other bird do they hold themselves up and
down and look flat against the sky.

A very famous French inventor of things that have to do with stabilisa-
tion in aviation told me that what I told him magpies did could not be done
by any bird but anyway whether the magpies at Avila do do it or do not at

least they look as if they do do it. They look exactly like the birds in the Annunciation pictures the bird which is the Holy Ghost and rests flat against the side sky very high.

There were magpies in my landscape and there were scarecrows.

The scarecrows on the ground are the same thing as the magpies in the sky, they are a part of the landscape.

They the magpies may tell their story if they and you like or even if I like but stories are only stories but that they stay in the air is not a story but a landscape. That scarecrows stay on the ground is the same thing it could be a story but it is a piece of the landscape.

Then as I said streets and windows are also landscape and they added to my Spanish landscape.

While I was writing the *Four Saints* I wanted one always does want the saints to be actually saints before them as well as inside them, I had to see them as well as feel them. As it happened there is on the Boulevard Raspail a place where they make photographs that have always held my attention. They take a photograph of a young girl dressed in the costume of her ordinary life and little by little in successive photographs they change it into a nun. These photographs are small and the thing takes four or five changes but at the end it is a nun and this is done for the family when the nun is dead and in memoriam. For years I had stood and looked at these when I was walking and finally when I was writing Saint Therese in looking at these photographs I saw how Saint Therese existed from the life of an ordinary young lady to that of the nun. And so everything was actual and I went on writing.

Then in another window this time on the rue de Rennes there was a rather large porcelain group and it was of a young soldier giving alms to a beggar and taking off his helmet and his armour and leaving them in the charge of another.

It was somehow just what the young Saint Ignatius did and anyway it looked like him as I had known about him and so he too became actual not as actual as Saint Therese in the photographs but still actual and so the *Four Saints* got written.

All these things might have been a story but as a landscape they were just there and a play is just there. That is at least the way I feel about it.

Anyway I did write *Four Saints an Opera to be Sung* and I think it did almost what I wanted, it made a landscape and the movement in it was like a movement in and out with which anybody looking on can keep in time. I also wanted it to have the movement of nuns very busy and in continuous movement but placid as a landscape has to be because after all the life in a convent is the life of a landscape, it may look excited a landscape does sometimes look excited but its quality is that a landscape if it ever did go away would have to go away to stay.

Anyway the play as I see it is exciting and it moves but it also stays and that is as I said in the beginning might be what a play should do.

Anyway I am pleased. People write me that they are having a good time while the opera is going on a thing which they say does not very often happen to them at the theatre.

So you do see what I have after all meant.

And so this is just at present all I know about the theatre.

Lorraine Hansberry
[1930–1965]

AN INTRODUCTION

WHEN LORRAINE HANSBERRY DIED at the age of thirty-four, she left two finished plays and one that was almost finished, one unproduced television drama, and a fable in one act she had intended to complete for the stage. Her first play, *A Raisin in the Sun*, was a Broadway success, winning for her the New York Drama Critics' Award of the 1958–59 season and establishing her as the most prominent woman playwright in the country.

Later made into a successful movie, *Raisin* is the story of a black family's struggle up from poverty and of the dreams and delusions which made that struggle possible. Her next play, *The Sign in Sidney Brustein's Window*, had for its main character a Greenwich Village white Jewish intellectual male who attempted to reclaim for the fifties some of the radical commitment of the thirties. The only black character in the play, Alton, a writer, has fallen in love with Sidney's sister-in-law. When he finds out she is not a high fashion model but a high-class white whore, he leaves her in repulsion. Sidney's other sister-in-law, Mavis, a suburban housewife, is trapped, as so many women are, within the confines of the double standard, marriage, and the family, but emerges—in one particularly beautiful speech—a courageous and compassionate woman.

Les Blancs, her third and final full-length play, reached Broadway five years after her death in a version completed by her divorced husband, Robert Nemiroff. James Earl Jones played Tshembe Matoseh, the Europeanized African returned to his village at a time of revolutionary uprising. Lili Darvas was the aged wife of a patronizing missionary. She encourages Tshembe to join the African freedom fighters because she knows the colonial way of life, exemplified by her husband, is rightfully doomed.

Both *The Sign in Sidney Brustein's Window* and *Les Blancs* opened to mixed notices. *Brustein* was kept alive for 101 performances by the concerted efforts of the professional theatre community and audience members who had seen and valued the play. It closed the night after its author died in a nearby hospital. *Les Blancs* never aroused the same support, but it, too, was deserving of a long run. *Raisin, Brustein,* and *Les Blancs* reveal a constant growth in the techniques of dramaturgy and, also, in the complexity of the author's human concerns.

In our heterogeneous society where people survive by ghettoizing others and clinging themselves to small, provincial groups, plays dealing with the complexity of relationships between the races (and, most currently, the sexes) are the hardest for critics and audiences to take in. Hansberry's progression was toward an increased layering of meanings, options, tensions, and possibilities. She was reaching out to embrace Pan-Africanism, questions of violence and nonviolence, political commitment in all its tragic and hope-filled dimensions. She was stopped by a cancer which killed her at an age before she could have reached artistic maturity. She was stopped, too, by a system of critical judgment-passing that can, and often does, work against playwrights who achieve commercial production, demanding always that they reproduce their past "hit," and that they limit their singular quest in order to be always, instantly understandable and barely challenging. In her notebooks Hansberry had planned female characters in place of Sidney Brustein and Tshembe Matoseh.[1] Did she censor herself, knowing she would be censured? Or did the forms of a woman-centered drama still elude her because the feminist community was not yet strong enough to provide the actual examples required?

In the following essay, Hansberry compares Walter Lee Younger from *A Raisin in the Sun* to Willy Loman in *Death of a Salesman*, Arthur Miller's tragedy of the "common man." While delighting in Younger's continuing life, a contrast to Willy's suicide, she criticizes herself, with modesty becoming a young playwright, for having been unable to create a central hero equal to Miller's. Yet the black communal structure, it seems to me, is precisely what has kept black people alive through generations of abuse. We might remember Willy Loman's mother, if we remember her at all, as a drain upon Willy's energy, a sap to his ambition—so neatly has the myth of the blameworthy mother been engraved upon white consciousness. Walter's mother, sister, and wife, on the other hand, are vibrant, assertive, caring characters. And if they are part of the myth of the black "superwoman," they are also, clearly, the conveyors of the life force.

Hansberry's ability to create not one central character but a network of many compelling personalities allowed her to end up, always, on the side of freedom and of hope. As it becomes clearer and clearer that women's theatre is about the interrelated lives of a community, true heroism may come to be seen as the strength in one that gives another strength. Then the single dominant hero and his sacrificial act will recede before the vibrant making of community.

The two letters on drama which follow her essay support the evidence in the plays that she had consciously put herself outside the contemporary dramatic tradition of despair and alienation. The letters also show Hansberry's strong, perceptive feminism, an abiding concern of hers which was never fully realized in her stage work.

The second letter, "Arthur Miller, Marilyn Monroe and 'Guilt' " was written to a friend after Hansberry had read Miller's new play, *After the Fall*. The play was published in the *Saturday Evening Post* (not *Life*, as Hansberry says) on February 1, 1964, on the occasion of the opening of the Repertory Theatre at Lincoln Center.

In his preface to the play, Miller had written: "No man knows himself who cannot face the murder in him, the sly and everlasting complicity with the forces of destruction," and described his play as "a way of looking at man and his human nature as the only source of the violence which has come closer and closer to destroying the race." In her letter, Hansberry pleaded for an indictment of the social order "which fashioned, warped and destroyed a human being such as Marilyn Monroe." She was angry, and rightly so, for in trying to tell the story of Marilyn Monroe, Miller had written a play about male *angst* that evaded all the crucial issues of Monroe's life and death. Yet Hansberry's rage at Miller might have been somewhat abated had she been able to do in her own plays the thing that Miller could not do in his. Hansberry also found herself continually telling men's stories while women characters wove a web of support around the edges of the drama, but never, never were fully heard.

As a black woman playwright, Lorraine Hansberry suffered triple oppression; the cancer that killed her prematurely is terrible proof of the tensions that infected her life. As a creative black woman, she combined the strengths of both her people and her sex, strengths that live on in her works, endowing them with compassion, complexity, and hope all too rare in American drama.

—K.M.

Lorraine Hansberry

[1930–1965]

SELECTIONS

From *The Village Voice Reader*

An Author's Reflections: Willy Loman, Walter Younger, and He Who Must Live

"*A man can't go out the way he came in. . . . Ben, that funeral will be massive!*"
—WILLY LOMAN, 1946

"*We have all thought about your offer and we have decided to move into our house.*"
—WALTER LEE YOUNGER, 1958

Some of the acute partisanship revolving around *A Raisin in the Sun* is amusing. Those who announce that they find the piece less than fine are regarded in some quarters with dramatic hostility, as though such admission automatically implied the meanest of racist reservations. On the other hand, the ultra-sophisticates have hardly acquitted themselves less ludicrously, gazing cooly down their noses at those who are moved by the play, and going on at length about "melodrama" and/or "soap opera" as if these were not completely definable terms which cannot simply be tacked onto any play and all plays we do not like.

Personally, I find no pain whatever—at least of the traditional ego type—in saying that *Raisin* is a play which contains dramaturgical incompletions. Fine plays tend to utilize one big fat character who runs right through the middle of the structure, by action or implication, with whom we rise or fall. A central character as such is certainly lacking from *Raisin*. I should be delighted to pretend that it was *inventiveness*, as some suggest for me, but it is, also, craft inadequacy and creative indecision. The result is

Originally published in *The Village Voice* August 12, 1959. Reprinted in THE VILLAGE VOICE READER (New York: Doubleday 1962). Reprinted by permission of Robert Nemiroff. Copyright © 1959, 1983 by Robert Nemiroff.

that neither Walter Lee nor Mama Younger loom large enough to monu-
mentally command the play. I consider it an enormous dramatic fault if no
one else does. (Nor am I less critical of the production which, by and large,
performance and direction alike, is splendid. Yet I should have preferred
that the second-act curtain, for instance, be performed with quiet assertion
rather than the apparently popular declamatory opulence which prevails.)

All in all, however, I believe that, for the most part, the play has been
magnificently understood. In some cases it was not only thematically absorbed but attention was actually paid to the tender treacherousness of its
craft-imposed "simplicity." Some, it is true, quite missed that part of the
overt intent and went on to harangue the bones of the play with rather useless observations of the terribly clear fact that they are old bones indeed.
More meaningful discussions tended to delve into the flesh which hangs
from those bones and its implications in mid-century American drama and
life.

In that connection it is interesting to note that while the names of
Chekhov, O'Casey, and the early Odets were introduced for comparative
purposes in some of the reviews, almost no one—with the exception of
Gerald Weales in *Commentary*—discovered a simple line of descent between
Walter Lee Younger and the last great hero in American drama to also *accept*
the values of his culture, Willy Loman. I am sure that the already mentioned primary fault of the play must account in part for this. The family so
overwhelms the play that Walter Lee necessarily fails as the true symbol he
should be, even though *his* ambitions, *his* frustrations, and *his* decisions are
those which decisively drive the play on. But however recognizable he
proves to be, he fails to dominate our imagination and finally emerges as a
reasonably interesting study, but not, like Arthur Miller's great character—and like Hamlet, of course—a summation of an immense (though not
crucial) portion of his culture.

Then too, in fairness to the author and to Sidney Poitier's basically brilliant portrayal of Walter Lee, we must not completely omit reference to
some of the prior attitudes which were brought into the theatre from the
world outside. For in the minds of many, Walter remains, despite the play,
despite performance, what American racial traditions *wish* him to be: an
exotic. Some writers have been astonishingly incapable of discussing his
purely *class* aspirations and have persistently confounded them with what
they consider to be an exotic being's longing to "wheel and deal" in what
they further consider to be (and what Walter never can) "the white man's
world." Very few people today must consider the ownership of a liquor store
as an expression of extraordinary affluence, and yet, as joined to a dream of

Walter Younger, it takes on, for some, aspects of the fantastic. We have grown accustomed to the dynamics of "Negro" personality as expressed by white authors. Thus, de Emperor, de Lawd, and, of couse, Porgy still haunt our frame of reference when a new character emerges. We have become romantically jealous of the great image of a prototype whom we believe is summarized by the wishfulness of a self-assumed opposite. Presumably there is a quality in human beings that makes us *wish* that we *were* capable of primitive contentments; the *universality* of ambition and its anguish can escape us only if we construct elaborate legends about the rudimentary simplicity of *other* men.

America, for this reason, long ago fell in love with the image of the simple, lovable, and glandular "Negro." We all know that Catfish Row was never intended to slander anyone; it was intended as a mental haven for readers and audiences who could bask in the unleashed passions of those "lucky ones" for whom abandonment was apparently permissible. In an almost paradoxical fashion, it disturbs the soul of man to truly understand what he invariably senses: that *nobody* really finds oppression and/or poverty tolerable. If we ever destroy the image of the black people who supposedly do find those things tolerable in America, then that much-touted "guilt" which allegedly haunts most middle-class white Americans with regard to the Negro question would really become unendurable. It would also mean the death of a dubious literary tradition, but it would undoubtedly and more significantly help toward the more rapid transformation of the status of a people who have never found their imposed misery very charming.

My colleagues and I were reduced to mirth and tears by that gentleman writing his review of our play in a Connecticut paper who remarked of his pleasure at seeing how "our dusky brethren" could "come up with a song and hum their troubles away." It did not disturb the writer in the least that there is no such implication in the entire three acts. He did not need it in the play; he had it in his head.

For all these reasons, then, I imagine that the ordinary impluse to compare Willy Loman and Walter Younger was remote. Walter Lee Younger jumped out at us from a play about a largely unknown world. We knew who Willy Loman was instantaneously; we recognized his milieu. We also knew at once that he represented that curious paradox in what the *English* character in that *English* play could call, though dismally, "The American Age." Willy Loman was a product of a nation of great military strength, indescribable material wealth, and incredible mastery of the physical realm, which nonetheless was unable, in 1946, to produce a *typical* hero who was capable of an affirmative view of life.

I believe it is a testament to Miller's brilliance that it is hardly a misstatement of the case, as some preferred to believe. Something has indeed gone wrong with at least part of the American dream, and Willy Loman is the victim of the detour. Willy had to be overwhelmed on the stage as, in fact, his prototypes are in everyday life. Coming out of his section of our great sprawling middle class, preoccupied with its own restlessness and displaying its obsession for the possession of trivia, Willy was indeed trapped. His predicament in a New World where there just aren't anymore forests to clear or virgin railroads to lay or native American empires to first steal and then build upon left him with nothing but some left-over values which had forgotten how to prize industriousness over cunning, usefulness over mere acquisition, and, above all, humanism over "success." The potency of the great tale of a salesman's death was in our familiar recognition of his entrapment which, suicide or no, is *deathly*.

What then of this new figure who appears in American drama in 1958; from what source is he drawn so that, upon inspection, and despite class differences, so much of his encirclement must still remind us of that of Willy Loman? Why, finally, is it possible that when his third-act will is brought to bear, *his* typicality is capable of a choice which *affirms* life? After all, Walter Younger is an American more than he is anything else. His ordeal, give or take his personal expression of it, is not extraordinary but intensely familiar like Willy's. The two of them have virtually no values which have not come out of their culture, and to a significant point, no view of the possible solutions to their problems which do not also come out of the self-same culture. Walter can find no peace with that part of society which seems to permit him entry and no entry into that which has willfully excluded him. He shares with Willy Loman the acute awareness that *something* is obstructing some abstract progress that he feels he *should* be making; that *something* is in the way of his ascendancy. It does not occur to either of them to question the nature of this desired "ascendancy." Walter accepts, he believes in the "world" as it has been presented to him. When we first meet him, he does not wish to alter it; merely to change *his* position in it. His mentors and his associates all take the view that the institutions which frustrate him are somehow impeccable, or, at best "unfortunate." "Things being as they are," he must look to *himself* as the only source of any rewards he may expect. Within himself he is encouraged to believe, are the only seeds of defeat or victory within the universe. And Walter believes this and when opportunity, haphazard and rooted in death, prevails, he acts.

But the obstacles which are introduced are gigantic; the weight of the loss of the money is in fact the weight of death. In Walter Lee Younger's life, somebody *has* to die for ten thousand bucks to pile up—if then. Elsewhere in the world, in the face of catastrophe, he might be tempted to don the saffron robes of acceptance and sit on a mountain top all day contemplating the divine justice of his misery. Or, history being what it is turning out to be, he might wander down to his first Communist Party meeting. But here in the dynamic and confusing post-war years on the South Side of Chicago, his choices of action are equal to those gestures only in symbolic terms. The American ghetto hero may give up and contemplate his misery in rose-colored bars to the melodies of hypnotic saxophones, but revolution seems alien to him in his circumstances (America), and it is easier to dream of personal wealth than of a communal state wherein universal dignity is supposed to be a corollary. Yet his position in time and space does allow for one other alternative: he may take his place on any one of a number of frontiers of challenge. Challenges (such as helping to break down restricted neighborhoods) which are admittedly limited because they most certainly do not threaten the basic social order.

But why is even this final choice possible, considering the ever-present (and ever-so-popular) vogue of despair? Well, that is where Walter departs from Willy Loman; there is a second pulse in his still dual culture. His people have had "somewhere" they have been trying to get for so long that more sophisticated confusions do not yet bind them. *Thus the weight and power of their current social temperament intrudes and affects him, and it is, at the moment, at least, gloriously and rigidly affirmative.* In the course of their brutally difficult ascent, they have dismissed the ostrich and still sing, *"Went to the rock to hide my face, but the rock cried out: 'No hidin' place down here!'"* Walter is, despite his lack of consciousness of it, inextricably as much wedded to his special mass as Willy was to his, and the moods of each are able to decisively determine the dramatic typicality. Furthermore, the very nature of the situation of American Negroes can force their representative hero to recognize that for his *true* ascendancy he must ultimately be at cross-purposes with at least certain of his culture's values. It is to the pathos of Willy Loman that his section of American life seems to have momentarily lost that urgency; that he cannot, like Walter, draw on the strength of an incredible people who, historically, have simply refused to give up.

In other words, the symbolism of moving into the new house is quite as small as it seems and quite as significant. For if there are no waving flags and marching songs at the barricades as Walter marches out with his little battalion, it is not because the battle lacks nobility. On the contrary, he has picked up in his way, still imperfect and wobbly in his small view of human destiny, what I believe Arthur Miller once called "the golden thread of history." He becomes, in spite of those who are too intrigued with despair and hatred of man to see it, King Oedipus refusing to tear out his eyes, but attacking the Oracle instead. He is that last Jewish patriot manning his rifle in the burning ghetto at Warsaw; he is that young girl who swam into sharks to save a friend a few weeks ago; he is Anne Frank, still believing in people; he is the nine small heroes of Little Rock; he is Michelangelo creating David, and Beethoven bursting forth with the Ninth Symphony. He is all those things because he has finally reached out in his tiny moment and caught that sweet essence which is human dignity, and it shines like the old star-touched dream that is in his eyes. We see, in the moment, I think, what becomes, and not for Negroes alone, but for Willy and all of us, entirely an American possibility.

Out in the darkness where we watch, most of us are not afraid to cry.

Two Letters on Drama

On Strindberg and Sexism

337 Bleeker Street
New York 14, N.Y.
Feb. 1956

To the Editor:

So!—[Your reviewer] has praises to give to this or that Off-Broadway group which turns to the "resuscitation of invaluable dramatic material"—! With this he dares to direct us to the Actor's Playhouse production of *Comrades.*

And with what are we rewarded, once there? An insufferably awkward, social travesty which has no reason taking up the time of actors anywhere— including the Village.

That the dead and buried Strindberg probed around in his madness and created such a horror is one sad thing; but that a critic would seize upon such stuff and wallow in it and assert that it is a profound piece of theatre—*that* is truly frightening.

The playwright clearly hated women with a depth and passion which defies reason or a mere expression of the *cute* "BATTLE OF THE SEXES: MALE POINT OF VIEW."

Socially speaking, the matter may be rather simply stated. Women are oppressed; women do battle against that oppression in the best ways they know how. And, at the moment, the worst way. The result of it all is emotional chaos for everybody. To try to artistically justify the ideas of the ancients about "woman's place" is tiresome, foolish, and dreadfully out of keeping with a general tendency on the part of world societies toward the ultimate recognition of the basic equality of all members of the race—male or female.

In this light, there is an overpowering sense of tragedy in watching the play. It is the feeling one might experience watching King Arthur and his knights diligently hurling their lances against, say—an atom bomb. This is war?!

I for one find the entire business of eternally trying to prove the varying degrees of inferiority or superiority of either sex to the other unbearably dull and quite pointless.

Yet it is probably true that if the play had had a reverse point of view it might have been dismissed rapidly as a badly written piece of "feminist" *propaganda*. Sometimes it almost seems that only when propaganda is propagandizing a return to a dead and useless past is it profound, "art"/avant-garde, etc.

Seriously, isn't there despair enough, aren't there neuroses enough from this still too popular misinterpretation of problems between men and women? And isn't it therefore rather terrible to salute such abetting theatre?

Strindberg, by the way, was incapable of answering or even dwelling on the truly main question which his play raises, in spite of itself. Namely: how did Bertha *get that way*? Axel tells Bertha that thereafter he cares to meet her only in the cafes where he meets his other "comrades." In his new life, "wife" will be a creature who knows enough to wear long hair and wait quietly and contentedly for him in the nights. Strindberg could not tackle the question of the "contented little wife" because from whence else have evolved the "Bertha Albergs"? Or, more important, the Nora Helmars? To have dramatically examined the woman to whom Axel thought he was fleeing, would be to once again realize the source of the problem. It would have possibly led him to move the whole business out of the realm of the disgusting "battle of the sexes" nonsense to an investigation of the nature of life as prescribed by society for a woman.

Instead Strindberg's message is flagrant and barbaric. "Slug 'em and throw 'em on the floor and raise your voice." Which is what Axel does to Bertha. It is mildly interesting to note, however, that this particular champion of man's sovereignty found it necessary to create a woman who was talentless in her field. Let us try his argument on another level: imagine in the home of the Curies one evening—Pierre seizes Madame by the wrists and flings her to the floor violently and forces *her* to promise that she will never come into *his* laboratory again! It might be satisfying to the male ego or something—but how dismal for humanity who needed their collective researches so much.

I suspect that, among others, one reason there have probably been more Bertha Albergs than Marie Curies is because there have been, as of yet, too many Strindbergs (in one degree or another) and too few Ibsens and Shaws.—Which is hardly a "feminist" statement.

The only answer, in drama, to Bertha Alberg is Nora Helmar. Ibsen apparently was able to see the whole; Strindberg saw only the misjudged shadows of individuals as he wandered about in that nightmare of his where the figure of woman eternally haunted his intellect, crying: "Adam—I am thy equal!"

I should love a personal reply from your reviewer.

Sincerely and with very best wishes for your remarkable publication which is a major positive development in our community,

Lorraine Nemiroff

On Arthur Miller, Marilyn Monroe, and "Guilt"

112 Waverly Place
New York 11, New York
Tuesday

Hi.

Here's the mag. Read the Miller tear from *Life*. Waaaallll. I *see* why you felt significance in it but am depressed I guess that you did. To me it amounts to little more than fashionable moumbliegoumbilie. It is the counterpart to this thing currently going the rounds when the European slave trade (of Africans) comes up: "Well, *Africans* participated in the selling." Which has what to do with what I can't imagine.

Bobby* said something funny and perceptive, I think, after he read the play and preface to it (dig that last sentence of it** which is a tip-off to the moumbliegoumbilie). He said Miller's trying to "pass" and it's got him turned around all whichaway. I wouldn't have thought to articulate it like

---

*Lorraine Hansberry's then husband, Robert Nemiroff. **The closing line from Miller's preface.

that—but I think it is *the* summary. In other words, he is trying like hell for the respectability of fashionable despair because nothing else, in the West, really is right now. Fashionable, I mean.

But, frankly, under analysis there is an emptiness in the statements that is more embarassing than anything. Please, what serious person has a right to expect that anyone who has ever studied the history of the human race can buy this stuff about "the destructiveness hanging over this age"? What in the name of God was hanging over the age of the War of Roses? Or the Crusades? Or the Byzantine conquests; the Civil War? Section out the tiniest place on the map and you will find a place where destruction seemed to have been the sole intention of the inhabitants. One of the reasons the Greeks and Armenians feel the way they do today about the Turks is that they were accustomed to being slaughtered by them by the tens of thousands for centuries. And reverse. Ditto the Russians and the Poles and the Russians and the Swedes and the Chinese and everybody in Asia and reverse. Ditto the Zulu against less formidable peoples as they swept South to get butchered by the Boers whom they shall in turn butcher and the Nazis murdered not only six million Jews—but twenty million Russians and on and on and on. You know all of this; my point is that the sentence [in Miller's preface] regarding the destructiveness of our age is meaningless; it is akin in rhetoric to that which we now despise as gingerbread in architecture—it serves no function, the house will stand without it. The house in this case being the truth.

We forget in our preoccupation with "our time" that the patrons of Shakespearean art rode to the theatre over bridges where the heads of those most recently fallen from Monarchical favor were set on spikes to drain dry. This too, the Renaissance! Presumably, Shakespeare, Jonson, Marlowe even felt they had to make their plays as bloody and heady and sexy as they were to merely compete with the life of everyday of the Elizabethans. The ages of man have been hell. But the difference was that artists assumed the hell of it and went on to create figures *in battle with it* rather than overwhelmed with it and apologizing and "explaining" their frailty.

Anyhow, about all this Camusian "guilt" and all, what does it mean? *Anne Frank and Adolf Eichmann were not both guilty of the crimes against the Jewish people.* I don't care what some of the Jewish leaders did by way of complicity or how many Ashanti chieftains sold some alien tribesfolk with whom they felt they had no more identity than the European slavers. It is a short step from this to the recognition of degree involved in seeing that those Jews who did comply to save their own skins, indeed, even to profit as that must have sometimes been the case, are individuals trapped in particular time and space and to speak of the equality of the "guilt" is incomprehensible. You and I have talked enough, long enough so that I know perfectly well that you would think that I had taken leave of my senses should I begin to rant and rail to you about the "guilt" of a child, brought up in the ghetto, because he engaged in anything so brutal and inhumane as gang fighting! *Or I shall presume that you would.* Naturally, his ethic of survival includes being able to fight good and—*fight dirty.* Now, are you or anyone going to be able to probe his own "guilt" about violence? That he should have any association whatsoever with that which insured his very survival as some abstraction called evil? Whaaaaaat? Do infants share in this universal complicity? Well, well. . . back to original sin again and Miller is trying to pass in more than one way!

Anyhow read the play. I think that it is fundamentally, a shameful work. A distinguished artist is kopping out when his culture most needs him. Miller has been punished and punished hard for seeing "too much" and now he wants in and I think that he has written a play which he thought would get the "thesis playwright" stigma off his back. I think it began with *View from the Bridge.* He has written beautifully in the past, *The Crucible*; *Salesman*; *All My Sons.* They are fine, fine plays and they had rather a great deal to say. They had so much to say that a sideways cultural attack was launched on their author: he was relegated a second place under the "poet"—T.W. [Tennessee Williams] and he wants up, up, up: if there's any wallowing going around here he aims to out wallow them all. . .

I know something about all this 'cause I have fiddled around with this universal guilt crap some too—and have always been forced to recognize that it is garbage which has just about nothing to do with nothing that is relevant in the world today. Things are very, very complicated. I don't believe that you think for a minute that I have a notion of black and white problems in the world. On the contrary. But—they aren't that complicated either. It is the painful confrontation with such as this which makes us want a universally applicable "guilt." The English are wrong, the Kikuyu are right; we are wrong, Castro is right; the Vietnamese people (there doesn't appear to be any difference between the Vietnamese people and the "Viet Cong" any more by our own account) are right and we are wrong; the Negro people are right and the shameful dawdling of Federal authority is wrong; the concept of "woman" which fashioned, warped and destroyed a human being such as Marilyn Monroe (or "Audrey Smith" or "Jean West" or "Lucy Jones"—*daily*) IS HIDEOUSLY WRONG—and she, *in her repudiation of it*, in trying tragically to RISE ABOVE it by killing herself is (in the Shakespearean sense)—right. Such a life as hers was an affront to *her humanity*. And if Miller had written a play that said *that*—the details of whether or not it was "too autobiographical" or not would be irrelevant. But he did not, because, enveloped as he apparently is in Catholicized "guilt" and all, he is incapable of indicting the social order which did that to her—choosing to wallow around in her "self destructive" will as if it were some kind of metaphysical lollipop she couldn't stop sucking (to return to some of the imagery of the play. . . .)

On that note. . . adios. See ya soon.

Lorraine

Producing & Directing: Theatre for the People

Hallie Flanagan

Judith Malina

Barbara Ann Teer

Hallie Flanagan

[1890–1969]

AN INTRODUCTION

ALTHOUGH IT WAS FUNDED by the United States government, Federal Theatre was, in fact, the vision of one woman, Hallie Flanagan, whose eyes were wide enough to take in the visions of many other artists of stature equal to her own. During the four years that the Federal Theatre Project existed, 1935 to 1939, Flanagan set a standard for theatrical producing that remains unmatched and she created a people's theatre across the land.

She was committed always to the artists—workers, as she called them—who made the plays and to the people of this country who had need of artistic sustenance. She never opted for quick or easy commercial success, never diluted her vision to serve the greed of Mammon or the need of some private demon of the ego. When Federal Theatre was abolished (by a Congress which feared, as reactionary people always do, the force of the created moment), Hallie Flanagan returned to the university world from which she had come, to continue staging daring modern and classic plays in innovative student productions.

Hallie Flanagan's address to the New York Federal Theatre staff, in the summer of 1936, shows her to be an inspiring theorist, capable of infusing dedication, purpose, and unity of vision in people who had long been on relief as well as in young theatre artists at the peak of their creative energy who were drawn to Federal Theatre because it offered subsidy for a dream they also shared. Unlike Eva Le Gallienne, Hallie Flanagan believed that a first-rate theatre might be created by people on relief. The raw energy of suffering and struggle compelled her as greatly as the most perfectly shaped aesthetic moment. In fact, she knew the latter was hardly possible without the former, especially if one were going to create new theatre works rather than restage a classic repertory.

Flanagan had been excited by the experimentation of Russian theatre workers in the teens and twenties, when the promise of a people's revolution still existed. She visited Russia and other European countries, including

Lady Gregory's Ireland, on a Guggenheim grant (she was the first woman to win one), then wrote of her experiences in a book called *Shifting Scenes*. After Russian theatre came the influence of the classic theatre of Greece, an enthusiasm she shared with her husband, and the popular puppet shows of Sicily. Bio-mechanical paeans to the machine and other modernist experiments in staging, the profound emotions of verse drama, and the robustness of folk plays were the aesthetic preferences contributing most strongly to her idea of a national federation of subsidized theatres. The plays issuing from these federal theatres would have been written and produced in response to immediate social needs; in form and theme they would be influenced by folklore, mythology, and history.

Soon after Federal Theatre was abolished, Hallie Flanagan wrote an essay in which she described the accomplishments of the 7,900 persons thrown out of work by the project's close.

> In four years they produced over twelve hundred plays, including an extensive classical cycle, an extensive religious cycle, Americana, modern plays, "Living Newspapers" and dance drama, vaudeville, musical comedy, marionette plays, pageants and circuses. They gave an opportunity to a hundred hitherto-unknown young dramatists, and the list of dramatists whose plays they performed includes almost every American playwright of note. . . . They built, equipped and manned stages in tents, on trucks, on showboats, on platforms in parks, schools and playgrounds, on overturned tables in remote CCC camps and in the wake of flood and disaster; they reclaimed, literally through their own labor, working long hours without watching the time clock, magnificent old theatres, which, before the government entered the picture, had fallen into disuse and often into decay. . .
>
> They traveled by truck through the rural areas, in Illinois, Michigan, Maine, New York, Oklahoma. In Florida they covered the turpentine circuit, and people came in by ox cart, carrying lanterns, came in barefoot to see Shakespeare. . . .
>
> They engaged in extensive theatre research on the origin, history, and development of American folklore, folk music and drama in the various regions of our country, research so important that it was sponsored by various state universities and requested for the Congressional Library.[1]

The following letters, written to her husband, Philip Haldane Davis, present an intimate, immensely likable portrait of the visionary woman who was then producing this mammoth project. The letters show her inseparable commitments to human needs and innovative art, her growing cynicism about the New Deal government as it succumbed to party politics, her nearly limitless compassion, keen humor, strong sense of self, and untiring energy—without which qualities of soul, service to an ideal as lofty as her own would scarcely have been possible.

Flanagan was also a theatre historian. Her history of Federal Theatre, *Arena*, is a spirited account, infused with fierce indignation that a theatre for the people could be abolished by elected officials. She did not believe, even when fresh from defeat in Congress, that the work would not live, that the land she seeded would not bear. In the final pages of *Arena* she wrote of a prophesy as yet unfulfilled, for, in fact, the end of Federal Theatre heralded the beginning of the McCarthy period, from whose bitter censorship the theatre of transformation and social justice has yet to recover.

The ten thousand anonymous men and women—the et ceteras and the and-so-forths who did the work, the nobodies who were everybody, the some-bodies who believed it—their dreams and deeds were not the end. They were the beginning of a people's theatre in a country whose greatest plays are still to come.

—K.M.

Hallie Flanagan
[1890–1969]

SELECTIONS

Opening Address, Federal Theatre Production Conference Poughkeepsie
July 1936

> Man is changed by his living; but not fast enough. His concern is for that which yesterday did not exist.

Ten months ago each one of us was individually concerned with his own aspect of the Theatre. We were fellow-workers only in the sense that we were all professionals, making a living in some form of theatre enterprise: writing, acting, designing or directing. Our conceptions of theatre were the result of varied training and experience; the commercial theatre (Broadway, repertory or stock); the semi-professional theatre; the foreign theatre; the university theatre—a varied background which should stand us in good stead now.

Suddenly we were plunged, almost without warning, into the creation of a gigantic theatre enterprise, with slight opportunity for consultation on policy, personnel or plays, and into the necessity of mastering, as we went along, a machine of governmental regulations so intricate that for months it seemed to take all the running we could do just to stay in one place.

The Birth of a People's Theatre

Due to a single economic fact—unemployment—the theatre in which we were individually working had been changed by its living. And today our mutual concern and the concern for our 12,000 fellow-theatre-workers throughout America is for that which yesterday did not exist—the Federal Theatre.

No doubt every one of us had thought at some time of some form of state or national theatre, unconsciously modeling such a theatre on institutions

182

in European countries. We had thought, perhaps, of careful planning by wise committees, of the greatest actors, writers, designers, plays, all housed in appropriately magnificent surroundings, of an academy of dramatic training for gifted youth.

If the loss of that dream still seems great, relegate it to the future or balance against its dignity its danger—the danger from which the American stage has always suffered—imitativeness. The pattern for our Federal Theatre was to be different—a pattern dictated by necessity, demanded for immediate use, utilitarian and functional. Any strength or significance the Federal Theatre may have must come from a clear understanding of that fact and a determination to turn the very liabilities of such a theatre into assets.

OUR AUDIENCE OF 500,000 WEEKLY

To the imagination, ingenuity and intrepidity of the workers on the Project from coast to coast, and to you their leaders, is due all credit for the fact that order is emerging out of chaos, that 12,000 people are working in 158 theatres in 28 states, playing to weekly audiences totaling 500,000. Indeed, so vast is this audience that our most pressing need is to decide how to justify its belief in the Federal Theatre. It is that audience which makes it not only appropriate but necessary for us, after ten months, to stop, take stock, profit by our mistakes and by each other's counsel, and decide what course we shall take for the future.

"RED TAPE" VERSUS PLANNING

The Federal Theatre has, as you know, two distinct lines: administrative and theatric. Since this meeting is called to discuss theatre rather than administrative matters, I shall not go into the latter, except to say that the administrative setup in Washington has changed very little.

We still are directly under Harry Hopkins through his administrator, Aubrey Williams. Mr. Hopkins has five assistant administrators. We formerly reported through one of these assistants, Mr. Jacob Baker; we now report, instead, through Mrs. Ellen Woodward, another assistant administrator, who has recently had her already extensive field of women's work enlarged to include all professional projects, including the four arts. Mrs. Woodward is an excellent executive who has worked with Mr. Hopkins since C.W.A. She is very friendly to the arts, and our recent conferences lead us to believe that she will do everything in her power to expedite our program.

You should also know that our program is not to be cut, that we have an expectancy of six months, when we will again be called upon to justify the ·

expenditure of funds on the double basis of relief and of professional excellence.

WHERE ARE THE "NEW" PLAYS?

It seems to me it is our job in the Federal Theatre Project to expand, as greatly as our imagination and talents will permit, the boundaries of theatre. Obviously, it is a dubious use of federal funds to do only those plays which have been already proved on audiences or our contemporaries. Obviously, it is a timid wasting of an unprecedented chance to regard the theatre only in terms of what we have hitherto experienced.

But where are the new plays? In common with the rest of you, I spend every available spare hour reading scripts, and such a dreary lot I never encountered. They cling forlornly to the skirts of the past. If I may mix my metaphors, they are the dull legitimate offspring of Henry Arthur Jones and Madame Vestris. Not only the plays, but the methods indicated for their production, class them as museum pieces—not as theatre pieces.

Architects today shatter facades and let the steel show; musicians shatter melody and experiment with dissonance; painters turn away from sentimentality to an objective or psychological view of nature and the economic scene—but the theatre still clings to melody, to the facade, to sentimentality.

LET THE THEATRE GROW UP!

If we want the Federal Theatre to become anything more than a temporary stopgap we must advance rapidly next year, using all the forces at our disposal—light, sound, kinetics, acrobatics. We must continue to experiment with dance movement and choral speech, not divorced from, but a part of theatre production.

We must see the relationship between the men at work on Boulder Dam and the Greek chorus; we must study Pavlov as well as Pavlova, Einstein as well as Eisenstein; we must derive not only from ancient Baghdad, but from modern Greece. In short, the American theatre must wake up and grow up—wake up to an age of expanding social consciousness, an age in which men are demanding that war and social injustice be outlawed, an age in which men are whispering through space, soaring to the stars, and flinging miles of steel and glass into the air. If the plays do not exist we shall have to write them. We shall have to work more closely with our dramatists. We cannot be too proud to study our medium.

By this I do not mean only the technique of dramatic writing; I do not mean merely the theatre itself, the lights, lines, playing space, and acoustics. I mean, specifically, our own Federal Theatre companies and our own Federal Theatre audiences. I mean, specifically, the problem of vaudeville and how the valuable techniques of the vaudeville can be reused. Our audiences want to laugh and so do we.

STUDY OUR MEDIUM

I should like to know how many of the hundred somewhat embattled dramatists who talked to me in the lounge of the Manhattan Theatre the other day, demanding with some asperity a "Playwrights' Theatre," really did not realize that that is what they are getting today in America. Every one of our 158 theatres is clamoring for scripts. Our vast new audience, untrained in theatregoing, is willing to take theatre on the terms we create. I should like to know how many of our playwrights have gone, notebook in hand, and studied performances and rehearsals of any definite group and the reaction of various audiences to that group, and then gone back and started to write a play for that playing group and for the audience?

Shakespeare was not too proud to write that way. Neither was Chekhov. Neither was Euripides. It is not going to hurt the imagination of any dramatist to cut his pattern to fit his cloth any more than it is going to hurt any designer to have to plan six weeks ahead to buy inexpensive materials instead of waiting until the night before the show and then buy gowns at Bergdorf Goodman's; any more than it is going to hurt any of us as directors and producers to find that we must enlarge our consciousness to include such economic facts as unemployment, taxation, the obligation of government to the unemployed and to art, the values and dangers of organization to the theatre worker, the effect of trade unionism on art, the spending of federal funds in relationship to censorship, the value of the theatre to recreation, education and therapeutics.

OUR STRENGTH LIES IN THE PROBLEMS OF THOSE WHO MAKE UP OUR AUDIENCE

It is the strength and not the weakness of the Federal Theatre that it is impregnated with facts of life commonly outside the consciousness of the theatre worker.

> *Tell your stories of fishing and other men's wives*
> *The expansive moment of constricted lives*
> *In the lighted inn.*

But do not forget that even as you tell that made up story you are part of a more crucial struggle, the struggle now going on within our labor organizations or around our peace tables. Doubtless we shall continue to write over the doors of our theatres the legend of *Ostnia:*

> *. . . Enter the street of your dreams*
> *All who have compounded envy and hopefulness into desire*
> *Perform here nightly their magical arts of identification*
> *Among the Chinese lanterns and the champagne served in shoes.*

But those same magical arts of identification on the Federal Theatre Project also make us one with the Kansas farmer surveying his blackened cornfields. The continuance of our theatre job, like the continuance of his farming job, depends upon the rainfall.

This consciousness that we are part of the economic life of America, that we are one with the worker on the stage and in the audience, is the very core of the Federal Theatre. If not, what does it matter that

> *The galleries are full of music, the pianist is*
> *   storming the keys*
> *The great cellist is crucified over his instrument*
> *That none may hear the ejaculation of the sentinels*
> *Nor the sigh of the most numerous and the most poor.*

EXTENDING THE BOUNDARIES OF THE THEATRE

Our first job, then, is to extend the boundaries of theatre. Our second is that we extend these boundaries together.

No matter how imaginative the plans each director has for his own season and no matter how successfully he carries them out, if each one continues to devote himself exclusively to his own group we become only a board of New York managers around a table. In that case it will be only a matter of time when jealousies and enmities will begin and we will become "isolated from each other like cases of fever."

During the first six months it was necessary that each director become egocentric. From now on egocentricity is the road back into the past. We must see the Federal Theatre, must see how our individual policies and plays fit the policies and plays of the rest of New York City, and increasingly, of the nationwide theatre.

OUR CONCERTED STRENGTH

This meeting I should like to think is only the forerunner of a regular monthly meeting—even if only a luncheon meeting, at which general policies and production problems can be discussed. More important, I should like to see producers occasionally attend each other's rehearsals, pooling ideas and suggestions. I should like to see each director, in weekly meetings with his own group, build up a feeling not only for his own theatre but for Federal Theatre. We cannot be too ambitious. We must do whole cycles of material of a nature to supplement the usual Broadway season. The Classical Theatre is a step in that direction—so is the Living Newspaper—so is the Dance Theatre, the Children's Theatre.

During the next year I should like to see the New York Federal Theatre Project live up to its place as head of our projects. I should like to see our best plays toured. I should like to see our directors offer their services interchangeably throughout the country. In other words, let us stress the very attributes of Federal Theatre which make it difficult—its size, its vast extent, and let us make these attributes serve us.

These things can only be done by concerted effort, and it is this concerted effort which alone can even begin to realize our vast potentialities.

Letters to Philip Haldane Davis

May 17, 1935
(New York City)

I have spent a day trudging from office to office getting various line-ups, from President Gillmore, of Equity, Motherwell for Stage, Mrs. Isaacs and Rosamond Gilder for Theatre Arts; then I called Philip Youtz and through him met Miss Gosslyn; she was very good and concrete; then at five, under the clock at the Penn Hotel, Elmer Rice materialized, very unpressed, rumpled, rosy and unkempt, accompanied by the inevitable Rachel Hartzel. We went in and had Manhattans and discussed theatre plans. Elmer read the plan E. C. Mabie [Midwest regional director of Federal Theatre] and I worked on in the garden with you and thinks it is wonderful. We talked rapidly and often in unison "plagiarizing each other," Elmer remarked. He described all the people he knew in the theatre down hounding Harry Hopkins [Director of the WPA]. "I was one," said Rice affably. "I went down to ask Hopkins for $100,000 for the Theatre Alliance. He said to me, 'Katharine Cornell has just been here, Frank Gillmore, Edith Isaacs, Eva Le Gallienne, and I don't know how many others. Each one wants me to finance his own independent idea; aren't any of you people interested in an American theatre? Isn't there any theatre in America with no axe to grind?'"

Hallie Flanagan's letters to Philip Haldane Davis used by permission of Shirley Rich Krohn.

"Out of my sub-conscious," Rice went on (of course he had had three Manhattans when he told me this), "I said 'Hallie Flanagan.' " At that he said Hopkins got up, shook his hand and said, "I should have known that, but I was afraid of being accused of favoritism. She used to stand on the backs of people and make Grinnell win football games with Chicago University (my own note is backs of the 'woikers')." Wouldn't it be wonderful, Phil, to have great regional art centers rebuilt out of the old opry houses, redone by unemployed architects and artists, housing plays and concerts. . . .

March 17, 1936

Phil, Bill Nunn, Dan Ring, and I met with Victor Ridder from 9 to 12. An organization called the "Veterans" is opposing the project. Why I do not know. They are tied up with the American Legion and the D.A.R., though their actions would seem to indicate that they are bought by the Hearst press. We found in this meeting that our scripts are being sold to the *Sun*, and at Mr. Ridder's suggestion we fired the two men on whom we have a case. The *Journal* carried a screaming headline "Federal Theatre in hands of Reds." Williams phoned in a panic from Washington and said we had better close the show. [She refers to the Living Newspaper "Triple A Plowed Under."] However, the *Times*, *Tribune*, *Post* and *News* all reviewed the play at great length and very respectfully. . . we must not be naive as to the political forces back of this. For instance, Brown, one of the labor department at 111 Eighth Avenue, had requested the dismissal of a Miss Hazel Hoffman who works in the mail opening department at 801. He accuses her of being a spy. I said I would have to see proof. Yesterday he showed me an affidavit from her made out to the Hearst press. She is rumored to have received $1000 for it, but this is only rumor. She swears that she has opened my mail for three months and found it "incendiary, revolutionary and seditious." Mr. Brown said she was purely a stool pigeon of the Hearst press. No wonder I have been saying that the New York office made me feel queer. It is a hot spot.

September 30, 1936

I got terribly mad at [Philip] Barber and [John] Houseman, both of whom maintain that the show [*Horse Eats Hat*] is flawless and that messy timing and clumsy curtains do not matter on such a show. Barber had the nerve to say that our shows had a higher standard of perfection than Broadway which is simply fatuous. They have more originality and power, but they are not expertly done and they must be. Why are my directors so easily satisfied? I think it is the unforgivable sin in a theatre person. I sometimes feel that I will go crazy not being able to make this project what it should and might be.

October 3, 1936

The high spot of the day was Herbert Price, a man with professional theatre background who was working with Miss O'Shea and then came to Washington and said "Give me something hard to do." Now he is back from his second month in the Black Ankle Belt organizing community theatres: "Their feet are still in the mud, they are still slaves. They live in indescribable want, want of food, want of houses, want of clothes, want of any kind of life." He talked to them about making up plays of their own life. Got an old barber shop turned over to them and they are all at it. They make their own costumes out of old sugar bags, dyed with the berries of the region. It seems that while down there Price got chiggers and "still have 'em, but they are not contagious. I itched so that I tore around and gesticulated and they thought it was the Holy Ghost descending upon me."

Black things of the day: Bill Beyer has resigned in Detroit; the state administration blew up about Sherry in Milwaukee and Miller has flown west either to defend or fire her; Thad Holt has frozen all employment; Malcolm Miller has forbidden John McGee to enter New Orleans. It is all like a great continued siege—funny, but tired-making.

Buy the current *Scribner's* and you will see that somebody has awarded the prize for the last six months for "the most outstanding theatre activity" to our Federal Theatre.

October 4

Washington is a curiously transitory place—the people look as though they had no roots. . .

Cahill and I felt pretty depressed this evening about the article in the *Times* in which the high proud critics are referring to our exhibits as "herd art." These critics seem to mistake quantity for quality. I don't think that we confuse them, but I think we are more apt to get something out of a great flood of people's experience than out of a precious, anemic drip of art theory.

October 12, 1936

No, my speech was not good, I am sorry to say—it was horizontal and gisty. . .

October 14

Mary and I are just starting off in the car for Williamsburg, after a day unparalleled even in WPA—Chicago negroes on the warpath and on the wire—Paul Green on the warpath and on the wire—Morris Watson down, storming the White House—a Baptist minister raising hell about an immoral play, *The First Legion*. Mrs. Woodward demanding that someone remove the bathroom humor from *Horse Eats Hat*, and 10,000 Democrats in Ohio (according to my superiors) wiring the White House to know how Hallie Flanagan is voting.

October 26

I feel sometimes I am looking at strange little creatures, myself among them, under a microscope. . .

November 8

I have just gotten out of the library, reading George Bernard Shaw's *On the Rocks*, in my frantic reading for new plays. It was turned down by the Guild and has never been done here and I think it is just the stuff for us. I have also run through a long scenario on money for the next Living Newspaper and have turned it down absolutely. It is just an adolescent, anticapitalist scream of hate, and I will not have such nonsense done on our stage. . .

Read the enclosed article by Burns Mantle. We immediately took up his plan with Mrs. Woodward. However, they point out that under no circumstances can we buy scenery and costumes or pay the royalties at present being paid. I wish we could do something to cooperate more fully with the commercial theatre, but every attempt I make is apparently against regulations. [This relates to Mantle's article of November 5 suggesting that Federal Theatre take over Sidney Kingsley's *10,000,000 Ghosts*]. . .

I do not know why I am thinking so much these days about Ibsen's remark about the majority always being wrong. I wish Roosevelt had not gone in with such a big one, and I do not like his rush back here with a rapturous up-turned grin and the remark about balancing the budget. I hope he won't forget that he was elected by the workers, and I certainly don't like Hearst and the *Herald Tribune* coming out for him.

November 10

I have thought up a way out of the cuts and have drawn it up in writing to present it at tomorrow's meetings. It is that all four art directors object to dismissing any qualified worker who will be turned from us back to relief rolls or destitution, and as a guarantee of our feeling we suggest that every person on our payroll getting $1500 and over, beginning with the four National Directors, take a proportionate cut, this money to keep the security wage workers on the payroll. . . . Later: they soon put a quietus to that!

November 11, 1936

. . . It has been another day of meetings and interviews—and another evening in bed reading plays—Barry's *Wild Harps Playing* is quite a lovely fantasy, but lacks the hard fierceness of Auden, and the sense of the economic world of Auden—and can fantasy really exist bearably without that sense? I just read that Chaplin said he was afraid of our humor today— the humour of Thurber and Frank Sullivan because it was so fierce and so definite—but I think fierceness is all that saves fantasy—did I tell you that Cahill and I want to write a play called *Bury the Living* to be a fierce one on what we are doing to youth in this country—no place to go and nothing to do after graduation. What in the devil do you think Roosevelt means by closing up the National Youth Administration? He has no real convictions and Peggy Bacon was right about the labels blurring the destination. Also you were, are and will be Right.

Phil Barber broke the news to the New York directors today about the reorganization and the break up of the small kingdoms—and I understand there is wild muttering and that Goodman resigned—my desk will be yellow with protesting telegrams. . . I love my new office and long to have you see it. I am to choose any of the Art Project pictures for it as soon as the exhibit is over. In the hall we're going to have a long line of pictures of productions. . .

I suppose by this time there is wild activity in said Green Room with Lester scowling away like anything. However—I wish more people had his sense of wanting a thing to be right. I agree with Brooks Atkinson in the Sunday *Times* that most of our productions are not very good. At the same time, the Martin Flavin letter, also in the Sunday *Times,* when he said "I take off my hat to the Federal Theatre Project" etc.—suddenly made me have a lump in my throat.

November 19, 1936

Sitting in Essex House, the first quiet moment of the day—a lull between a seven o'clock cup of tea after the last delegation and an eight o'clock meeting with [Virgil] Geddes, [James] Light, and the designer of *Native Ground,* Howard Bay, in my opinion definitely a genius. At ten Bill and I are going to see a rehearsal of the negro dance unit in *Bassa Moona.* The day has included a survey of Kreymborg's unit, a rehearsal of *Mr. Jiggins,* our Irish company, a run-thru of *America, America,* a mass recitation, very moving, then Pierre [Rohan, editor of *Federal Theatre Magazine*] and proof of the magazine, lunch with Bill and Colonel Somervell. Tomorrow I see a run-thru of the Negro *11 PM,* the children's theatre and *The Emperor's New Clothes,* and at night the Resettlement show, *200 Were Chosen* . . .

Wednesday night, December 3
[Regarding WPA Arts Project's job cuts]

Have you any idea what this is like? Of course you have being you and feeling all that I feel. Picket lines and the terrible banners: "Mr. Roosevelt, what do you mean?" Men and women, screaming and fainting. A sit down strike with people barricading themselves behind desks when the police break in. I saw two riots yesterday, not at our office but at 39th Street at the Art Project. The people slept in over night. The whole thing was unbelievably horrible. No one seemed to be in control. The police were clubbing people, who were spitting in their faces. A woman knocked down and the crowd rushed right over her. . .

When Eddie Cahill and I tried to get in the side street a man was battering his head against the wall, screaming that his wife was pregnant, that they had two children and that he had to have his $23 a week. Bill, Phil Barber, and I had a consultation. They thought I should go back to Washington, since this same condition exists everywhere. Miller wires riots in Denver and Seattle, not on our project but on the WPA. . .

The supervisors unanimously refuse to submit lists of those to be fired, so Barber is making the cuts himself, and Bill says he is doing a good job. In the meantime the morale on the project has been wrecked, and people in the cold and snow are picketing the WPA. . .

Friday, December 4

I got to Washington and could not reach either Hopkins or [Mrs. Ellen] Woodward but I did succeed in getting hold of Dave Niles. He says nothing can prevent a big Congressional appropriation—over 50,000 telegrams to the White House on the subject of the arts. He says that the cuts on the other WPA projects cause no ripple compared to the arts. . .

December 6

It is raining, a long, horizontal day of rain and fog. But a wonderful thing happened. I saw *Rembrandt.* It is as exciting as truth is apt to be (remember your discovery about historical plays) . . . only two other people I know have voices with the characteristic of Laughton, that is, vibrant, personal and disturbing. One of the other people is T. S. Eliot. The other one is you. He is a great actor. I mean he acts with his mind and emotions as well as his body. The settings made to resemble Rembrandt paintings did not quite come off in the ordinary sense of background, but achieved wonderful moments—*The Reading of the Bible, The Women Sweeping, King Saul, The Bakers,* and *The Night Watch.* The first speech in the play about loving a woman is one of the most wonderful things I have ever heard.

Part of the reason I felt this picture so was that I was forgetting the cuts. I do not believe they can be made. . . .

The Guild has bought out from under us the play I wanted so much, *But For The Grace of God,* the one on child labor. We signed with Sidney Harmon on Wednesday, Atlas saw the Guild that night and used our desire for a nation-wide production to get a good deal from the Guild.

December 9 (Washington)

We are still in this state of horrible suspense. As I see the bureaucratic stupidities and weaknesses here, my sympathies are constantly with the workers, especially when I see their courage in trying to get up curtains. Surely artists have never worked under such terrible conditions. . .

December 17

. . . I must see *Johnny Johnson* over again with you. Feeling as you do about Paul [Green], you would love his hero. The rather dumb country boy, the tombstone maker who enlists because he is sick of tombstones, and reads Wilson's speeches and believes in them. He is so like Paul Green that I kept remembering the night in his livingroom. To me this is the most potent of all the plays against war because it is funny and sad and infuriating and inevitable. . .

May 10, 1937

. . . I am nearly crazy reading plays. I just finished one which looked exciting, *Cuban Scene,* but I am sorry to say it turned out to be one of those plays where you cannot tell whether it is Pedro who is speaking or Ramon. It is all atmosphere and no plot except an offstage strike. It is all background and no foreground. It is just no play. . .

Please, Muses, deliver unto us a play. We will sacrifice a young heifer, a black one, and the little cow in amber without its left ear. Let it be a play full of singing and dancing and the sound of timbrels. . .

May 13 (Wardman Park Hotel—Washington, D.C.)

Everything here is focused on Congress. Hopkins is taking a terrible drubbing everyday, with all the forces of reaction within and without the party. Hard upon him. Between attacks he lies down and drinks hot milk. In the face of all that he is going through and all that our workers are going through, I got pretty disgusted listening to the luncheon speakers of the National Art Federation talking about art. "I don't worry about hunger," said one large-paunched gent, "artists have always been hungry. The greatest art has been created in garrets, etc." There was a lot of sneering at those of us who were full of "apostolic zeal" to have the theatre say something. . .

November 6, 1937 (Portland, Oregon)

Football in the river and honk-honking going on in Portland streets because Portland is playing Montana tomorrow, and in New York *Julius Caesar* is opening and in Washington apparently terrific procedure battles are going on, while up in Maine our intrepid company is playing their same old vaudeville for at least the 90th time to the inmates of various asylums. (I wonder how we are really affecting people in the asylums—I know if I had to see some of these shows very often I would be in one.)

And in Poughkeepsie someone is writing about Spartan boys combing their long black hair before going into battle.

We came down from Seattle by the noon train yesterday, arriving at six, and being rushed at once to a dinner and then to a rehearsal of *The Taming of the Shrew,* done with our vaudeville actors. Pretty terrible, I am very sorry to say—hammy and corny, but they are all trying so hard. Then to a reception given by the stuck-up Civic Theatre. After a horrible night in a horrible hotel, I went out all nerved up to close the project, and then what do you think happened? These very same actors, vaudevillians, circus clowns, tab show people, came in and did a play about Flax; they had written it themselves, and I want to tell you that although crude it was really something. Then they proceeded to do a part dance-part Living Newspaper show called *Bonneville Dam,* and if anybody thinks I am going to close this project now he is crazy. I got so excited that I went down and told Griffith, the state administrator, that he ought to build us a theatre, and he said if you say that these people are worth it, I will. I think he is the best state administrator I have ever met, and I believe we are really going to get a theatre.

November 9, 1937 (San Francisco)

We were rushed at once to our theatre, the gold and red plush Alcazar, where we saw the *Warrior's Husband,* a thoroughly professional job, though a play I particularly dislike. The theatre is fresh and beautiful, the ushers in good-looking maroon suits, gold-lined capes, etc. The orchestra excellent, the audience enthusiastic. There is too much floridity in acting and design, and above all, in advertising. However, this is perhaps rather carping, for after all, isn't it rather like a miracle to see these people, who when I was here before were just a crowd of anxious, frightened, insecure, actors meeting in a dirty, old hall, now at work rehearsing and producing with an air of stability and professionalism? Perhaps it is too much to hope for high inventive imagination in every production.

After a morning of calling on administrators, I saw something much better than the *Warrior's Husband,* a really exciting rehearsal of Galsworthy's *Justice* by a new director, Ralph Freud. Then a run-thru of three marionette shows, *Alice in Wonderland, Emperor Jones,* and *Twelfth Night.* Not since Sicily and our expeditions to that puppet theatre in Athens opposite the Parthenon have I seen such humor as in the Dormouse, the White Knight, and the twitching of Malvolio's mustachios. And it was to me an entirely new experience to have a marionette theater affect me emotionally as I was affected by the jungle shadows as the O'Neill drums beat.

November 19, 1937

California is full of palms and politicians, both overgrown. I am waited upon by a delegation asking me to look into the moral life of our actors, but in spite of this one cloud in the horizon we are doing the nativity plays in the Episcopalian church and we are doing Shaw's *Caesar and Cleopatra* in a theatre which might have been designed for it, the Mayan, with a marvelous musical score written on the project. We have a good Negro *Androcles and the Lion* in rehearsal; *Ready, Aim, Fire* is breaking all box office records; our dance group in *American Exodus* is thrilling, more wholesome and clean-cut dancing than the New York variety and just as good technically; and above all Hauptmann's *The Weavers,* almost ready to open, is magnificent. How is this for a project?

Judith Malina

[1926–   ]

AN INTRODUCTION

JUDITH MALINA'S DIARIES begin on her twenty-first birthday and continue to the present moment. Somewhere in a dressing room, a restaurant, a hotel, or in the back of a Volkswagen bus moving from theatre to theatre across the continent of Europe she is writing the events of today in a small composition book.

From this wealth of mostly unpublished material, I have excerpted freely from the early years, 1947–50, when the Living Theatre was struggling to become a reality and Judith Malina and Julian Beck were growing into the artists who would birth this dream. The essence of one's creative life is present from the beginning, inchoate, unlearned, blocked by the obstacles of what already is, pertinent for us to understand. Process is the essence of creation, and these early years, unadorned by constant accomplishment, are process, pure and easy to behold. Here, already, are most of the themes and desires which continue to metamorphose into the plays and collective creations of the Living Theatre: pacifism, anarchism, a need to speak of human suffering, to break the chains that bind us to our punishment; a love of ritual, myth and image; a wish to make the theatre immediate, alive, living, a moment in the here-and-now that leads to change.

By the time the diaries excerpted here begin again, in Italy in 1976, Judith Malina, Julian Beck, and the Living Theatre are known worldwide. Judith's direction of Jack Gelber's *The Connection* (1959) and Kenneth Brown's *The Brig* (1963), her adaptation and staging of Brecht's *Antigone* (1967), and her mise en scène with Julian for the collective creations *Mysteries and Smaller Pieces, Paradise Now,* and *Frankenstein* (1965–68) altered the course of modern theatre through their innovative staging and the strength of their radical consciousness.

The Italian diaries do not chronicle major works created by the Living Theatre, but focus instead on the street plays that happen almost daily, in public piazzas, at factory gates, schools, in psychiatric hospitals. The plays are antiwar, antirepression, pro–sexual liberation, feminist. They combine the startling physical images and group movements Judith has developed out of Meyerhold's theories of bio-mechanics with terse recitations of facts and poetic statements of the Living Theatre's transformative beliefs.

Many of the plays are staged with a mixture of Living Theatre company members and factory workers, students, hospital inmates, school children. The nonactors are integrated into the pieces within one or two rehearsals. Because the verbal and physical images the Living has developed are so clear, the performances achieve instant power. No other theatre company I know works more effectively on the street or has pursued so diligently the complex problem of audience involvement.

Based since 1975 in Rome, but touring almost constantly, the Living recalls the wandering theatre troupes of the Middle Ages who roved through Europe bringing an outlawed libertarian energy to people officially bound by the strictures of the Roman Catholic Church. In 1979–80, the Living toured politically wounded Greece with a new work, *Prometheus,* and their classic version of *Antigone* which they restaged on the public square of a small fishing village. "Eh, Antigone!" the fisherfolk would call after Judith as she walked about the town; and they stood to cheer the dress rehearsal. The same year, Judith directed the company in a German-language production of Ernst Toller's expressionist masterwork *Masse-Mensch.* The play was performed in Munich, the same city in which the failed revolutionary uprising Toller writes of had occurred. The Living would like to return to their home in New York City and create a new work here, but the economic problems of supporting a large noncommercial company are awesome in a country which provides major subsidy only to those institutional theatres which strive to develop plays for Broadway. Yet if the U.S. has a national theatre it is the Living, our longest-lived, most consistently controversial and influential theatre troupe.

No other theatre, after all, has achieved the selfsame blend of political commitment and artistic mastery. For the Living is a theatre of moral passion and visual splendor. Julian Beck's settings for works like *Prometheus, The Destruction of the Money Tower,* or *Frankenstein* are among the finest designs of the modern stage. Judith works with actors' bodies, sculpting a Greek chorus for *Antigone* that seems to bring to life an ancient frieze or, in a work like *Seven Meditations on Political Sado-Masochism,* creating group images of oppression that cannot be erased from the mind of the beholder. No other contemporary theatre, except, perhaps, that of Genet, has explored the relationship between political and sexual bondage in such depth, with so many insightful images.

For all of her creative life Judith Malina has been an exceptional woman in a world of men. The Living Theatre has made plays from male archetypes and patriarchal myths in which women, like Antigone or Emma Goldman (both roles Judith has played), are the moral standard bearers, the rebels against a continuing history of violence and penal codes. The vast scenarios of *Paradise Now, The Money Tower,* or *Prometheus*—in which the two great, defeated dreams of liberation, the Greek myth and the Russian Revolution, are juxtaposed—contain a cry for human caring which comes from Judith's persistent identification with all victims of every wrong.

In 1972, when the Living Theatre performed in the slums of Brazil, she wrote of the poverty, "Everyone is appalled. I'm not. I'm here all along. I remember the boy in Taxco [Mexico, 1949, with the bleeding sockets where his eyes had been] and the choice when I ran away [to fight his misery with her theatre work]. And now I demand paradise for him out of all proportion to my ability."

> *He would be almost thirty now. . .*
> *if he survived.*
> *O little blind boy of Taxco, I*
> *will fulfill the promise yet*
> *that I made to you in my broken*
> *heart twenty years ago.*

Concealed within that awesome promise so few have dared to make was a need grown ever more decipherable as she's remained faithful to the memory of the child. A need, felt in the sorrow of her heart, that has become the passion of her work: to reveal the violence of all forms of slavery, and then to strive to break the bonds of submission and despair. Her passion is the passion of our age.

—K.M.

Judith Malina
[1926–   ]

SELECTIONS

From the Diaries, 1947–51

June 4, 1947

"Schon einundzwanzig, und noch nichts für die Unsterblichkeit getan."

Secretly, I expected a sudden and decisive change.

I wake early and my mother has set out the traditional birthday table laden with dainty things and gifts.

Birthday feelings at twenty-one. I dress in new clothes. I feel a certain sense of freedom at leaving the bookshop, quitting the job where I have not been happy working.

Julian comes and brings birthday presents: Cocteau's *Thomas the Imposter,* an album of the finale of *Götterdämmerung,* and of César Franck's Symphony in D Minor.

Then I go to Harald.

When I came in Harald had a tall red candle burning on a cake and blue crepe paper covered his baggage and the dresser. Somewhat worn but still extant were the orange crepe paper streamers that I had hung. But our love is saddened by the knowledge of our coming separation.

For my birthday he gives me these notebooks, and asks me to keep a record of my thoughts and actions. I promise to show them to him when completed, but I realize I must try to avoid writing as he would have me write. A journal kept for someone else is a letter and not *ein Tagebuch.*

In the evening, to the Cherry Lane Theatre where I am rehearsing *Ethan Frome* for the On Stage Company. After a long evening we rough-blocked one scene.

I struggle with the character of Zenobia Frome. But there's comfort in playing in a theatre in which I have played before. It was two summers ago that Lola Ross and I played here in *By Any Other Name*—and now Lola too is with the On Stage Company.

When I was waiting for Julian to return from his Sierra adventure last summer it was Lola, my old schoolmate from Piscator's, in whom I confided all the earliest plans for the Living Theatre, and with whom I shared the dreams of the most important work of my life for which I am now preparing.

June 9, 1947

A rehearsal is canceled and I spend the morning studying my first act lines with Harald and then I accompany him to various offices and consulates.

Now he is at the Dramatic Workshop where we met and studied and worked and rehearsed together during his brief stay in this country. He's gone inside but I have to wait for him in the Ritz Coffee Shop across the street. Because I'm not allowed to enter the Workshop until I write Piscator a letter of apology.

I've put it off from day to day. It's difficult because I'm in the wrong and don't have an adequate excuse.

We were rehearsing Sartre's *Flies*. The rehearsal was strained and late. Harald had quarreled with me and I was crying. I was not in costume and not in a human humor when Piscator scolded me. But that's not a legitimate excuse for responding so rudely to a director and a teacher—and a loved and honored one at that—as disrespectfully, as I did. I must write him before it is too late.

June 16, 1947

Yesterday I bought Hallie Flanagan's *Arena*. In the first exciting chapters she describes how she created a nationwide theatre movement to speak to the people, to the workers. A theatre using all the forms, new and traditional, verse and prose, in all the languages that are spoken in the USA; in every city and village, and on wagons for the country people and for the poor. . . And I look at the scope of the book and I think pridefully: "It can be done. She did it. So can I."

Looking for a theatre. Julian and I go to see the former Labor Stage which is occupied by the Experimental Theatre of Equity and to the Belmonte, now showing Spanish motion pictures. No hope.

In the mail I receive a diploma from the Dramatic Workshop for Acting instead of Directing.

Now I'll have to go and protest, and they'll say I wrote Acting down on my scholarship application and I'll have to tell the whole story: how I entered the Dramatic Workshop fervent to be an actress and after a few days of watching Piscator's work I knew I wanted to do the more encompassing work that is called Directing.

Piscator regarded me coldly: he does not have a high regard for the staying power of women in the masculine professions. He expressed his suspicion that I would "get married and forget about the theatre," that for this reason I had better study acting. I pleaded with him, swallowing my humiliation at his low opinion of my qualifications because of my sex, and he, somewhat reluctantly, allowed me to take the directing course. Thus I was able to study not only acting, but stage design, theatre management, lighting, and above all take invaluable directing classes with Piscator.

Now they've sent me an Acting diploma, and Piscator is not even in New York for me to protest to. I've tried through all my school years to prove my worth to him and I haven't yet.

I will go and ask for the Directing diploma even if no one ever sees it, because I worked for it.

July 14, 1947

We begin rehearsals of *The Dog Beneath the Skin.*

For years I have refuted Stanislavsky's sense memory theory. In Raiken Ben-Ari's class I played the last scene of *Iphigenia in Aulis* in a conscious attempt to demonstrate that I could play the famous tearful plea with my mind empty of all but the most prosaic thoughts. I said: A painter does not weep when he paints a weeping figure.—Yet I exploited my own emotional turmoil when I played Cassandra. And in the role of Mildred Luce, driven mad by the loss of two sons in the war. . . What alternatives can I find to the sense memories of grief?—Does the actor exhibit his peculiar emotion the way the freak exhibits his distorted physique?*

I'm reading *Back to Methuselah.* Julian, who is ambitious, thinks it could be a Living Theatre production.

July 17, 1947

Finished *Back to Methuselah,* Shaw's cycle of plays. I have always been uncomfortable in utopias. From St. Augustine to Thomas More, from Huxley to Shaw, the utopias are ugly because they are not human and our only crite-

---

*I only understood years later, when I had taken diverse trips into the actor's possibilities, that it was not "realism" I was protesting against (however futilely) when I was 21, but the fake mimicry of the real moment that is fictional acting. What I was looking for was the non-fictional reality of the here and now (Ouro Preto, 1971).

rion for beauty is a human one. Mohammed's paradise is perhaps the most pleasing because of its sensuality.

July 20, 1947

We rehearsed *Dog Beneath the Skin* all day, from 10 A.M. to midnight. It took eight hours to run through the play once. I watch from the house. Technically everything is very confused but the quality is astounding.

Alexis works keenly, unsmilingly, impersonally, like a knife, with short, thorough strokes. Piscator is a sabre who slashes through to the meaning of the play in one clean cut. I'm afraid I will work like a saw, arduously and laboriously. What makes the best cut?

May 15, 1948

Mother is having a birthday party from which I have momentarily escaped.

Bobbie Jastrow's parents are here proudly describing the progress of their boy. Just having received his doctorate in nuclear physics, he is going to do a year's study in Europe and then go to the Princeton Institute for Advanced Studies where he has been invited on a fellowship.

The boy who played handball with me when I saw him last and who explained (with many scientific charts) the mysterious ways of sex to me at his Bar Mitzvah party the first time I wore high heels, is now one of the wise men in the country. Wise, that is, in the technological horrors of our time.

With the Jastrows we were discussing the coming elections, Wallace and the split vote, and I am suddenly trembling with all sorts of emotions. War and the atom and the frail hands of men holding such mighty weapons. I feel sick and wonder.

I have come here to the bathroom, the only quiet place in the apartment, to think of what within my tiny scope I can do. I feel how small I am, and yet how strong. I know that it is not beyond my power to make choices to make my life useful. That at least I can do. Yet that is so difficult, so insurmountably difficult. I must stop. I can't yet think deeply enough about it.

June 1, 1948

Yesterday: Julian's 23rd birthday! We were together most of the day. He says he feels old.

I am as one possessed today. Anxieties and hopes set off by thoughts on politics, on my reluctant place in the political structure, my immense dissatisfaction with all existing orders.

The mail brings *Resistance,* the anarchist newspaper, which I have been receiving for years. I am surprised to find it full of pertinent material.

Till now I had hardly paid attention to the magazine even though Paul Goodman writes for it. Because I distrust militant politics. Though Kropotkin writes splendidly on the future society, I don't know how to share his faith. I have tremendous respect for the anarchist ideal. Yet all the anarchists I know except Paul seem to live such disordered lives.

Paul writes an aritcle in *Resistance* on vegetarianism. In it he examines the problem of free choice and the intellectual insight that free choice demands. He looks into the causes of behavior, he realizes the frailty of people and loves them because he understands the genesis of their failings. His honesty makes me look with horror at my own self-deception and the treachery that my right hand commits against my left. He is wise like an elder.

His intellect is one of the most positive things I have encountered.

There is, after all, only one problem no matter where we begin our wondering, the old and only problem of good and evil.

September 9, 1948

Julian and I have a long conversation about having a baby. I do not wish to marry, but there seems little else left open for me and in the end I admit it. Yet what I am afraid to lose is my struggle to assert my "person" as an individual distinct from Julian and any other.

I will find a way. Even in this.

September 12, 1948

Julian is going on a five-day trip to Vermont with Pierre. How can he do this under present conditions. I am aghast that he can leave me now.*

Finished *Lotte in Weimar*.

An appalling revelation in Mann's essay on Goethe.

Goethe, according to Mann, when he was a member of the government in Weimar in his late years, sat in judgment on a court case trying a young girl for killing her baby. There was a plea from the court for mercy, but Goethe *signed the death sentence* because he placed justice above mercy.

Mann defends Goethe's monstrous cruelty by an appeal to order. Mann writes: ". . . it bears witness to a stern self-disciplining of his own kindliness and pity and their suppression in favor of established order.

"For order the mature Goethe held in such honor that he openly declared it to be better to commit injustice than tolerate disorder."

This from the author of *Faust*!

So much for the value of literary morality.

Farewell to the moral teaching of Goethe or Mann. Goodbye to literature. . .!

---

* I suspected that I was pregnant. I was afraid to write this in my journal lest my mother see it.

October 11, 1948

I try to be sociable. But when Julian's father defends every reactionary cause I can't stand it. In the middle of a hard argument I find myself so enraged that I say hastily that I have a headache and tearfully leave the house.

Out on the street Julian confronts me. Why am I not tactful?

I can't. I can't. I cry out against the whole way of life.

Julian asks me what I really want. And I tell him the other side of the fantasy, the dream I have of being in the real world doing something useful.

"I want to go to Detroit. . . and I want to talk to the men who work on the assembly line. . . and I want to find out. . . "

But I did not know what I wanted to find out. Something about why he lives in a real world I do not know, about the world of the factory worker.

When I worked in a factory I thought I would be trapped there forever. But I don't belong on West End Avenue. I don't belong to the bourgeoisie.

Can Julian understand this? Not now. He looks at me blankly when I say: "I want to go to Detroit . . ."*

October 14, 1948

Julian doesn't know about the horror, neither its workings, nor its causes, nor its manifestations. He is unaware of the minuteness of the individual in the universe. In his own concentrated self—which he imagines to be eternal—he conceives the universe. All things revolve around his consciousness, even the distant stars.

October 16, 1948

The imbecile pettiness of the forms through which I must pass in order to exist within "the social group." How narrow all the passages are.

November 18, 1948

Am I married? Is this my home? Is the child I am expecting a reality, a living person-to-be? Are these strange, cool people now "related" to me? Is this my life that I am living? My only, dreamed of, planned-for, anticipated life? Is it for this that I prayed and hoped through all my childhood? For this emptiness, this meaningless existence? What of my dreams? What of the woman that I was to be?

Enough of these haunts and spirits. It is morning and it is well that I should try to use the day.

---

*In 1974 the Living Theatre went to Pittsburgh, where they presented *The Money Tower* and other plays for the steel workers and their families, performing on streets, in yards, and in front of the factory gates.—ED.

February 2, 1949 (Taxco, Mexico)

I walk cautiously among the cobbles in my high heels. Julian was looking in a shop window. A boy approaches me to beg.

I look into his face and see his sightless eyes. They are two sores that bleed a pus like tears along his cheeks.

I want to give him, not a few centavos, but all my care, all my devotion, to cure his eyes—to stay in Mexico and cure them all—the entire plan of my life lies open in his sore eyes—and I realize what I have to do—because of what I am able to do and what I am not able to do—and where my devotion to him is—and I screamed—

so that I frightened the poor child, and I ran, with my eyes closed, because he could not see—

and I knew that the boy thought that I screamed in revulsion, but that was not true—

I screamed because I was leaving him, and I had already promised myself to him, and to do the work that I had to do for him, because in that pain and blindness he made it clear.

September 21, 1949

In a sudden spurt of straw clutching I am making the rounds of theatrical offices while mother watches Garrick.* I have inordinate love for the crowd, which is so distasteful to Julian, and for the racetrack atmosphere of Broadway. I walk myself weary, meet old friends or acquaintances. After a time I shall come to despise it again, but now I love it.

December 1, 1949

Again at work on The Living Theatre. Each time with fresh hope. Now the costliest project of all and entirely unfeasible.

We plan, since no theatre seems to exist, to build one. And in order to do this inexpensively to build it with a quonset hut, one of those metal sheds that the army developed.

But the price of property in New York City is fantastic. The whole thing is fantastic.

Paul Goodman will speak about it to his brother, Percy, who has built a quonset synagogue in Long Island.

At least I am married to an optimist.

December 13, 1949

Recollections of the wild days of our youth. I think I still love that free,

---

*Her newborn son.—ED.

insane, outrageous, and beautiful Julian, the mad, unfettered, homosexual poet who has disappeared so completely that he himself does not recall him, not even as well as I do. And when he does, it is without any love for his lost liberty, without any realization of his love for his need for liberty. Julian forgets that his old crudeness was only the cuttingness of glass being shattered to let in the air.

But now? We find ourselves in a kind of life in which contentment is supposed to replace the ecstasies of misery, but. . .

December 15, 1949

Reading of Dick Gerson's play *The Thirteenth God* at the Dramatic Workshop. Rehearsal with Chouteau Dyer* is always enjoyable. Robert Carricart read Alexander with such passion that I was moved, though not to tears, by his passionate looks. I read Statira, Alexander's Persian wife.

Yet it was so gratifying to read a role, to use again the range of my voice, the gestures of the eye or the clenched or open palm, to live that life, even so tentatively and so temporarily—the life before an audience. Oh yes I do want to act, though there is no intellectual rationalization for it. I do want to act.

December 28, 1949

Read Gertrude Stein's *Doctor Faustus Lights the Lights*. A marvelous play. Her words are symbols, a quality that becomes her theme. She derives from the legend with insight and beauty. I want very much to do this play.

Also read Brecht's *Good Woman of Setzuan*. Although it is a good play, it is difficult to do parable-propaganda theatre.

January 30, 1950

Last night Julian read to me from the *Times* about the hydrogen bomb, H-Bomb, Hell Bomb, and all night I was obsessed with dreams of war.

I want to work. I am almost ready to begin.

Last night at Martha Graham. How little it meant. She is a noble artist. I am too impatient with the spectator's role. I am impatient with the aesthetic. Graham's *World Pictures* are moving, but I am involved in a search in another direction. All things extraneous to it become diversions.

February 14, 1950

The play, *A Member of the Wedding,* is about loneliness. It should have

_____

*One of Piscator's collaborators at the Dramatic Workshop, a woman for whom Judith has deep respect.—ED.

been a good play. This new poetic realism is a style as expressionism was a style and it will meet the same doom because it only reveals a psychological state idealized by distance and falsifying the reality by sentimentality.

February 19, 1950

Old faces at the New School Alumni Meeting.

Piscator talks. Some flame that is not forgotten revives. His voice is calm and sardonic and alive with an inner excitement. Among all the small voices, a clear and strong voice. And that silver head, a very medallion of a head.

He speaks of the disappointment he feels that the Dramatic Workshop has not become a vanguard army of Political Theatres across America. He speaks derisively of certain students who have not followed his political inspiration. Of Tennessee Williams. Piscator says he wishes "to make of every actor a thinker and of every playwright a fighter."

And his regard and intentions seem to select me, to accuse me, to want to force me into willing action.

August 15, 1950

In our search for some kind of action, we begin a letter writing campaign and a system of distributing labels, and beyond that we can only "trouble deaf heaven with our bootless cries."

August 16, 1950

Friday, the Becks will take Garrick overnight and we hope to deluge the city with 6,000 labels reading: "Answer war Gandhi's way" and "War is hell. Resist it."

Until 2 A.M. I type these on gummed stickers.

August 18, 1950

Midnight: We meet Robin at Columbus Circle and divide our labels. Julian is in his white suit and I am wearing a long black net dress and white cape. We walk along the streets seen by too many, too conspicuous. It is too early. To waste an hour or so we go to a soda place and sit for a while. More NoDoz. Then out to our work.

On every street, the police car passed us several times. Curious passersby begin to look like plainclothesmen. In the gutters and on the sidewalks there are dozens of revolting waterbugs, some scurrying, others crushed, dead, dying.

At 3 A.M. we start at 59th Street from Eighth to Madison Avenue. Then we go east to west and west to east through 57th Street. The whole world seems awake.

We feel criminal, moving through the streets. At Fifth Avenue and 57th Street a police car pulls over to us. Fortunately we have rehearsed all possibilities. Our object was not to be arrested, therefore not to provoke the policemen.

We answer quietly, respectfully, innocently. We resist the temptation to argue. The police—or any legal authority acting on the assumption that they are superior by virtue of delegated authority—always present a challenge to the victim to prove that he is in fact not inferior.

The precinct was telephoned and asked about the labels we were putting up.

Fortunately we had left most of them in the car and had only a few hundred with us. We were not arrested. While the older policeman phoned, a young, innocent one stood with us.

"Do you think you'll stop the war by putting those up?"

How we wished we could have said yes.

"If we can save one life. . . " said Julian.

He argued as he must.

November 23, 1950

When I feel that I can do all that I want to do, I become elated and industrious. Then, in my ardor I work faster and faster until the ardor exhausts itself into nervous energy. The jitters are followed by a terrible letdown. I have just experienced such an elation, but the cycle hasn't yet run its course. Now I write nervously, gripping my pen so hard that my fingers ache and I can't write quickly enough. My anxiety mounts. Impatience takes over. I'll scream. Then I don't.

Instead of turning away from the theatre, I have to approach it in a different way, a way frowned on by most people in the theatre, but the only way that I am able to take.

I have forgotten that I am an artist. I have forgotten that I am a woman.

Daily on my rounds I become a "character ingenue" and I'm ashamed of that because I can't really be that because I'm inherently something else.

I hope to act if only here and with a few people as an audience so that I'll be able to keep doing the thing rather than dreaming about it. To act means to have an audience.

May 9, 1951

For a long time I've talked about doing a Yeats play in our front room (perhaps with the glass tabletop as the Well of Emer) and other plays for a small invited audience. These could sit on chairs and cushions: 10 to 15 people per performance.

Then this plan became the Wooster Stage with a much more elaborate program being planned: Noh plays, new plays, and some of the fine chamber plays that are available. When that failed the idea was abandoned.

Now Harold [Norse] is keen about it through his Yeats study. Yeats advocates small theatrical works in private rooms in a *Theatre Arts* article appropriately called, "Instead of a Theatre." Dicken [Richard Stryker], who wants to compose for such small performances, has many ideas. The purity of Dicken's values is amazing and instructive.

From impatience I am swept toward enthusiasm. At last we have other artists to work with us and we may finally materialize a small, inventive theatre in a room.

May 28, 1951

Robin was talking about the theatre, or the theatre that Robin knows and understands.

And I felt that the theatre is thoroughly corrupt. Not in intention, but by inbreeding of the tradition that has begun to destroy the roots of theatre.

To enact for another.

There is an absolute need for spontaneity. Everything else has been replaced by the film and other mechanical mediums.

Plot is not theatre though theatre can include plot.

Theatre work has been specialized till no one is permitted knowledge of another's activity. The stagehands paint the flats; the actors stand in front of them.

The only ones who are allowed to be involved in all the aspects is the omnipotent and power-corrupted director and the non-artist producer.

There can be a *living* theatre only in the work of small groups of people interested neither in effect or success—except for the successful action.

Plays should be short enough to be easily rehearsed so that they do not deaden in the process. The plots, simple. The style, pure, direct; the theatrical elements of music and dance carefully included. Too much scenery and in some cases too much music or pure dance could be out of proportion.

Poetry, but not too many words.

Perfect tempo. Arrived at by learning to feel the play each time spontaneously. Sacrifice some of the perfection of the production to perfection of immediacy.

The Noh is a perfect medium, but Noh is only the beginning. The Noh is too rigid.

Beyond the Noh's strictness lies the short enacted poem, the active living poem. Gertrude Stein has clues.

It may be possible to work on this. But then Robin asks me: "Why do you want success on Broadway?"

And I answer: "For a need which is only a sickness; but I doubt that I can ever cure myself of it."

July 1, 1951

In the midst of our planning for the Theatre in the Room, the larger plans for the Living Theatre which we have struggled with for four years now, suddenly emerge.

We can't wait. We can't put off the Living Theatre until we have a theatre building of our own.

We decide: we will rent the Cherry Lane. With permission of the authors and publishers and estates, we will put on *Faustina* by Paul Goodman, *Beyond the Mountains* by Kenneth Rexroth, and *Dr. Faustus Lights the Lights* by Gertrude Stein.

We make a deal with Leo Shull with whom the simplest transaction becomes a game of smart moves.

For $1,800 we can have the Cherry Lane for two months.

I will direct *Faustina* and *Dr. Faustus*, Julian will direct *Beyond the Mountains* in which I want to play the triple role of Iphigenia, Phaedra, and Berenike (Electra).

I would like Dicken to do the music for *Faustina*, and if I imagine the ideal music: Lou's [Harrison] "Beyond the Mountains" and John Cage's "Dr. Faustus."

July 3, 1951

The Theatre in the Room which is going to begin rehearsal soon still needs a major opening play.

Crying Backstage will be the curtain raiser followed by the three minute *Ladies' Voices* for Helen and me. But the substantial play of the evening? We consider Brecht, Yeats, and Masefield.

We drive to Lou Harrison's hoping to ask him about *The Only Jealousy of Emer* for the Theatre in the Room and possibly about music for *Beyond the Mountains*.

Julian, now that the theatre is in motion, cannot talk of anything else and never relaxes nor allows me to relax.

July 6, 1951

Complete program for the Theatre in the Room for the 15th of August.

Goodman's *Crying Backstage,* a comic invention; *He Who Says Yes and He Who Says No,* a didactic piece by Brecht; Stein's *Ladies' Voices*—Helen and I; and two scenes from Claudel's *Satin Slipper:* the shadow forms and the moon.

July 30, 1951

At this late hour we drop our plans for the Claudel piece for the Theatre in the Room. It's too sentimental, too much heavy cream. Instead we will do a scene called "The Young Man and the Mannikin" from Lorca's *If Five Years Pass.* Julian and I will play it.

Remy [Charlip] has gotten (I think from Jean Erdman) some fine Hawaiian lava stones for the percussion music in the Brecht play. They are like any other black stone, but make a more vibrant thud when struck together.

August 9, 1951

Rehearsal yesterday of the Brecht play. Open hostility from the cast and condescension from Bill Keck. It is easy to love when you are loved, but otherwise.

The Room plays are a demonstration of our intentions. We invite 20 people for each performance. A row of 10 on benches against one wall; in front of them, 10 cushions on the floor.

Remy helps write out invitation cards to friends and artists. Julian and he do a crayon and ink drawing on each one, and Remy writes with his pretty script.

The Lorca is not yet learned and not yet blocked, and this evening is a dress rehearsal. Madness. But, I am in good cheer.

August 15, 1951

"I hate the theatre," I say to Dicken.

His shocked expression like the look of a child discovering some grim actuality.

"Why?"

"Because she is cruel to me."

Cruel? Like a nightmare beast, with a lash and tongs, for piercing and striking. Like a man enamored of a vampire, I follow her fatally.

Too romantic an image? It is. Isn't there some way to break out of the spell of a fairy tale and its distorted landscapes?

August 16, 1951

Everything went better than I could have dreamed.

Remy [Charlip] arrived with Merce [Cunningham] and John [Cage] while we were still at dinner. Their presence terrified me. I felt trapped. I felt unready, even unwilling, but there was no way out.

A thunder storm broke out.

Rain is a good omen as is a bad dress rehearsal.

I listen from the bedroom door to *Crying Backstage* and fret because it is going too quietly and without enough tempo.

Then I went out for the Brecht. Suddenly the sanctuary of one's home is full of judging eys. I felt too closely observed.

It will never again seem hard to act on a stage where the distance is so great, the lights so protective, where the audience can't see every flick of the eyelash, the motions of the tongue in speech, the tense trembling of the fingers.

Remy stands beside me at the opening. When I trembled he put his hand on my shoulder, and when it did not calm me he pressed tightly against my shoulder so that it hurt. As in some potent therapy the tension vanished in that moment of pain.

The staging as austere as the play. The striking of the lava stones and Remy's movements support the argument of the story. And the bare wood construction of Julian's stage set it perfectly.

The Stein was liked and encores were called for, but we did not repeat it.

During the Lorca under the blue light, Julian and I scarcely recognized each other. I wore a heavy veil which protected and hid me. But I regretted my ill-timed steps in the presence of Merce and Sudie Bond and Shirley Broughton.

The music served as a screen. Dicken played Bill Keck's harp, and Bill, his bamboo flute. After our exit, the dying fall of the pavane ended the evening.

Then a whole happy hour of talk and the pleasure of being liked.

John Cage and I continued the talk we had at the Ninth Street Gallery when he said that the painters were getting away from the art world and the musicians were getting away from the concert world and Julian and I began to plan the Theatre in the Room.

Other inspirations were Robert Edmond Jones who had advised us to work in a room without money, with no money at all—as was done—and finally Harold's reading to us Yeats's ideas on chamber theatre.

Also the night at Fred Mitchell's when, in a drunken daze, Robin and I discoursed, lying on Fred's carpet. As Fred played the guitar I insisted that a play could consist of an actor walking across a floor once, or making one perfect gesture, and that a play could be ten to fifteen minutes long, a growing idea which was implanted by the satire on theatre that Valeska Gert did in the Beggar Bar.

Out of that talk—in spite of its exaggerations and limitations—and out of the advice of Jones and Yeats, the enthusiasm of Harold Norse and the ideals of John Cage, came this evening.

But John Cage said: "It grows out of a need more than anything else."

August 21, 1951

The Theatre in the Room is over. Immediately we go on to other things. We are scheduling The Living Theatre for December, 104 days from now. The amount of work is colossal.

October 20, 1951

[Julian and I visit] Aline Bernstein.* In a large, ill-furnished apartment on Park Avenue, the beautiful lady lies in a small, sunny bedroom. She was able to smile through her many troubles. In one hand a hearing aide stretched towards us, and the other went frequently to her face to shield the eye which is temporarily sightless from a hemorrhage.

She, too, has a backlog of remembrances: the Civic Repertory where she designed Eva Le Gallienne's plays; the Neighborhood Playhouse and the events there of which Tom Wolfe wrote so innocently when he loved the lady.

She praised and was impressed with Julian's work.

She was sad to be as she said "indisposed and out of things," but she chatted about the book she was writing and the sets she was doing, and the rehearsals she had been attending. Next to her bed is a dictaphone (to which she says "excuse me" when she is interrupted) and she dictates to it. This work she considers "not working."

Framed above her bed are the famous designs for *The Little Clay Cart* and, in a rack, designs for a book of costumes which she complains no one will publish.

Again, the most striking presence was the energy and strength of this woman who so ill and handicapped is yet capable of so much activity.

She gives us warnings and advice. She agrees to be a sponsor.

"Beware of light on the stage; it dims the actors, makes the text fade out into silhouette."

---

*Aline Bernstein was resident designer at Eva Le Gallienne's Civic Repertory Theatre. As part of the preparations for the Living Theatre, Judith and Julian were visiting designers.—ED.

The Living Theatre opened at the Cherry Lane with *Dr. Faustus Lights the Lights* and Kenneth Rexroth's *Beyond the Mountains,* but as the work of the theatre accelerated, Judith's diary entries stopped. Her program note for Goodman's *Faustina,* which opened May 25, 1952 follows. —K.M.

Notes on a Ritual Tragedy

How shall I convey the emergence of power out of what has in itself no power? To underline the passion of the playwright and the priestess when they say (in holy concord):

"It's a lot of shit, but that's how we do it."

That is how we do it. Because the play is a ritual. Any play is a ritual, but in this play the ritual is overt and we speak out about it with real brazenness, saying over and over: we haven't the strength and yet we can give the strength.

Here is the eastern ritual called the Taurobolium in which the initiate is bathed in the blood of the sacrificial bull and emerges from the pit reborn. This story* places us again in the pit and calls us again to partake of the rites that our sophistication long discarded, and then. . .

The arrogance to require the audience to partake! That is, to admit the *presence* of these hundreds of people.

We are the creators in an art where every night hundreds of people are ignored; a pretense is made that they do not exist; and then we wonder that the actor has grown apart from society; and *then* we wonder that the art itself staggers lamely behind its hope of being part of life.

How shall I convey my belief in what the playwright says? The *I Ching* says, "It is the Creative that begets things but they are brought to birth by the receptive." And it says of me further, "The person in question is not in an independent position, but is acting as an assistant. This means that he must achieve something." I consulted this book of ancient Chinese oracle not only for myself but for my audience. To allow ourselves to be led, all of us assistants in the ritual, which hasn't any power, but from which power is derived. The play does not take place in pagan Rome. Believe me, believe me that it takes place in the theatre. In this theatre and *tonight.* How shall we (in concord) derive power from the action? When the priestess says:

Notes on a Ritual Tragedy copyright © 1982 by Judith Malina. Used with permission.

*Taken from an incident reported in Kurt Seligmann's *Mirror of Magic.* —ED.

"Where is the power to come from? I haven't got it,"—say that it comes from the art of the play, and that it comes out *to* us, and now we have got it.

That's how we do it.

From the Italian Diaries, 1976

Since 1975 the Living Theatre has been based in Rome, touring Italy and other European countries. Sections of the Italian diaries reprinted here record two street theatre performances and the audiences' responses.—K.M.

October 1, 1976 (Cosenza)

A *Meditations** performance on the street of a remarkable little city called "Castrovillari" at the foot of the Polluia Mountains, just south of the plain which we view from our hillside in the Bellavista Hotel. Here there's no regular plaza, just a wide space on the sidewalk, where a light is rigged up onto the wall of an adjoining building at Jose's instructions.

A large crowd, all ages, sexes; students, mothers and children, young women in groups of three and four, aged men, both refined and of the streets, groups of serious faced businessmen, in short, all kinds. This play always inspires me in the streets. I feel the spectators are observing very critically, in the best sense. *Acting Note:* I try to show the audience that I really believe what I'm saying so that they will listen carefully to what I'm saying to see whether they are in accord with it.

In order to be in accord with me they weigh their opinions against mine and thereby examine their own argument critically.

In the torture scene** (it's clearly this scene that draws out incident) a *carabinero* pushes his way through the circle of people and watches a moment, sternly, looks at the naked figure on the parrot's perch, reads the crowd as too friendly to the event for him to interfere alone. He leaves and returns with two white-uniformed police. There's a buzz in the crowd. Maria is still reading about the police, how ruthless they are, how they come

---

Excerpts from the Italian Diaries copyright © 1982 by Judith Malina. Used with permission.

Seven Meditations on Political Sado-Masochism, the oldest piece in the repertory, created with college students in the U.S. in 1971–72.—ED.

**In which a naked actor is hung from a parrot perch, and electric shock torture delivered to his genitals and anus is simulated. The scene derived from Judith's and Julian's three-month prison experience in Brazil. When they were released, the other prisoners asked them to speak about the torture. The scene is a brutally naturalistic moment in an otherwise imagistic play; Judith says it is meant to wake us from our trance and make us face the reality of daily torture in prisons around the world.—ED.

from among the people. As Julian takes up the text about torture, two
police cars arrive; skipping past the screams of the man on the torture rack,
many leave the circle and go towards the police cars. I could see this much
only. I could hardly hear what kind of confrontation between some of the
spectators and the police dissuaded them from a bust, which the first
carabinero certainly had in mind, to depart. There were no police at the end
of the play. The raps I had were the most intelligent; a friendliness, even in
the most challenging questions. "What's the difference between com-
munism and anarchism?" The sense of anarchism in a Christian culture?
What happened under Mussolini? The women: (we were asked to perform
at 6 P.M., so that the women could see the play—could be out in the
streets, but it is 10 P.M. when we are rapping, and the women are still
there). They are glad when I praise them, not only for being independent of
this restriction, but for *demanding* respect from the men for their choice; the
men, standing around, nod their approval.

Talk also, in those few minutes—half hour of theology, of Jesus as Jewish
Pacifist Anarchist, of the ongoing textile workers strike in this city, of the
city, history, striving to be self-governing since feudal times.

November 11, 1976 (Faenza)

The Women's Play: At the OMSA Factory: Ten women of Faenza and
Living Theatre women: Taking the theme from our discussion: The inability to speak—and even the unwillingness to speak in what Dimitra called
"the male rhetoric," I realize here for the first time the long expressed and
never before fulfilled desire to create a work out of the encounter and treating the situation of those who collaborate in the collective creation.

Nor are they able to be enthusiastic, their fearful reluctance only another
indication of their subject matter. Till afterwards when they are glad and
proud.

We face the entrance to the workers' cafeteria, standing in a line in which
we cannot see one another. At a sound cue we raise our arms in the Delta
symbol of the Feminists: We are silent, a tape speaks for us. It's a tape of
Women's stories, complaints, abuses. . . It speaks alternately of the abuses
of daily life, and of the local and locally known dramatic incidents—of rape,
abortion, deaths, lost jobs. . .

We try to take a step forward, silently, our symbols over our heads, and
we balance slowly and precariously, but we do not speak—cannot, will not,
do not speak . . . Tape speaks. . .

And then the tape stops and we strain in a chorus of non-verbal sounds,
we stretch forward and our mouths move and our faces are contorted with

the years of our oppression and we want to speak—but we have no voice. . .
As in the common dream.

With the grating sound of our preverbal speech, we reach and fall forward—we tumble down together and, our alienating line broken, we reach
to one another and as we touch our broken sound turns into a chord and we
rise, helping each other up and our chord rises and stops suddenly and one
after the other we speak. We say all sorts of things about our lives as women,
hopes, fears, demands, resolves, analysis, outburst, communication. I'm
amazed at how well they finally speak, and they too are amazed at themselves and each other: at how strong their voices are when they finally break
the silence.

And with our words we approach the women who work in the stocking
factory, standing at a small distance around us in little groups in their white
work-smocks. The group I approach giggles defensively and disperses but I
question one young woman, who looks haughtily at me and says, "My husband understands me and I don't need this nonsense." I say she is fortunate,
as am I, who also has a husband who is good to me, but that we have some
obligation to all those women not so well off as we are, and she says
peevishly, obviously speaking from the most superficial defensiveness, "I
don't give a damn for the others. . ." One of the Faentina women joins us
and asks about the treatment of women in the factory. She says the working
conditions are wonderful; she has nothing to complain of—"Would you say
it's a model factory?" asks our friend. "Yes," she answers aggressively, "it's a
perfect factory." I try a third time. I complain of the comportment of the
men on the streets and she opens a little to our common complaint, and before we part she has softened as much as she can, given her initial hostility.

We eat lunch in the *mensa* and compare our raps and experiences. It's almost by the book, what everyone says. . .

I had expected the play to go poorly because it was so unfinished and im-
perfectly rehearsed, but I was glad that on the scene it worked, and I was
sorry Hanon [Reznikov] is sick abed and didn't see it.

Barbara Ann Teer

[1937–   ]

AN INTRODUCTION

I MET BARBARA ANN TEER, founder and director of the National Black Theatre, in the office of her Harlem brownstone. Located about ten blocks away at 9 East 125th Street, on Harlem's major cultural thoroughfare, is the performing space of the National Black Theatre, which attracts actors, students, and audiences by the high and focused energy of the performing achieved through Teer's Pyramid Process of actor training.

After enjoying considerable success as an actress and director in the New York theatre of the late sixties, Teer abandoned the commercial scene and moved uptown to Harlem, where she founded a theatre in which all the "levels of energy housed inside Blackness" might find full expression.

She went to the gospel churches for inspiration. Attention to the rhythms of spirituals led her further back to her African roots, until, without consciously knowing it, she was touching elements of the Yoruba religion in order to free the energies of the people in her workshop sessions. Then the National Black Theatre began creating rituals, and the American present became one with the African past as a new black theatre was born.

Teer is surrounded by co-workers who share her devotion to NBT, which is a devotion to unleashing the spiritual powers inside of people. She is aware of the force of her personality, of her talent, of the strength of her vision. She is aware, too, that her theatre's continuity depends upon the close, familylike structure she and her theatre staff have created. No work that truly liberates the spirit, she feels, is possible without a community to support each person's perilous journey inward to the sources of his or her strength.

Teer envisions her theatre as effecting a marriage between East and West. Because of this, NBT has toured extensively, both in America and in Africa. Over the years NBT's aesthetic has shifted from one that encompassed only a black identity to one that today, influenced by Werner Erhard's est, is part of the human potential movement. NBT's philosophy is best expressed, perhaps, in their mantra:

> *I got to love myself so much*
> *that I can love you so much*
> *that you can love you so much*
> *that you can start loving me!*

—K.M.

Barbara Ann Teer

[1937–   ]

AN INTERVIEW

Karen Malpede: First of all, what black women have influenced you?

Barbara Ann Teer: My grandmother, my mother.

KM: Tell me about them.

BAT: I come from a family in East St. Louis, Illinois, that is very active in community service. My father was, at one time, a schoolteacher, a coach, and then principal of an adult education program, and now he's assistant mayor of East St. Louis. My mother is very active in all kinds of executive positions with universities and—excuse me, I can never remember all her titles—but she has dedicated her life to serving other people. She has been a starter and initiator of social services, a developer of people. My grandmother was the same kind of person. My grandfather was also very active in black lifestyle. I grew up in a black community, and actually it wasn't until I was fifteen and in college that I had racial confrontations because that's what they were. My sister Fredrica Teer* also is an organizer, an organizational developer. She's the executive director of the National Black Theatre. So you can see my whole background comes from service. My parents weren't satisfied with me being just an entertainer or an actress or a dancer, so I went to a lot of universities and schools in this country, five to be exact, and I finally graduated magna cum from the University of Illinois with a degree in dance education. Then I went to Europe and studied in Germany, Switzerland, and Paris. I came back, went to Sarah Lawrence to work on my master's degree, and that's when I just had it with the educational system. But I had to have all the credentials so my parents would know their daughter wasn't just hanging out.

KM: Are there black women performers or black women writers who have influenced you?

BAT: It's really very funny. I don't think I've been influenced by any-

---

*Since this interview was held, Fredrica Teer has died of cancer.

body except by my old man, Adeyemi, and my two children. I think that—
I'm sure that—any theatrical influence—and I sound corny—has come
from God, and I mean it comes from within, it comes from out of nothingness, out of no way, nothingness. I think if there's anybody I admire it
would be Nina Simone because of her absolute craftsmanship and her love
for her craft and the spirit and the energy with which she projects her craft.
Nina, people like Aretha Franklin, Maya Angelou, Diana Sands, a close
friend whose work I admire—I think if there's any thread running through
all of them it is their absolute love for the art, their magnanimous talent,
their commitment, and their ability to magnetize people. I admire them
all, but I don't study or emulate them.

KM: You were quite successful as an actress when you gave up the commercial theatre to start your own theatre. Why did you do that?

BAT: I was trained to be an artist first of all and a fine artist. The discipline is different from being in show business. I was trained as a dancer.
Dance is something you eat, drink, and sleep. The art fed you and made you
feel alive and made you feel purposeful and that you were making a contribution, and you felt cleansed and healed when you finished performing.

When I came to New York I went to the Henry Street Playhouse. I was
dancing with Alwin Nikolais. Then I hurt my knee. I had to relook at what I
wanted to do with my life. My father flew out, and he did a lot of therapy on
my knee. As a result of the injury, I started studying acting. Again, I
studied with the masters. I studied with Sanford Meisner and Philip Burton
and Paul Mann. Robert L. Hooks, with whom I was close friends, was
doing *Dutchman* at the Cherry Lane Theatre. A lot of young people were
coming to see the show. Afterwards we'd talk with them, and they would
want to know how they could get into the theatre. So we started to teach
these teenagers. We worked in his house. We called it the Group Theatre
Workshop. I trained the performers and created the work.

It was then I realized that all my training didn't matter. Nineteen-year-
old black people didn't need all that technique. I got to see that acting technique was really not necessary to create aliveness, and, in fact, it was a handicap. Those young people taught me a lot because I had to give up all the
things I had learned and be with them and experience who they were and
create from their "I am"-ness.

The first production we did was based on an eight-line poem by Gwendo-
lyn Brooks, who was a Pulitzer Prize winner. The poem's title was "We
Real Cool." Improvising imagery on the eight lines, we created an evening
of theatre which was two and a half hours long. It was very successful. Joe
Papp put it on a mobile unit and sent it around New York City for the sum-

mer. It was at that point I realized that these children—and they weren't children, they were young adults—had this need to be "stars." It was then I realized that show business didn't work.

Okay, by this time I'm working a lot, I'm directing, I'm starring, I'm winning awards, and I'm not satisfied at all because of the value system. I found that people were very competitive, people were not loving, people were waiting for you to drop dead so they could get your part. Show business was not a nurturing situation. My idealistic life ideology didn't work in show business. It was a business.

A series of disillusioning things happened to me. I remember when *The Great White Hope* came to Broadway. It had a cast of sixty some black people; they wanted to hire me for one of the leads. I said I will only do it if I can be assistant director. I was told that I wanted to be the black thermometer for the show. I said, "Well I can't see how you can direct sixty black people, and you have no experience of black life style." Again, there it was —and it just kept happening like that for me, and I realized that this is not the place for me, that I had a particular point of view about how I wanted to move, that people don't go to Chinatown and tell the Chinese how to run the theatre, you know. There was an arrogance I couldn't deal with. I mean, how dare you tell me how to do what I'm brought up—you know—to do.

Anyway, I left, and when I left, I left everything. I left the Group Theatre Workshop, which was the genesis of the Negro Ensemble Company. I wanted to come to a black community to start a theatre; I wanted to develop the black community economically and create an art form that fit the sensibilities of black people. I was not interested in proving to white people that I could do their technique as good as they could. I was not interested in any further reciting of the European forms. I didn't get very much support. In fact, I got no support—I was working against the traffic.

KM: The black arts movement was at a peak when you started the theatre?

BAT: It was '68 when I started the theatre. The black arts movement started around '64 to '65 with Leroi Jones (Amiri Baraka), you remember. We were all down in the Village together, I was directing an Off-Broadway musical which was called *The Believers*. It was very successful. It ran for about nine months. There was a woman in *The Believers* who was an opera singer—extraordinarily gifted. She was on her way to Germany for her opera career. She had a Master's degree in opera and a minor in piano. I was writing a lot in those days, and I wrote an essay in a book called *The Black Power Revolt*. This woman read it. She wrote a note in the book and sent me the note. It said, "I would like to study with you, what do I have to do." She was my first student/collaborator. I was sort of amazed. I didn't think adults wanted to study with me.

Her name is Zuri McKie, and she's been with me for ten years. She's associate producer of the National Black Theatre. I started teaching. I told her that she couldn't study by herself, she had to get a group of people. So basically the people from *The Believers*, there were eight of them, started to study acting with me. We moved uptown to the Elks Lodge. Suddenly I had about fifty students, and the Lodge was not large enough so we got a loft. We started working twice a week from 7:00 till 2:00 in the morning. We did this for two years, and that's how the National Black Theatre Workshop evolved.

I didn't attract performers—you know, I attracted people who were committed to expressing themselves in a way that was not oppressed or "less than"—people with college degrees, people of all sorts; we called ourselves the Liberators. These people had a mission, a purpose, a commitment that went beyond day-to-day survival. For two and a half years we went behind closed doors, and we experimented. There were no books, there were no films, there was no model.

KM: Can you tell me a bit about how you started to experiment?

BAT: I started clearly wanting to discover what I call now, for commercial reasons, the Secret of Soul. The science of celebration.

KM: How do you think you came to that as an oppressed person, as a black woman in America?

BAT: Because in every show that I was ever in, I was always told, "You have too much energy. You have too much energy, Barbara, sit on your hands." If it was TV, "You're too plastic, Barbara." I couldn't understand why I had all this energy. I knew it turned me on, and whenever I saw somebody with that kind of energy perform, I felt an organic relationship to them. Technique kills that, you know. I wanted to create a place where I could be who I was, the way I was, and not feel that it was a handicap. I also knew that gospel music was a universal turn-on for everybody. As soon as those rhythms hit the piano, people just go out, and I would go out. So I wanted to know what this was about, because nobody knew, and everybody thought all black people can sing and dance, which is a joke. I wanted to discover what this thing was and make it a science so that people would stop saying, you know, it's just by accident or everybody who was anybody always came out of the church.

KM: Did you come out of the church?

BAT: No and yes. I started in church but not that kind of church. Baptist churches, holy roller churches, Pentecostal churches are the churches where the form is the most pure. I came from the church, but I didn't come from that kind of church. I think I got it—I was born with it, and I used it to dance a lot when I was young. I used to go to dances and dance until I couldn't stand up, you know. And you see movement—dance and music, we say, is the language of God. I also feel that we brought the fine arts to this planet. So that we know organically how to activate the spirit, and that is a gift that is beyond everything. Yet because it comes so easy to us, we take it for granted, and we don't worship it and appreciate it.

KM: When you say we brought fine arts to this planet, is a there an African ritual that has to do with the beginning of the fine arts?

BAT: I got very involved in occult discipline when I started the theatre. I had to because I was dealing with invisible things. One of the women who came to the theatre as a guest lecturer was called Her Majesty Masaketa Facinto, the Empress of the Gheez Nation. She had a very large movement in upstate New York. Her Majesty introduced me to many concepts I began to develop. One was that we volunteer ourselves into a serving position. We were not slaves. It was impossible to bring hundreds of thousands, millions, of people across the water to an unknown destination. Africans came to this continent to learn the ways of the West—to master form. Her Majesty said we brought fine arts to this planet.

There are many mythologies that support this that have not come to America. But they're not the way I want to present them. So I'm writing one. I'm working on the combination of the East and the West.

But all you have to do is look at black people and observe them and be with them and experience them, and you'll see that this is so.

You know I was a gym teacher in a New York City school for one year. I used to be responsible for dance classes. I was in a junior high school, and they had about sixty little girls in one class, and we were not supposed to play music. One day after lunch they were all silly, and they asked if I would play this record. I said no, and they said please just play, we'll sit down and be still. I said okay now, you know, I'll get in trouble if I play this record, and you make any noise, so I'm going to play it, and you just sit there. So I put it on, and they went wild, you know, they went all over the place. I said, "I thought you all said you were going to sit still." "Oh, we can't sit still," they said. That's what happens, you know. When the spirit hits, you can't sit still. It just shoots you right out of your seat.

But now I'm a scientist, so since I'm a scientist, I know how it works, I practice it every day. It's my business, I'm a master at it, and I know that

that's what the gurus call the self. My ancestors said, "There is something within." I cannot explain, all I know is that it's something within—it banishes all pain. That energy—that life force—that's inside us *is* there. It's given, and it's in everybody. Some people worship it and honor it and make love to it and make it work for them, and some people ignore it and just hang out in their minds. Hanging out in your mind doesn't bring you very much aliveness, doesn't bring very much happiness, and eventually once those in the West have acquired material well-being, which is what we came here to learn, they always go back to the spirit.

KM: Backtracking a little bit, the black theatre of the early sixties was heavily dominated by men. In fact, you were one of the lone women. It seems to me that the roles that were being written in plays by black men were not conducive to the life force of women. Did that situation contribute to starting your own theatre?

BAT: What a loaded question. Yeah. I had written an article for the *New York Times* geared toward that question. I realized that in my lifetime I could look forward to being a maid, a matriarch, and a prostitute, and I couldn't really play the matriarch until I got to be a certain age. Working on those parts there was no space to make the person a human being. That was true of the whole Western mentality. It didn't have to do with blacks and whites. It was just a, you know, a male-oriented country, and women were relegated to housework, and menial things, behind-the-scene things.

I've had big brawls and fights, you know, but I'm just saying it doesn't matter. I refuse to change because of somebody's rules—'cause rules were just made by somebody to control. But I found a tremendous support base—people who were committed and had an undying love and who felt good being around me. The groups without that kind of base have gone by the wayside . . . are falling by the wayside. I really admire and respect the men in my theatre because they caught quite a lot of hell, you know, 'cause here I am a woman, and they're men, and how could they be in an organization that's run by a woman. The women were all very much like me, very assertive and clear and powerful. We developed what is referred to as a family organization. Most of the people in the theatre now after ten years have children. We keep expanding and going out, but we have a family base. We just couldn't let anybody stop us because the vision was more powerful than the day-to-day crisis stuff, you know. I knew that I was developing a black arts standard—in those days, that's what we called it. And I was about maintaining and developing or perpetuating what I call the richness and beauty inherent in black lifestyle.

Everybody wants to experience well-being, everybody wants to experience themselves as wholesome, healthy, able to generate their power and to experience the validation of that power. I don't address myself to the mental condition. I address myself to the being inside of a person. When being speaks to being, all beings want to love.

This country is known for separation—separation of dance from the singing, from the writing, separation of producers from performers, separation of men from women, separation of scientists from artists. It's a separate kind of thing, and it is one of the main reasons we have so much conflict.

I start from the whole, and coming from the whole, you may end up finding what specific thing you enjoy doing, but the whole is the thing from which everything comes. I train my people to create spontaneously and fearlessly from within and not to be taken off their purpose by or for anything. So the men probably felt very inspired for the same reason the women felt inspired because we were all considered *oppressed*, you know.

KM: I want to go back to church gospel music and ask you how you began to work with the sense of the spirit you described.

BAT: It happened by going to church and sitting there all the time, being with the people, talking with the minister, talking to the ushers, talking to the deacons, watching people enter the spirit, seeing how they handled it. My mind started creating the science of it. I went back to the theatre and tested some of those things myself with my own people. It worked, and basically through trial and error. I always had a drummer— my drummers were always very good, and they were always very much trained in the religion so they knew the rhythms that would activate the certain deities, vibrations that would awaken the sleeping giant.

KM: You're talking about African drumming?

BAT: Well, everything is African. Everything comes from its roots, and it's been defined or it's been altered in some way, but basically the source of it comes from Africa. It's in our genes, and once certain rhythms are played, the spirit is activated whether you like it or not. That's what happens in voodoo in Haiti and in African religion. In any black country, it's the same thing. It's often the same thing in any church where rhythms—certain rhythms—are played.

We didn't do our first piece until '71. But before that the standard of art was created. The standard was basically what I call the five cycles of evolution. We went through what I call the "nigger" cycle, "negro" cycle, and militant, nationalistic, and revolutionary cycles. We analyzed each of those cycles from a social point of view, a religious point of view, a political point of view. We found out about the colors, the foods, the lifestyle of the fam-

ily, the relationships of people within each of those cycles. Each performer
was required to go through each cycle. Each person had to keep a notebook
of pictures and experiences when they went into each cycle. They would
have to dress their cycle; they would have to live around those people. It was
a total educational process. Then when we got to the revolutionary cycle we
found it was all the same. That's when we decided we wanted to perform.

KM: How long was this period?

BAT: Two years. In the meantime, we were having symposiums on Sunday where we invited all of the major figures in the black world to come and
address themselves to the community about whatever was going on. Rap
Brown, Stokely Carmichael, James Foreman, my sister Fredrica Teer, and
Congressman Charles Rangel all spent a Sunday afternoon with a hundred
people or more. We would rap and talk and exchange and try to get in touch
with what this overwhelming force was that was called blackness. It wasn't
simply a skin color to me, it never was, but it was what made me unique.
We decided to perform after these two and a half years. We realized that we
had a standard, but we didn't have a form to hold the standard, and that's
when I started creating rituals. Ritual is the theatre. Our first production
was *The Ritual* and it was done on Channel 13. It was so popular they got a
thousand phone calls, and the show was aired three times consecutively
back to back. That caused the show to go national. We then got a lot of different job offers, none of which I took because they were all too commercial,
and I thought it would water-down this thing.

In those days people used to get possessed, just go right out, you know.
The drums would take them out. They would talk in tongues, and they
would tell stories, and they would share with me all kinds of things when
they came back. They experienced a freedom I had never seen before. I was
just loving every minute of it. I couldn't sleep at night I was so turned on. I
began creating exercises and processes and techniques to handle the energy
and I continued to go to my mentors, who were church people.

Ritual got us a semivisibility in the black world. We started touring college campuses and black studies programs performing *The Ritual to Regain
Our Strength and Reclaim Our Power*. During the performances people would
get so turned on they would spontaneously start running up and down the
aisles just celebrating themselves—you never saw anything like it. By this
time I had changed all the standard theatrical titles. I said we were not actors, we were liberators. Our theatre wasn't a theatre—it was a temple. Our
techniques were in a form I called ritualistic revival—we were doing revival
form, we weren't doing play form.

Somewhere in '71–'72 the Ford Foundation sent a man to this country named Ulli Beier, who had the reputation of being the foremost authority on African art. He was the head of the African studies program at the University of Ife in Nigeria, but he was German. He walked into our theatre one night, with his dashiki and African sandals on, which took a lot of guts to wear in Harlem, and when the ritual was over Ulli came to me and asked if I knew what I had done, and I said, "Do I know what I've done?" He said, "What you've done is very major and could transform, if you use that word, the whole of not only American theatre, but African theatre as well. African theatre is almost wholly European, you know." He said, "You being an American coming to Africa with these ideas would allow African people to go back to their original tradition because they think Americans know what's happening." I said, "I don't want to go to Africa."

KM: You said you didn't want to go?

BAT: I didn't want to go to Africa. I said, "I didn't pay my way to come over and I'm not going to pay my way to go back." He said, "Okay, meet me at the Ford Foundation tomorrow." Ford gave me a fellowship to go to seven countries and to do research. I went to one small village in Nigeria and I never left that place. I lived there. I traveled extensively through the bush areas. It was that experience that totally turned me around 'cause I really got to be validated. I got to legitimatize myself. I got to see that I was not crazy. I got to be treated like a queen, and a powerful woman. I met kings, emperors, and priests.

KM: This happened in the village?

BAT: It happened all through Nigeria. My base was in a village called Osogybo, which is the major cultural Mecca of Nigeria. I had created a production that used the deities of the Yoruba religion. I wasn't really sure what I was doing, and I was asked, "Where did you get this from?" I said I got it from my head. Ulli said, "Do you realize that there is an actual village that houses this deity in the form of a river called Osun?" He said, "I want you to go there." Well, I did.

KM: Did you go alone?

BAT: I went alone. It was very painful because I didn't want to go alone, so I said I was going alone in order to establish a base for the theatre company to come, and that's what I did. I brought them back the next summer, and we built a base over there, and then I brought six Nigerians back to stay with us for six months. We set up what we call a human chain—marrying the East to the West, and I started training Africans in my form. I went to Africa, and I got initiated into the Yoruba religion, and I learned how to divine. They taught me everything I could ever want to know, and I felt secure in who I was and not threatened by all the so-called American experts. I wouldn't be intimidated. I would stick to my purpose and that worked.

The love that I experience from within me, the love that I experience in the people around me—the commitment and the absolute respect, appreciation for what I am and what I'm doing—keeps me going. The force, I mean, black people exist because of that force. They have tried to kill us. They have tried to bomb us. They have tried to starve us. And we still are here thriving. It's because of the foundation that was laid when you listen to the spirituals. They are called spirituals because they are spiritual. They feed the spirit. They fed the Europeans all these years. The energy and vibration which the country rides on comes from that spiritual force. If there were no black people in America, it would long have crumbled. That's not even discussable—it's not even an arrogant statement. You can't have anything without a life force.

The history of the National Black Theatre is phenomenal. The places we've been, the people who have wined and dined us, the gurus all over the world who have acknowledged us—and yet the theatre is still a baby. We want to transform theatre so that people can get back into the experience of what theatre is all about. Theatre is here to support this country, not just to take some money for its tickets for an evening. It's a celebration.

We can turn you on instantly, but people don't value this because it's not coming from cocaine, it's not coming from drugs, and it's not coming from alcohol. It's coming from a natural science. We are masters at that, and I'm glad about that, and it took ten years for me to be able to clearly say what I am—without being called a voodoo lady or an occultist.

KM: In the community?

BAT: Everywhere, you know, I'm known for that. I'm the voodoo lady of the world. What can I tell you?

And it has served me well, I mean. I would love people to learn about the Yoruba religion and love it. Ours is an incredible religion. It has no rules, it has no rights and wrongs or goods or bads, no formal churches—just create, create from within, create. We don't have to put it into a form 'cause there's a million of them where that one came from—new dances; every time one gets stale, we create another one. We don't stick to one dance for centuries and centuries. Nothing is sacred and holy because everything is just created, spontaneous.

KM: You call your training process the "Pyramid Process of Performing." Why?

BAT: I made a transformation in myself. My sister came here from Hawaii, and she said, "Barbara, you got to take a thing called est." I didn't know what she was talking about. She said, "The only way I'm going to work with you is if you take a training called est." We had tremendous resistance to the idea. Werner Erhard came to New York and conducted an all-black training. It was through that training that I got clear that I wanted to be totally responsible for my oppression, that I created it, that I was responsible for it, and that nobody did it to me. Then we started changing the whole look of our educational workshop. We started doing workshops that were beyond oppression. We're doing one now called Master Liberation Workshop, which is very successful.

I had to take all of that eight years of researching and put it into a technique, too, you know, like Stanislavsky. I don't want to call it "Teer," so we call it Pyramid Process of Performing, and we call it God-Conscious art, which means art that is conscious of life, art that is conscious of love, of energy—you know, art that comes spontaneously and fearlessly from within and allows you to be in the now and experience yourself moment to moment without having to hold onto a form.

Feminist Plays & Performance: Ending the Violence We Have Known

Clare Coss, Sondra Segal, Roberta Sklar

Eleanor Johnson

Karen Malpede

Dolores Brandon

Edwina Lee Tyler

Feminist Plays & Performance: Ending the Violence We Have Known

GENERAL INTRODUCTION

WE SPEAK FOR OURSELVES on the following pages. I attempt only a general introduction.

The feminist theatre groups and artists represented in this section, while all working in very different ways, are each redefining the nature of dramatic conflict. This mysterious essence of the theatre is not, we think, an outgrowth of the primitive hunt or tribal war, nor a relic of the pagan (and Judeo-Christian, and nuclear age) customs of ritual murder, nor a memorium of the ancient *agon,* or battle, between the forces of "good" and "evil," nor the supposedly cathartic violence of the theatre of cruelty.

Dramatic conflict—or, more accurately, dramatic tension or complexity—is the *process of change* in which we as women, and men of nonviolent courage, are currently engaged.

The process of change and of creation takes many shapes as befits a healthy, growing culture. The Women's Experimental Theatre attempts a direct connection with an audience of women who become collaborators in the event. Emmatroupe de-eroticizes rape by eliminating the presence of the rapist and focusing upon the inner anguish of the victim and upon her courage. At New Cycle Theatre the work centers around the complexities of intimacy, trust, and tenderness.

Each of these theatres, again each in our separate modes, seeks a way of speaking that is also a way of hearing. The audience for each is meant to see the actor understanding, as if for the first time, the new truths she or he has uttered. The shock of recognition unites audience and actors, and each group is simultaneously moved toward an emotional understanding of the next world action.

It's too early yet to say whether any or all of the three theatre groups represented here will become part of the history feminist theatre is sure to make, or whether others will seem more compelling at a later date. Women's Experimental Theatre, Emmatroupe, and New Cycle Theatre share some roots in the Open Theatre. Historically we represent three separate evolutions of the experimental theatre of the 1960s and early seventies.

Women's Experimental Theatre keeps up the work with personal storytelling and direct presentational techniques. Emmatroupe combines carefully sculpted physical images and an inner musicality with texts taken from a variety of feminist sources. New Cycle Theatre wants the poetry of dialogue, character, and deep psychological exchanges to be part of the theatre again.

Two performers are represented here alongside the three theatre groups. Dolores Brandon is an actress and director committed to what is new and difficult; her passion, craft, and intelligence are startling upon the stage. Edwina Lee Tyler is a conga drummer who, like an ancient priestess, performs works of healing with her drums.

—K.M.

Clare Coss

[1935–   ]

Roberta Sklar

[1940–   ]

Sondra Segal

[1941–   ]

NOTES ON THE WOMEN'S
EXPERIMENTAL THEATRE

THE WOMEN'S EXPERIMENTAL THEATRE creates and performs theatre by and for women and brings it to the general public. We are dedicated to the evolution of a feminist theatre aesthetic and to the establishment of women's theatre as a form of expression within the arts. Our program includes the creation and performance of collaborative works, the development of experimental methods of acting through workshops, and public research with women on themes relevant to our experience. Based in New York City, the Women's Experimental Theatre performs and offers workshops throughout the country.

The founders and artistic directors of the Women's Experimental Theatre are Clare Coss, Sondra Segal, and Roberta Sklar. Each of us participates in the conceptualization, research, writing, and directing necessary for the work. *The Daughters Cycle* by Coss, Segal, and Sklar is a trilogy of plays exploring the roles, relationships, and possibilities for women in the family.

The Women's Experimental Theatre has been in residence at the Women's Interart Center, New York City, since 1977. *The Daughters Cycle* was produced by the Interart Theatre during the theatre seasons 1977 through 1980.

Why do we need a feminist theatre?
Is there such a thing as a universal?
What is worthy of our artistic attention and philosophic consideration?
What is the place of woman's experience in the theatre?
Is childbirth as worthy of artistic consideration as concepts of time and
    space?
Does the mother/daughter relationship have less impact on the culture than
    the father/son relationship?
Are the experiences of women universal experiences?
What would make acting a feminist act?

235

Who is the audience for feminist theatre?

What does a feminist performer look like?

What is the sound of her voice?

Can you approach any material from a feminist perspective or is there a feminist content?

Does feminist theatre have a history?

Do you feel represented by and interested in the women in *King Lear?*

Was Sarah Bernhardt a feminst actress when she played Hamlet?

Must we have an all women audience?

Must we have all women performers?

Is feminist theatre art?

Is feminist theatre dangerous?

To whom?

What is the relationship between the performer and the witness when they are both women?

Whose interests does a woman's theatre serve?

Why does taking care of yourself so often feel like you are betraying others?

The work of the Women's Experimental Theatre is predicated on the belief that women have a separate and distinct experience. Our plays give testimony to the uniqueness and stature of that experience.

We see through feminist eyes. We rigorously focus on women's lives and are engaged in developing forms of research and presentation that reflect and create women's culture.

We call upon the woman in the audience to experience herself as a woman at the center of her own life, to acknowledge the validity of her experience, to feel her commonality with the other women in the theatre, to reflect upon her separateness, to consider change, to celebrate.

Most theatre is male theatre—men talking to other men about what is important to men.

Our theatre is by, about, and for women. It derives from a deep regard for women and is a continuously deepening regard for every aspect of who women are, will become, have to be.

The feminist actor gives testimony to the ability of women to change. We witness the woman performer as she applies consciousness and choice in her presentation of self and character at the same time and as she demonstrates the capacity to shape and choose her own emotional experience. We see a woman in the playing space who is just herself. Then we see her enact another and also herself at the same time. We also see her comment on it. All of these levels are a testimony to our own capacity to do the same in our own lives. The woman in the audience also recognizes publicly the validation of her own experience, the commonality of her experience with other women. There is something in this process that enables all of us, the performers and the audience, to risk looking into our separateness and our differences.

The woman in the audience is the acting partner of the woman performer on the stage. In the course of the play, the woman in the audience reaches "a point of recognition." She not only empathizes with what she sees, but she is stirred into self-recognition. What occurs between the woman in the audience and the feminist actor is disequilibrating to both. It is disequilibration which moves towards reorganization—in how the woman sees herself and in what the woman feels about herself, now that her own experience has been named and given life. The actor demonstrates transformation, and the audience woman considers transformation in her own life.

The woman performer and the woman in the audience have an intimate nonverbal exchange. Intimate, charged experiences occur between performers, between people in the audience, and between the women on either side of the performing line. It is emotionally logical that when we invite women to join us in naming the matrilineage at the end of each performance, almost everyone stays because intimacy and trust have been established between the performer and audience member. There is a desire and a need for a more equal exchange between them. It occurs in the matrilineage where we are all performers, all "actors" naming our matrilineage. We are all witnesses to one another.

The feminist actor is not intense and in a world of her own. She is intense on a plane that is completely interactive with the woman who is watching her. This is so different from most theatre.

There are two kinds of theatre, the kind in which you pretend the audience is not there and the kind in which you acknowledge and act knowing the audience is there. In the kind of feminist theatre we are involved in now, there is a mutual acknowledgment that the other person is in the room. In our daily lives, so many of our experiences with other women have not been visible. In *The Daughters Cycle* we have never denied the visibility, the existence, the importance of all the women in the room.

We recognize that in any situation where a man is present, that presence may be an intrusion on the potential intimacy experienced between the women. There are a variety of ways that the presence of a man may be an intrusion. One way is that women worry about him, how he's taking it in, how hard it is for him—all those things that a woman is expected to worry about whether it is her man (husband, lover, father, brother, son, friend) or just a man there in the room. And our theatre is not about how he feels, if he is taking it in hostilely or painfully or empathetically. The worried woman has a diminished experience. We want her to have a full experience. She does not have complete access to herself to be a full audience member because she is in part being an audience for the man, as she is in so many other contexts. We need her. We need this audience woman, the active witness. The reality of our theatre depends upn the availability of the audience woman as well as the performer woman.

An all-woman audience has the space for an unfettered response, and it can take off in celebration of itself. And it does. This is one of the great rewards of creating and performing women's theatre. Events that are for, by, and about women are the hard won results of a very serious effort and struggle that has gone on by women in this decade. It is thrilling to be part of one of these events. They are so special—so much an affirmation of one's self as a woman.

Why do we collaborate? Theatre is an inherently collaborative art form. We do not do it out of principle but because we love it—it is exciting, stimulating, and forces our personal and artistic growth at an amazing rate. Our collaboration is with women. This is the time of our lives—the three of us are crazy about women. We love thinking about women. We love seeing the vastness of women's experience. Our collaboration is based on an interweave of our three voices through dialogue, writing, and improvisation for the duration of a project.

One of our ways of working is to go to other women beyond the theatre context with carefully structured theatrical research forms. First we name a specific need within the play that we are working on. Then we select or design research forms and go to other women, not simply to glean data but either to challenge or corroborate something we suspect is true. This work form expresses both a sense of responsiveness and responsibility to other women.

Because the relationships between sisters are so multi-leveled and varied, we held a series of workshops attended by over 150 women to research *Sister/ Sister*. Thematically these workshops centered on family rule that relate to the socializing of sisters and the experience of sibling position. One exercise, devised specifically to elicit testimony on these themes, called upon each participant to present a description of, condemnation of, and a plea for understanding of the baby, the middle, and the oldest.

We use a lot of humor in the work—a deliberate choice to ameliorate the pain of seeing the experience of women in the patriarchy. We have the intention to disturb, stimulate, challenge, call upon ourselves and other women to change. And we have the intention to create good times. We are not dedicated to pain. We do not offer reparations for childhood. We do not erase our experience, but we do seek to find and celebrate the positive aspects of our lives—and we find humor where we can.

There are forms that are traditionally used to blind and to dull insight or even to obscure reality. In theatre, very great emotions can be stirred up and humor can be used to put a finish to them. We are very careful, when we raise something, that we use humor to reinforce what is there, not to wipe it out. The way we juxtapose requires the audience to remember rather than forget.

The family is the central theme of *The Daughters Cycle*. Every political movement has a major institution to focus on and be critical of in a way that either dismantles it or significantly changes it. The patriarchal family is a powerful institution that depends upon and perpetuates the subjugation of women. Feminists know that we must dismantle the internalized structures of family relating that have been so debilitating to women. Women want to be able to choose their actions, not repeat familiar survival techniques that once served in the context of the original family but no longer serve in adult life.

Women have been historically relegated to the domestic sphere. We have chosen not to turn away from that sphere but to look into it as thoroughly as we are psychically willing and able to do. We seek to name the experiences and relations of women in the family, analyze what has gone on there, take claim to the women who have existed in the roles of mother, daughter, sister. We bring the setting of the plays into the domestic sphere where so much of what happens between women happens—the kitchen, the shared bedroom, the dining table. It is a deep entry into the familial experience.

Women are socialized to live the major part of their lives infantilized in the family of origin and in a romanticized family of the future. Our analysis of the family leads us to a clear vision that we must give up the family romance.

I am a separate person
I did not wage war
I did not rape women
I did not murder my daughter
I am not my father
I did not kill my husband
I am not my mother
I did not slay my mother
I am not my brother
I did not commit acts of violence
I am a separate person
I am Electra

I am a separate person
This is my body
These are my thoughts
This is my mouth
My voice
These are my words
I speak for myself

—From *Electra Speaks*

We could go on forever creating on the themes of women's lives. As women working within the male tradition we did not know that the world of women's experience was so vast, rich, and exciting. We didn't really understand until we became woman-identified that our experience is infinite. Anything you can think about you can think of from a woman's perspective.

Sister/Sister, Part II of the trilogy, reveals the mercurial relationship between sisters within the context of the family and reflects realities common to all sibling relations. The play presents struggles, defeats, and triumphs sisters experience over issues of loyalty and betrayal, competition and support, closeness and distance, sameness and difference. It is a mourning for the death of the family romance and a celebration of choice.

Electra Speaks, the culminating play in this trilogy on women in the family, is a study of the women in the *Oresteia*—Clytemnestra, Electra, and Iphigenia as mother, daughter, and sister; Cassandra as the other woman; and Athena as Daddy in the guise of a woman. It is a feminist retelling of one of the major myths of western culture and an analysis of the ways in which the lines of demarcation are drawn between women in the patriarchal family.

In *Electra Speaks* we pose the question: "Whose interests are served by the institutionalized division between women in the family?" We seek to project previously ignored experiences of women in the archetypal family. If something goes unspoken, it becomes unspeakable. In Part III of *The Daughters Cycle*, Electra sees what happens to her sister, her mother, herself—sees what happens to women in the House of Agamemnon—and chooses to speak. Her speaking takes her toward separation and survival.

Daughters, Part I of *The Daughters Cycle*, is a ritual that moves through themes of birth, the ambivalent and interchangeable nature of mother/daughter roles, the underlying contracts negotiated between mothers and daughters, the commonality of all women as daughters, and a naming and reclaiming of our matrilineage. *Daughters* is the founding play of the trilogy.

The Matrilineage

(A standing circle is formed for the naming/reclaiming. One by one each woman enters the ritual by speaking her own name. There are four rounds)

> *I am Sondra*
> *daughter of Lille*
> *daughter of Sarah Rebecca*
> *daughter of Tzivia*
> *daughter of a woman from Austria*
>
> *I am Clare*
> *daughter of Alistine*
> *daughter of Marie Josephine*
> *daughter of Marie Josephine*
> *daughter of a woman from southern France*
>
> *I am Mary*
> *daughter of Chew Kwong Ping*
> *daughter of Nok Yip Lee*
> *daughter of a peasant woman*
> *from my ancestral village of Soy Woy in Canton,*
>   *China*
> *whose name I don't know*

I am Debbie
daughter of Arlene
daughter of Frances
daughter of Celia

I am Mary
mother of Jennifer
daughter of Agnes
daughter of Mary Regina
daughter of Eva

I am Roberta
daughter of Rose
daughter of Golda
daughter of Ruchel
daughter of a woman from Odessa
whose name I don't know

I am Sondra
daughter of Lille
daughter of Sarah Rebecca
daughter of Tzivia
for whom I was named
Tzivia had five daughters
Chaicha, Roncha, Bette, Esther, and Sarah
each of these women came to this country in her
    teens
Tzivia never saw any of her daughters again
she was the daughter of a woman from Austria

I am Clare
daughter of four women who brought me up
daughter of Alistine
who gave birth to me
daughter of grandmother Josie
who took care of me my first four months of life
daughter of Dolores Dobrosky
who came to work for my mother when she was
    sixteen
and I was seven months old
my earliest memory is Dolores leaning over my
    crib

smiling
daughter of Aunt Clare
who taught me artifice and survival

I am Mary
daughter of Chew Kwong Ping
when I was growing up I was fortunate enough
to have my own room
My bed was right under a large picture window
Whenever my mother heard me coughing in the
 night
she would come into my room right away
lean across my bed and close the window
because she didn't want me to catch a cold
she was the daughter of Nok Yip Lee

I am Debbie
daughter of Arlene
daughter of Frances
when I was very young I used to sleep
in the same room as my grandmother Frances
before I went to sleep she'd always say
pleasant dreams
I remember never knowing what she meant by
 saying that
until I was much older

I am Mary
mother of Jennifer
daughter of Agnes
on June 26th my daughter Jennifer graduated
 from high school

I am Roberta
daughter of Rose
when my mother died five years ago
as the rabbi spoke a eulogy for her
he named her repeatedly as Rose
daughter of Aden, her father
he never mentioned her mother
since that time I have had the opportunity
to name my mother publicly

Rose
the daughter of Golda, her mother
the daughter of Ruchel, her grandmother
the daughter of a woman from Odessa
whose name I don't know

Eleanor Johnson
[1947–   ]

NOTES ON THE PROCESS OF ART AND FEMINISM

Eleanor Johnson and Judah Kataloni founded Emmatroupe in 1975. The following essay is an account of Johnson's artistic maturation, as she grew from a student to a director who would integrate feminist ethics into an avant-garde aesthetic. The company occupy a loft theatre space in Greenwich Village where they continue their explorations of the theme of violence against women.—K.M.

> Feminist art is not some tiny creek running off the great river of real art. It is not some crack in an otherwise flawless stone. It is, quite spectacularly I think, art which is not based on the subjugation of one half the species. It is art which will take the great human themes—love, death, heroism, suffering, history itself—and render them fully human.
>
> —Andrea Dworkin[1]

BACKGROUND

As an experimentalist, a woman, and a theatre director, what was my tradition? To where and to whom did I look for inspiration? In addition to my many years of formal training in theatre, the most important influences on me were the works and theories of Stanislavski, Piscator, Brecht, Meyerhold, Copeau, Grotowski, Chaikin, and the European tradition of political theatre, and avant-garde theatre. I had/have a deep "connectedness" to the notion of the artist with a mission, the "unwanted questioner of truth, the unsolicited inquirer into action" (Maria Piscator). The male artists I named above were my models, and their work/vision had the most lasting effect on my own process and expression. To me, the avant-garde must be as Maria Piscator describes:

> Avant-garde is a revolt and a liberation. It is a movement and not an isolated experience. . . .

Avant-garde is the synthesis of many experiments, sometimes even of several generations. Preoccupied with the meaning of life, and not only with the observance of human law, it restores true meaning to the word "religion."

. . .the avant-garde is never a result; it goes back to the roots, the roots of a culture, a country, or a generation.

Avant-garde doesn't live by interpretation. It is essentially creative; it communicates a new way of doing.

. . .we could say that every avant-garde is an invasion into society, a spearhead; in a literal sense it is backed up by many formal forces and machinery which have been refined by years of experimentation. . . .

It enrolled the most daring experiments and innovators and produced the most startling contradictions—pursuit of newness, desire to shock, eccentric behavior, scandal and charlatanism, as well as courageous attempts to plough one's way through the thick haze of decaying values and to inaugurate, on a higher level of sincerity, discipline and organization, a self-sufficient reality.[2]

This is the tradition I claim.

In 1967, after several years of study in America, I went to Great Britain to study classical theatre and to establish a base in Europe for my research into the avant-garde, especially in France and Germany. Like many artists, I came to understand that my creativity was deeply connected to my country and my generation and so I came home. The turmoil in the United States and the apparent vitality of theatre in New York City drew me back to America and it seemed like a new beginning. I arrived in New York City in the fall of 1970. Little did I know then that I was too late—by 1970 only the embers of a vision with half-truth seemed alive and it took several years for me to realize that the fires had gone, and emptiness, despair, and absorption with self remained.

The creativity of the male artist was passing into the "Me Decade." Simultaneously, the Women's Movement was born, was thriving, was ignored.

FEMINISM

. . .humanity is male and man defines woman not in herself but as relative to him; she is not regarded as an autonomous being.

—Simone de Beauvoir[3]

This goes right to the core of female invisibility in this culture. No matter what we do, we are not seen. Our acts are not witnessed, not observed, not experienced, not recorded, not affirmed. Our acts have no mythic dimension in male terms simply because we are not men.

—Andrea Dworkin[4]

Women have always lived in a situation of extremity, salvaging life as best we could out of wars, holocausts, massacres, violence against us and our children so daily as to have been made almost invisible. I believe we will continue our struggle for self-determination, dignity and freedom in the face of planetary extremity, because we have come to see that our struggle, radically understood and radically pursued, is the struggle against planetary extinction.

—Adrienne Rich[5]

I arrived at the second major turning point in my life—Feminism—and suddenly my life was exploding inside of me. I began reading everything I could on women's social and political history and I went back to women's literature, all the while reading every feminist author of my own time. Without realizing it, my center had been tied to an intrinsic integrity and "woman centered consciousness" (Mary Daly, *Gyn/Ecology*) and yet, for so long in time, I was blind to the vital and most important political movement of my generation and my world—the women's movement. It was not until my encounter with feminism that I could clearly voice that which I knew and yet was unable to name. The very avant-garde tradition I had honored would always exclude me because I was a woman with a woman-centered sensibility and commitment. The knowledge that I had worked so very hard to acquire would never be honored because my vision was antithetical to male values. As a result my aesthetic achievements are simply invisible—what I do is not perceived because it falls outside the misogynistic framework that is the norm.

Now that feminism had become the pulse-beat of my life and the life of those close to me, I realized I must take a political/moral stand against the all pervasive obsessiveness with male violence against and misrepresentation and degradation of women. By refusing to accept these standards of woman-hating I was completely exiled from the mainstream of art. My ideal, dream, and theory of art and feminism lead me into the most painful and solitary battle against the whole of male culture. It became an amazingly bitter and yet powerful awakening. And so I made the only life-affirming choice possible: I pulled away from the world of male art and committed myself to a very new kind of education. My struggle with self and the reasons to live my life in art gave birth to Emmatroupe.

When will the question of form no longer replace the question of art? When will one really understand that art does not come from form, but form from art? How many thousands of years will it take . . . for men [and women] to realize that each new content demands its own form and that form without content is a sin against the spirit?

—Kandinsky

I.

In the fall of 1975, Judah Kataloni and I founded Emmatroupe. Since 1972, Judah Kataloni and I had worked as colleagues in various projects, including the first New York production of Karen Malpede's *A Lament for Three Women*. Kataloni's growth into feminism essentially paralleled mine. As a result, our partnership deepened aesthetically and politically. In the same year, Emmatroupe went into seclusion, a necessary exile from the dominant avant-garde that used its influence, prestige, visibility, and money to glorify the sexual exploitation of women. We needed time, space, and freedom if we were to succeed in creating an experimental theatre company committed to the exploration and investigation of a feminist ethic and aesthetic. Strong in the wake of this political and creative energy, Kataloni and I built this new vision into a reality which soon had a unique life of its own. I wrote in my workbook, winter of 1976:

Why theatre and if theatre—how can we continue to support systems or methods of work which render women falsely? How can I, and other women artists, and the few brave men with feminist consciousness, search/grasp/and shape new ideas if the environment in any way chokes female expression? How do we begin to model and structure an alternative way of "be-ing" and working? To rediscover the power and function of theatre in our society, we must go back to the very roots of theatre—we must "begin at the beginning."

I wrote in my workbook, spring of 1977:

It is becoming clearer that my experiments with the actor and form, the actor and content, and the actor and technique need to be continually checked with honesty and rigor against my old *romanticized* ideas about aesthetics and theory. I must not be afraid of "female identified self" as I search with the entire company for the connectedness needed in order to link the form-imagery to this new and powerful understanding.

Judy Chicago in *Through the Flower*,[6] in one of her essays about her struggle as a woman artist, wrote:

Studying women's art and literature made it clear that most female creators
. . . had embedded a different "content" in the prevailing aesthetic mode of
their time, and in so doing had rendered their point of view invisible to
mainstream culture. Only in the twentieth century was there any attempt to
express the idea that the "form of art itself" would have to be different if it was
to communicate a female point of view.

2.

I am forever encouraged by the artists of a generation who grow through
education and inspiration towards moral and meaningful actions both in
their art and in their life. Ibsen and Piscator, each in his own time, did this,
and women are the ones doing it now. Today women must be the heroes of
art and life.

3.

I have moved away from the structure of the well-made play, although I
still think one day I might again like to direct a Brecht or Chekhov or Ibsen
play. I was once asked if I would be interested in directing a feminist version
of Shakespeare's *King Lear*. This offer left me somewhat confused as to why
anyone would want to do a feminist *King Lear*. It's an absurdity to think that
anyone would think feminism is about women "liberating" themselves in
order to be able to play the "great themes," rooted in roles originated by and
for men. If there is one play of genius in the Western world which exclusively deals with the utter calamity of patriarchy, it is *Lear*. I myself am only
interested in works of art that speak with the same depth and genius about
the tragedy of women under patriarchy. But where are these texts that reveal the woman's human condition? Women have always made great art but
this art has been consistently blackened out of the historical and social consciousness of every era. The "background" of time is so filled with the
shadows and sorrows of women's genius-courage-life that it is time, once
and forever, to "break the silences and deception of history" (Mary Daly,
Gyn/Ecology).

4.

I think of myself as a conceptualist in mind and a composer in spirit and
method. I am interested in the laboratory process through which the actors
and directors work together in search of all that is expressible and meaning-

ful. The most important part of our laboratory process is the developmental phase known as the research stage. This means reading, analyzing, studying, discussion, consciousness raising, and especially it means exploring the hidden past of women. At the same time, we are developing original methods of work which integrate training and acting technique and styles of performance with collective research on our theme. The research stage is a period of preparation of the actors—intellectually, artistically and technically. The creative potential of each actor is explored fully both in private workshop sessions with the directors and advisors and in group seminars and in workshops. The focus is on exchanging skills and the mutual investigation of the meaning of acting; its relation to gender, and its potential to express a point of view which combines: the actor as herself/himself, the actor as character, and the actor as commentator. The research stage emphasizes maximum artistic and intellectual responsibility on the part of each member of the core unit of actors. This stage usually takes us six to eight months into rehearsal and it is from this intense exploration and study of theme and technique that the collaborative relationship between director and actor is established. Without this shared knowledge the actor would not have a context of thinking or perceiving necessary in order to move consciously between subjective and objective reality which eventually allows the actor to reveal h/her audience personal and political correlations. In other words, this gives the actor the key to what s/he is doing, as well as how and why s/he is doing it. I believe, as Brecht did, that "true art is stimulated by its material." How else to create but from a place of deep understanding and passionate concern for the material one works on: how else to speak with total simplicity and honesty of the social inequities of one's own world? If one is to proceed in this direction, it becomes essential and necessary to create one's own text from scratch. Through this laboratory process we search for all that is possible, all that is expressible, in order to say as best we can that which feminist artists must say. This rootedness in women's lives allows us to break down the mystification surrounding the process of making art. "Once one steps outside the images of Madonna and whore, mystification is impossible" (Andrea Dworkin, in conversation).

5.

The Emmatroupe company worked very closely with the written word. The sources of our text/scripts came from women's literature, poetry, theory, and from the social-sexual-political analysis of history past and present. The major feminist writers/thinkers of our time—whose books change lives—became central to our work and purpose. Kataloni and I took on the roles of dramaturg as well as that of director/conceptualist and producer. It took over two years to find this new approach to theatre and acting which both illuminated and examined, on the personal level, the psycho-emotional realities of feminism and, on the political level, exposed and challenged the social-sexual view of women in a world where the actions and values of men define the lives of women.

With *A Girl Starts Out . . . A Tragedy in 4 Parts* with texts by George Eliot and Andrea Dworkin, we succeeded in creating and communicating a new expressionism voiced through language, image, symbol, myth, and story. The scenario is one of female persecution, but in its mode it steps outside of the pornographic: the female character is victimized as women in life are victimized, but the actor's body is not sexualized for a male viewer and the rape is never sentimentalized, *romanticized,* or glorified. Instead it is shown for what it is, what it does, and what it means. It is the presence of the actor that affirms womanhood and female potential as primary and essential and at the same time makes visceral what rape does to women. Ruth Wolff wrote:

> Emmatroupe wants us to know that rape has always happened, and it is time to cry out against it. Emmatroupe also claims an ethical responsibility in their presentation of violence—a desire not to exploit actors by physically debasing them nor to rob women actors of their dignity.[7]

In 1978, after seeing an open rehearsal of *A Girl Starts Out . . . ,* Kate Millett wrote to Emmatroupe:

> Working a long time in secret, Emmatroupe has reached back and touched fire with the primitive power in theatre to create a fierce and terrible cycle of the ages of woman, allegory, farce, murder, wake-building on literary texts, music and the language beyond words, further back: gestures, cries, whispers, chaos.

A Girl Starts Out . . . , made it clear that, once again, it is possible in theatre to give an ethical picture of the world as complete in its artistic vision as in its politics.

Karen Malpede

[1945–   ]

"**K**aren Malpede is the creator of an oneiric, mythic theatre where people speak as if in dreams," critic Rosette Lamont wrote providing succinct and suggestive categorization of my plays. Most of them were originally produced by New Cycle Theatre, which Burl Hash and I founded in Brooklyn in 1977. The first two notes appeared in programs for New Cycle productions of *The End of War* (1977) and *A Lament for Three Women* (1978). The third note is from the introduction to *Making Peace: A Fantasy* (1979). Other plays of mine produced by New Cycle are *A Monster Has Stolen the Sun: Part One* (1981) and *Sappho & Aphrodite* (1983).

Program Note to *The End of War*

A theatre that alleviates pain. This is what I most wish the New Cycle Theatre to be. We cannot alleviate pain by ignoring suffering or by accepting violence against ourselves or others as the natural order of things. In the theatre we relive together, in community, the personal sorrows of our past lives, the permanent sorrows of humankind in history. This shared recognition of what is not to be endured alone might free the energy inside us which is transcendent and aspires toward the good.

In the place that pain has left there is a reservoir of joy which comes, as Elena says in *The End of War*, "from making the hard choices for the first time." The theatre might also alleviate pain by putting images of comfort and of caring, of exchanges of compassion and knowledge into our minds' eye.

In rehearsal for *The End of War* we have found the violent choices, the hostile ones, and, for women, the helpless choices, too, are often the first ones we act out because they fill some preconceived notion of what "drama" is. But as we have not wished to make a graven image of what is, our struggle in rehearsal has been to see beyond the sado-masochistic dynamic so as to loosen its control over us. We work to find within our selves ways to make compelling the complex realities of growth and of gentle love. In the cycle plays our task is giving shape to moments when one person takes in another's feelings and, through taking-in, gives back the compassionate response.

To us there seems to be no other dramatic experiment worth making. The shapes of violence have been so deeply etched upon our consciousness they threaten to control nearly all our actions in the world. We long for a theatre that gives shape to the good, for we are no more than what we dream we might become. In the revelation of each new becoming lies the hope for nonviolent social change.

Welcome.

Program Note to *A Lament For Three Women*

I am a city person but once I lived in a small log cabin set between a wood and tiny meadow at the end of a dirt road in Woodstock, N.Y. I had spent two summers there before I stayed to see one of New England's magnificent autumn shows and then to watch the winter's winds and cold wipe out the wood's and meadow's luxuriant growth, laying bare beneath me the ground upon which I had been walking all this time. The shapes of the gullies, the rise and fall of the hills that had mystified me on many summer walks suddenly made perfect sense once they appeared without the rich, green camouflage of leaves and grasses. It was as if, through the death of the growth around me, I came to understand, for the first time, the shape of the world. By seeing, at last, the contours of the land, I came to realize the reasons why I had been lost so often in the summer. The summer was deceptive, I thought, for the cover that had seemed so comfortable was actually the means through which I had been kept ignorant. The winter, with its seeming harshness, revealed the truth of the landscape and made me feel an intimate of the land around me, one of nature's trusted and trusting friends. The earth asks of us that we live through the winter with her if we seek to know her as she truly is.

A Lament For Three Women is my first play, written over four years ago about the dying time of life in order to reveal the contours of the inner landscape. *Lament* falls into a long tradition of women's mourning plays, but the hope is that it breaks with that tradition, too, because the women are not merely vessels filled with grief at other people's deaths, they are, also, harbingers of a new life, one in which past pains are mitigated. This play of nearly unrelenting sorrow reverberates with the hope that follows upon clear sight of what is gone and what might come to life.

Watching the first rehearsal of this new production I saw, through the beauty of the bodies and the voices of the actors, that while the text of *Lament* reveals instance after instance of the lack of love, the action of the play gives image after image of love's transforming use. For as the women, each one alone upon the cold, bare landscape of her former, dying life, begin to give each other the mothering they never had, they grow strong together. As each woman recognizes the past's abuse of love, they come together to a moment when they can imagine a future, as yet unlived but through its sight made possible, where love will do the work of healing and of giving strength. In the midst of winter they catch sight of spring—a spring whose contours they now understand and whose wild release of passion they need no longer fear.

Welcome to the New Cycle Theatre.

Introductory Notes to *Making Peace: A Fantasy*

Innocence and exuberance: the two qualities necessary to perform this play. And, within each character, a passion that is innocent, exuberant, and urgent. We must lose our fear of approaching ecstasy. The play is a fantasy, by which I mean that what should happen does happen: that what might happen will happen. This is not a realistic play. It is a play in which each leap beyond the known is taken.

Vulnerability and strength: these are the alternating motions in the play. Each action sanctions vulnerability because strength is impossible without it. Being vulnerable allows another person to be strong and to care for you. And being vulnerable allows one's own strength to reform: to reissue in yet another form. Yet to be vulnerable in a situation that does not permit trust is suicidal. We need to create on stage situations in which trust is possible. This is the actors' job and the play will fail unless they accomplish it.

Heroism: The play is not a heroic play since heroic drama does not sanction vulnerability. But it is a play about heroism, nevertheless, a heroism within the reach of those who are alternately vulnerable and strong.

The play is not a sentimental play. But it has elements of sentimentality in it. The love of love, for instance. And enlarged emotions. Emotions enlarged because it is like the characters to feel passionately at all times. In production I would like: close attention to American sentimental-religious art of the 1840s. As a source, not as a style. I envision a style of costumes, of scenery, lighting, and of movement that is wondrous and innocent. Again, innocence. Transcendence is impossible without it. The innocence of the fool and of the saint. The spirits will wear angels' wings, small ones that bob around as they walk, that can be covered by their shrouds and yet pop up again. Small, irrepressible wings. The spirits [Mother Ann Lee, Charles Fourier, and Mary Wollstonecraft] will be dressed in angels' long white gowns. I see the innocents dressed in green and the escaped slaves [Harriet Tubman and her parents] in brown. There is a hierarchy in this play in which the highest are also the lowest and the meekest the most powerful. For the spirits are incapable of working the magic that comes quite naturally to the escaped slaves; and the innocents [fictional characters—two from a Shaker, two from a Rappite utopian community], impervious to the demands of the spirits, are awakened by the insights and by the needs of the slaves.

The heavenly mound, whereon the ardent spirits dwell, should be simple and beautiful. There is no need for it to be very high, the spirits are not so far away, and, yet, for the longest time they can't get down. Nor does it have to be very big—a certain crowding upon the heavenly mound will help the action there, perhaps. To become familiar with the spiritism of the time in which the play is set, one might want to read Emanuel Swedenborg's *Heaven and Hell*. The entire theatre space ought to be transformed from the dark and somberness of *The End of War* to a light, festive, almost sentimental, but, especially, innocent and exuberant environment.

Music: Shaker songs and dances and black slave songs and dances. The dance continues throughout the play. At first, only Mother Ann knows how to dance but at the end the innocents, spirits, and escaped slaves all dance: the Shaker circle dance and the ring shout. The spirits above dance the Shaker dance; the escaped slaves lead the ring shout below.

Miracles: all the miracles in the play can happen. The flowing of blood and of milk, the turning of blood into milk, renewable ecstasies—these are commonplaces of female sexuality. In this play, female sexuality works miracles. The play is a celebration of female sexuality; of strength in vulnerability and vulnerability in strength.

Racism and sexism: these two worst modes of oppression are directly addressed. But, as befits a fantasy where what might happen will happen, racism and sexism are addressed in the process of their undoing within the minds of those most directly affected, i.e., the victims. Racism, that mode of ill-logic, of fear, whereby non-Aryan men are reduced to the status of women, and non-Aryan women become the sexual, emotional, and physical servants of all others. Sexism, that mode of illogic, of fear, whereby all men find themselves superior to all women. In racism, in sexism, the primal fear and terror, the cause for the violence against the feared, is abhorrence of the passion seen in the oppressed: sexual passion, intellectual passion, emotional passion, spiritual passion, fecundity of all sorts—they are all connected. Once all fecundating passions are allowed to surface, the boundaries between the sacral and the profane tend to disappear; spirit and material worlds merge. The moment of this merging becomes the world of this play.

Fantasy is, quite simply, another way of perceiving what is true. Fantasy is how we see those longings which persists in us but which have not been adequately realized in life. Among the deep, persistent, unrealized longings held in common by the human race two must surely take precedence: the wish to feel that we are born good and are capable of much goodness; and the wish to see others this same way. The purpose of our fantasy is to rouse these ancient longings and so increase the hold they have on us; and on the audience.

Dolores Brandon

[1945–]

ON ACTING

Dolores Brandon is a feminist actor and director, born in Toronto, who trained with Katherine Sergava and Sonia Moore (both practitioners of Stanislavsky's system). In 1977 Brandon became a founding actor/director of New Cycle Theatre.

Elsewhere, Brandon has conceived and acted the one-woman show, *Women of Ancient Greece,* conceived and directed *In Praise of the Common Woman,* and with Rebecca Rovner as video director, conceptualized and acted the one-woman video version of *Utinam,* a dramatic poem by French Canadian writer Cécile Cloutier.

The following essay on acting, written in the summer of 1980, connects Brandon, and the feminist theatre, to the acting theories written by women which begin this book. In fact, Brandon has been a student of Angna Enters's writing on character creation. But unlike Enters, who worked alone, Brandon envisions the actor's true fulfillment in those moments of breathing together, when each member of the ensemble gives-and-takes alongside each other and the life rhythm of the community is created on the stage.—K.M.

Feminism and the Art of Theatre

The Director of the Soviet Film Office halts work on Sergei Eisenstein's film *Bezhin Meadow,* contending "the work continues to emphasize the passion for destruction." Eisenstein bravely searches his purposes:

> How could it happen . . . I had worked for two years. What was the mistaken viewpoint? . . . the mistake is rooted in one deep-seated intellectual individualist illusion, an illusion which beginning with small things can subsequently lead to big mistakes and tragic outcomes . . . the illusion that one may accomplish truly revolutionary work "on one's own" outside the fold of the collective . . . the error is philosophical. Philosophical errors lead to mistakes in method. Mistakes in method lead to objective political errors.[1]

Let not my citing this incident in any way suggest I condone or support the Soviet censorship activities. I do not. I am completely in awe of how this great artist received the criticism. The ability to stand outside his work, view it with absolute selflessness, is extraordinary. The complete wish that his art serve to create a better world leads me to think of trends in our theatre. Yes, the theatre is a political agent. It never escapes. Relationships created on the stage reinforce existing social relationships, affirming some, condemning others, pointing the way for the new. What we choose to do on stage can never be too carefully considered, for there we present models of what we believe to be possible or impossible. In its curious, magnetic way theatre encourages imitation, and for this we are responsible.

In this context I would like to examine aspects of our contemporary theatre that trouble me. One is the sudden proliferation of one-wo/man shows. I do not wish to condemn or discourage the form. I have chosen it for myself in the past and have seen several entirely enjoyable, brilliantly performed solo works. It is difficult to be an actor. Rarely does s/he work regularly and continuously, rarely does s/he really choose the work s/he does, rarely can s/he look back over the work of five or ten years and say "I truly wanted to do that role, it had something to say, I needed to say it." The one-person show offers this opportunity. The actor chooses a character s/he has some deep feeling of connection with; usually the character will be one who epitomizes an age, a folk or mythic hero/ine, artist, revolutionary, et cetera. S/he, the actor, really occupies the skin of this being, transforms her/himself visually, vocally, and indeed spiritually. This is the dream every actor starts out with—the wish to be for a moment someone other; to breathe, walk, talk as if an other. In becoming other s/he guides the spectator deeply into another human soul, the world of other.

Yet something is amiss. We have not experienced the whole of this wo/man represented. We cannot. We see her, hear her only with herself. S/he does not relate to an other. We lose dialogue and in some peculiar way must experience the character as neurotic, someone cut off and alone. A viewpoint to be sure, valid, common perhaps, but ultimately disturbing, hopeless, and often untrue to the reality of the particular character's life. In this form the actor lives deeply within a character and shares the inner life with the audience in a very focused and intense way. It is a pleasure to experience this sharing. But the great joy of theatre for both performer and spectator is not achieved. For the real joy of theatre occurs when two, three, or more actors give themselves wholly to the imagined situation, breathe together, trust, abandon all fear, all resistance, and commune deeply with each other. In such moments we truly "act." All pretense flees and we *are*. We affect and are affected. This act we can take into our lives for it has been true, lived. We have altered our selves and are changed. The truth of our act stirs something very deep in the audience. Acts of profound personal exchange are within the reach of every wo/man. The wish to commune deeply with an other is greater than the wish to be alone. The effort to speak and be heard, to listen, to touch and be touched, held, in conflict, even, is the very nature of life. If we do not do this on stage, we are permitting ourselves and others to give up; we are saying we no longer expect or believe we are stronger and more beautiful when we work and share this life with others.

I do not think actors are choosing to work alone because they prefer to. Rather, this is the most economically viable form. So what seems a free act, an act of choice, is, in fact, not. For women this is particularly serious. (I address women particularly because the one-person show has always been the form most available to her and one in which she has excelled.) We play into the arms of those who wish to see us alone, neurotic, and small. Our largest imaginings are effectively eliminated, discouraged. Women have never existed separate and apart. She has always been at the very center of collective work and ritual. It is her breath, her blood that brings forth life. It is her sharing that brings forth knowledge. The roots of feminist theatre exist in nature rites, rites of passage and initiation, ceremonies in which we were tutored in the ways of life and communed with spiritual guides who aided us to heal ourselves and others, ceremonies in which great pain was endured but great joy was shared.

These forces are struggling to emerge in our contemporary feminist theatres. Often trampled upon, the little shoots are growing, pushing their way up through the debris of human life shot, mutilated, raped, wasted, and beaten in a theatre of alienation and cruelty, a cinema of fascism and decadence. The feminist theatre we know emerged when women began to share experiences in consciousness-raising groups and helped each other grow. These groups effected real change in the lives of women as well as men. Women's expectations for themselves and their "families" changed radically. When we decided to bring this new consciousness to our theatre something peculiar happened. Our method was to be collective. Some of us, wishing to eliminate all shadow of hierarchy, chose to work without a director, without a playwright. We collectively conceived a text and collectively made decisions regarding form. Curiously, we frequently arrive at forms in which there is no dialogue. We are no longer speaking to one another. The characters are highly abstracted, "presented" rather than lived, their inner lives are underdeveloped and they have no unique, defining characteristics. The text is spoken in a monotonal manner, face front. The collective spirit is absent from the stage. As spectators we find ourselves in court, members of a jury. We listen to case histories, reports on crimes against women. A trial in which the jury is asked to remain silent, the witness and prosecution are present, there is no defendant, and there is no judge. We leave the stage, theatre, knowing more, perhaps understanding the situation better, but again something is missing. The actor did not act, did not become other. Nothing changed. There could be no changing; we had no dialogue, we did not touch, we did not see into an other's eyes.

I think with fondness and optimism on the lines from Karen Malpede's play, *The End of War:*

GALINA

We did not speak, nor could we,
not from fear of being caught
but because cold hatred for the other body
that we
touched had silent hold on all our thought. . . .

OLD MOTHER

My lost daughters, speak no more,
it is the cry, unadorned and pure,
the cry of the wounded heart I hear.
In a wild flight let the cry soar,
turn, be transformed and changed until
forgiveness comes to pulse in the same spot
where once the wound was all that could be felt. . . .

This is a night for our rejoicing,
this is a night for our rebirth. . . .

For one moment all is different
all is changed
all is as it could have been
had women not suffered other's pain.

This is the miracle theatre will work. The alchemy is in the method. We must reexamine the word "collective." What does it mean? It must mean more than simply having a group of people working together on a particular project. Certainly Eisenstein was doing that. He was not working alone; nor is our solo actor, nor is our feminist troupe. It was not the process of work on that film that came under attack. It was the content, the world he created on that screen. I quote Eisenstein:

. . . the socially false emphasis in the situation led to a false psychological interpretation. The situation is solved in psychological abstraction, that bears no connection to a realistic investigation of actuality . . . since attention is not fully centered on man, on his action, the role of accessory and auxiliary means becomes excessive, hence . . . the settings instead of the actor.[2]

So it is the world we create on our stages that must be true to the collective essence of humankind. To ignore the relationships that weave in and through each life, to ignore the processes of decay, growth, and change is to perpetuate a false notion—that our lives are lived outside the "fold." This is the lie that can render our theatre impotent. We are free when we recognize an other in our selves, our selves in an other; when we choose to be "multiple and various." At some level actors know this or they would not choose to act. To create worlds on our stages in which we talk only to ourselves and do no affective acting is to disown our power and to rob the theatre of its greatest purpose. Hannah Arendt says it best.

In judging these affects we can scarcely help raising the question of selflessness, or rather the question of openness to others, which is in fact the precondition for "humanity" in every sense of that word. It seems evident that sharing joy is absolutely superior in this respect to sharing suffering. Gladness, not sadness, is talkative, and truly human dialogue differs from mere talk or even discussion in that it is entirely permeated by pleasure in the other person and what he says. It is tuned to the key of gladness, we might say.[3]

Edwina Lee Tyler

[1944–   ]

AN INTERVIEW

Edwina Lee Tyler, founder of the women's African percussion group, A Piece of the World, is a young performer of magical presence who, since January 1979, when her group began to play at women's and black music concerts around New York City, has enthralled larger and larger audiences. She plays conga drum, cow bells, and the shekere, and she dances as if possessed by some vibrant life-giving force. As a whole, the group she leads gives out a strength, warmth, and harmony that lifts women's music into the realm of the sacred—back, that is, to where it all began.

—K.M.

Karen Malpede: How did you begin to play the drums?

Edwina Lee Tyler: It was in me. It was never a thing of "when I grow up I'm going to play the drums and get a teacher." It was already in me. I was already playing beats when I was three. I didn't know the technique, but I was playing the beats that I heard inside me—and that had to come out. I've been playing the drums so long it's just as natural as going to the bathroom or getting a glass of water.

KM: You speak about the beats being in you and having to come out. It sounds sacred, and the drums are the most sacred of instruments . . .

ELT: It's a sacred instrument for me because it lights me up. When I'm sad and there's something in me that won't light up, I go to the drums. When I'm finished playing, I'm a satisfied person. I also have to move, to dance; but the drums, it lights me up. It keeps me happy. It keeps me very happy.

KM: When you perform you seem to have a very clear idea of what your relationship to the audience is and of what you want to create in them. Could you talk about that?

ELT: I used to play in Washington Square Park. All different types of people would be walking by, and they'd come over while I was playing the drums. I would be in my own world, but I would also be aware that they were there and I'd see them patting their feet. I just gave out me. I just gave out me, but, then, when they would get tired of me I would perform to them. I would get up and perform to them. Sometimes people have a story inside them, and if you give to them that story comes out. I like to get close to the audience, so I can feel their vibes. I can't explain it, but I can feel their vibes when I'm close to them; they just bring their vibes on out to me.

KM: So then you play the rhythms you get from them?

ELT: From them, yes.

KM: And what effect does it have on them when they hear their own beat, even though they don't know consciously that's what you are doing?

ELT: I've had people come up to me and say, "Thank you, I feel much better," or "You know, I wanted to go home because I was in a rotten mood, but thank you because you gave me something and I feel better." People have said, "You gave me inspiration." I've had that done to me and I want to do it in return. I have to give them something. You can't perform and not give somebody something. It's a must. You can't keep it to yourself. Then you're being stingy. I give them me; in return they are giving their selves to me. And it's a wonderful combination.

KM: The first time I saw you perform was in Prospect Park, on quite a big stage. Your ability to go right up to the audience, to achieve intimacy with them, seemed amazing to me then. How did you become able to do that?

ELT: Sitting in Washington Square Park, I had my audience so close to me that I could hardly breathe, but I also got a closeness. I could feel them. I like performing to the ones who are sad. So I say, "Turn the house lights on." I have to see faces, to see what they're about. That night in the park, I saw a gentleman with his face straight. I mean his face was really straight. All of a sudden I started to play just to him. I wanted to let him know I understood and that I was going to give him my feelings anyway. I saw his face go from being so tight he couldn't move it till it opened right up. That made me so happy I could play to the rest of the folks.

KM: So when you give you often choose someone who looks like he or she can't take in.

ELT: Yes, a healing, maybe it's a healing. First, I have to give before I can enjoy myself.

KM: Let's go back to the beginning. How did you learn to play the drums?

ELT: My parents, Edward and Ruth Gibbs Tyler, were singers. They performed together, giving concerts in Carnegie Hall and places like that. They traveled on the road in musicals. Music was in our house. We had all sorts of music. My brother was a percussionist, and he started teaching me. When my mother moved uptown from 116th Street to 145th Street there was a fellow who used to play in the park. I was the only girl just standing around while the young fellas were playing the drums. One day I asked him, "Could I play your drum?" He looked up at me and said, "Oh, sure." And he saw something in me because he said, "Hey, wait a minute, let me teach you the right way." He started teaching me different rhythms. I've only seen him about three times since I was kid. Each time I see him, I thank him. He always asks if I'm still playing and he says, "Good."

KM: So you learned this ancient African instrument on the streets of New York City.

ELT: Yes. Right now my message is that the ethnic and black in America are not far apart. They are together. I am Afro-American even though I've never been to Africa in my life. Most people can't believe I'm not from there. My soul and my heart are from there. Black people don't have to feel separated from Africa. I'm from Harlem on 116th Street and I feel exactly what's happening over there.

KM: Is there a connection between your performing and the feminist movement?

ELT: For quite a while women didn't feel they were supposed to play the drums, in any field, whether it was jazz, Latin, any field. Especially in America it was not considered cool for women to do this. Women had to wait. We had to wait and this gave us time to practice and to get to know ourselves on the inside and to bring it out. Its time has come. I don't mean to say, "Oh, men, stay away from men," because I've learned from a man. His teaching helped me bring the strength I already had inside, out. Women are going to be with women. This is an automatic thing. But when you find an audience of all kinds of people joining together and saying, "Thank you, hey, I understand," then it's even greater.

KM: Where is your music taking you now?

ELT: My music has expanded more and more, leading me somewhere. It was right there all the time, only I couldn't put my finger on it. Now I know I want to put the classical into the ethnic because that's a part of me also. Before I really got into ethnic, classical music was there in me. And I played it. We always had classical music around because my father was a classical singer and composer and so was my mother.

KM: Right now "A Piece of the World" is composed of women who play drums, bells, and shekere. Will you add instruments to the group?

ELT: Yes. When I add an instrument, it's going to be a cello. I already know a woman who's going to rehearse with us on flute. She's very, very good. She's an improvisor. She knows African music but she's a reader of classical, also. Then, I'm going to add a violin. I'm going to add these instruments in because classical music is something I can't get away from. It was brought up in me. I have to have it, too.

KM: I don't think there's an incompatibility. The ethnic music presents a holistic world view.

ELT: Oh, yes.

KM: And so does the classical.

ELT: Yes, it gives out.

KM: Have you ever worked under words, with actors?

ELT: I have. The experience is great because it teaches sensitivity. I started because my father was an actor. He acted with his music. I worked with him. He was a hard teacher because he was hearing things so way out. I had to come up to him. He couldn't come down to me. He had to bring me up to him. So even before I knew the whole technique of percussion, I knew the sensitivity of what it is about. It's not about staying up there so loud but about bringing it down—'cause that's what we're about—we're not all the way up all the time. I say this for all percussionists—they should work with singers and actors because you learn sensitivity. It's so great when you can know the singers you're working with. That's what you're about—you're an actor, you're a singer. Even if you can't sing, you sing. You have a mouth, you have heart, you have words to say. And it's combined.

KM: It becomes a way of living then.

ELT: That's what it is—a way of living—that's what it is. And people don't realize. Oh, it's a way of living. Everybody's feelings are going to come out. Just by talking, I'm understanding things a little bit better. I couldn't understand how come I was hearing these things—these different sounds—but now I know. I'm a modern artist also connected to my roots. I have to give that modern stuff right now. It's inside me, it's going to come out.

Notes

Introduction

1. Lorraine Hansberry, "Willy Loman, Walter Younger, and He Who Must Live," in *The Village Voice Reader,* ed. Daniel Wolf and Edwin Francher (New York: Doubleday, 1962), p. 199.
2. Judith Malina, "From the Diaries, 1947–51" In *Women in Theatre: Compassion and Hope,* ed. Karen Malpede (New York: Drama Book Publishers, 1983), p. 208.
3. Danny Staples, trans., "The Homeric Hymn to Demeter," in *The Road to Eleusis,* ed. R. Gordon Wasson, Carl A. P. Ruck, and Albert Hofmann (New York: Harcourt Brace Jovanovich, 1978), p. 64. The Homeric Hymn records an already late version of this tale. It seems likely that in the original Persephone was not abducted but went into the underworld of her own free will, thereby establishing herself as the energy corridor through which life returns.
4. Jane Ellen Harrison, *Ancient Art and Ritual* (Bradford-on-Avon, Eng.: Moonraker Press, 1978), p. 157.
5. Theodor H. Gaster, *Thespis: Ritual, Myth and Drama in the Ancient Near East* (New York: Norton, 1950), pp. 276–77.
6. Rosamond Gilder, *Enter the Actress* (New York: Theatre Arts Books, 1961), pp. 1–2.
7. Jessie L. Watson, *From Ritual to Romance* (New York: Anchor, 1957).
8. Gilbert Murray, Foreword to *Thespis,* p. 9.
9. Jane Ellen Harrison, *Themis* (New Hyde Park, New York: University Books, 1966), p. xli.
10. It is significant that in the Homeric Hymn, Demeter leaves Olympus and walks upon the earth to mourn her daughter. She returns, that is, to where she had come from, for she was originally a nature spirit and arose among her people on the earth.
11. Edvard Lehmann, *Mysticism in Heathendom and Christianity,* trans. G. M. G. Hunt (London: Luzac & Co., 1910), p. 293.
12. Isadora Duncan, "The Dance of the Future," in *The Art of the Dance,* ed. Sheldon Cheney (New York: Theatre Arts Books, 1969), p. 63.
13. Martha Graham, "Notes on 'Voyage'," in *The Notebooks of Martha Graham* (New York: Harcourt Brace Jovanovich, 1973), p. 130.
14. Katherine Dunham, *Journey to Accompong* (Westport, Conn.: Negro University Press, 1971), p. 133.
15. Roswitha, *The Plays of Roswitha,* trans. and ed. Christopher St. John (New York: Benjamin Blom, 1966), p. 133. Different scholars have used different spellings. In the text I have maintained Gilder's usage, Hrotsvitha.
16. Ibid.
17. Ibid., p. xxix.

18. Augusta Gregory, *Collected Plays II* (Gerrards Cross, Eng.: Colin Smythe, 1971), p. 283.
19. Hallie Flanagan, "What Was Federal Theatre?" in *People's Theatre in Amerika,* ed. Karen Malpede Taylor (New York: Drama Book Specialists (Publishers), 1972), p. 171.
20. Judith Malina, "From the Diaries, 1947–51" in *Women in Theatre: Compassion and Hope,* p. 205.
21. Judith Malina and Karen Malpede, "Judith Malina Chooses Life" and "The Bonds At Last Undone," *New Women's Times Feminist Review* (November and January 1979).
22. Barbara Ann Teer, "An Interview," in *Women in Theatre: Compassion and Hope,* p. 225.
23. Eleonora Duse, in *Actors on Acting,* ed. Toby Cole and Helen Krich Chinoy (New York: Crown, 1970).
24. Ellen Terry, "The Pathetic Women," in *Four Lectures on Shakespeare,* ed. Christopher St. John (New York: Benjamin Blom, 1969), p. 129.

Ellen Terry

1. Ellen Terry, *Memoirs* (New York: Putnam, 1932), p. 23.
2. Ibid., p. 302.
3. Ellen Terry and Bernard Shaw, *A Correspondence* (New York: Theatre Arts Books, 1949), p. xxv.

Eva Le Gallienne

1. Eva Le Gallienne, *With a Quiet Heart* (New York: Viking, 1953), p. 19.
2. Eva Le Gallienne, *The Mystic in the Theatre* (Carbondale, Ill.: Southern Illinois University Press, 1965), pp. 125–26.

Angna Enters

1. Angna Enters, *Artist's Life,* (New York: Coward-McCann, 1959), p. 6.
2. Ibid., p. 56.

Isadora Duncan

1. Sheldon Cheney, ed., *Isadora Duncan: The Art of the Dance* (New York: Theatre Arts Books, 1969), p. 41.
2. Isadora Duncan, *My Life* (New York: Liveright, 1955), p. 162.
3. Cheney, *Art of the Dance,* p. 43.
4. Emma Goldman and Alexander Berkman, *Nowhere at Home,* ed. Richard and Anna Maria Drinnon (New York: Schocken Books, 1975), p. 126.
5. Duncan, *My Life,* pp. 196 and 188.
6. Ibid.

Augusta Gregory

1. Lady Augusta Gregory, *Seventy Years* (New York: Macmillan, 1974), p. 100.
2. Lady Augusta Gregory, *Our Irish Theatre* (New York: Capricorn Books, 1965), pp. 80–81.
3. Ibid., p. 83.
4. Ibid., p. 92.
5. Elizabeth Coxhead, *Lady Gregory* (London: Secker & Warburg, 1966), p. 138.
6. Gregory, *Seventy Years*, p. 309.

Lorraine Hansberry

1. Adrienne Rich, "The Problem with Lorraine Hansberry," *Freedomways,* vol. 19, no. 4 (1979): 249. According to Robert Nemiroff, "The Sign in Jenny Reed's Window" dropped its title character after the first draft as Hansberry turned from the story of a young idealist persecuted for her beliefs, to the problem of the disillusioned male intellectual. Early notes for *Les Blancs* indicate the author thought of giving Tsembe a twin sister, Candace, also a European-educated African.

Hallie Flanagan

1. Hallie Flanagan, "What Was Federal Theatre?" *The New Republic* (October 1939), reprinted in Karen Malpede Taylor, *People's Theatre in Amerika,* (New York: Drama Book Specialists (Publishers), 1972), p. 171.

Eleanor Johnson

1. Andrea Dworkin, "Feminism, Art, and My Mother Sylvia," in *Our Blood: Prophesies and Discourses on Sexual Politics* (New York: Harper & Row, 1976), p. 9.
2. Maria Ley-Piscator, *The Piscator Experiment: The Political Theatre* (Southern Illinois University Press, 1967), pp. 123–25.
3. Simone de Beauvoir, *The Second Sex,* trans. H. M. Parshley (New York: Knopf, 1953).
4. Andrea Dworkin, "The Sexual Politics of Fear and Courage," in *Our Blood: Prophesies and Discourses on Sexual Politics* (New York: Harper & Row, 1967), p. 9.
5. Andrienne Rich, speaking at a support rally for Mary Daly, Boston University, April 8, 1979.
6. Judy Chicago, *Through the Flower: My Struggle as a Woman Artist* (New York: Doubleday, 1975).
7. Ruth Wolff, "Theatre: The Aesthetics of Violence: Women Tackle the Rough Stuff," *Ms.* Magazine (February 1979): 34–36.

Dolores Brandon

1. Léon Moussinac, *Sergei Eisenstein* (New York: Crown, 1964), pp. 160–62.
2. Ibid., pp. 160–62.
3. Hannah Arendt, *Men in Dark Times* (New York: Harcourt Brace World, 1968), p. 17.

Selected Bibliography

General

Chambers, E. K. *The Medieval Stage*. Vols. 1 and 2. London: Oxford University Press, 1978.

Chesler, Phyllis. *About Men*. New York: Simon & Schuster, 1978.

Daly, Mary. *Beyond God the Father*. Boston: Beacon, 1973.

—————— *Gyn/Ecology*. Boston: Beacon, 1979.

Deming, Barbara. *Revolution and Equilibrium*. New York: Grossman, 1971.

—————— *We Cannot Live Without Our Lives*. New York: Grossman, 1974.

Dinnerstein, Dorothy. *The Mermaid and the Minotaur*. New York: Harper & Row, 1977.

Figes, Eva. *Tragedy and Social Evolution*. London: Calder, 1976.

France, Rachel, ed. *A Century of Plays by American Women*. New York: Richards Rosen, 1979.

Gassner, John, ed. *Twenty-Five Best Plays of the Modern American Theater*. New York: Crown, 1949.

Gaster, Theodor. *Thespis: Ritual, Myth and Drama in the Ancient Near East*. New York: Norton, 1977.

Griffin, Susan. *Woman and Nature: The Roaring Inside Her*. New York: Harper and Row, 1978.

Harrison, Jane Ellen. *Ancient Art and Ritual*. Bradford-on-Avon, Eng.: Moonraker Press, 1978.

—————— *Epilegomena to the Study of Greek Religion & Themis*. New Hyde Park, N.Y.: University Books, 1966.

—————— *Prolegomena to the Study of Greek Religion*: Cambridge: Cambridge University Press, 1903.

Murray, Gilbert. *Euripedes and His Age*. London: Oxford University Press, 1965.

Orenstein, Gloria. *The Theatre of the Marvelous*. New York: New York University Press, 1975.

Rich, Adrienne. *Of Woman Born*. New York: Norton, 1976.

Wasson, R. Gordon, Carl A. P. Ruck, Albert Hofmann. *The Road to Eleusis*. New York: Harcourt Brace Jovanovich, 1978.

Weston, Jessie L. *From Ritual to Romance*. New York: Anchor, 1957.

Isadora Duncan

My Life. New York: Liveright, 1955.

The Art of the Dance. Edited with an introduction by Sheldon Cheney. New York: Theatre Arts Books, 1969.

Katherine Dunham

Journey to Accompong. Westport, Conn.: Negro University Press, 1971 (reprint of 1946 edition).

Island Possessed. Garden City, N.Y.: Doubleday, 1969.

Angna Enters

Artist's Life. New York: Coward-McCann, 1958.

First Person Plural. New York: Stackpole Sons, 1935.

Silly Girl: A Portrait of Personal Remembrance. Boston: Houghton Mifflin, 1944.

Love Possessed Juana (Queen of Castile): A Play in Four Acts. New York: Twice a Year Press, 1939.

On Mime. Middletown, Conn.: Wesleyan University Press, 1965.

Hallie Flanagan

Arena: The History of the Federal Theatre. New York: Benjamin Blom, 1968 (reprint of 1940 edition).

Can Your Hear Their Voices? in *A Century of Plays by American Women.* Rachel France, ed. New York: Richards Rosen Press, 1979.

The Curtain, a play. New York: Samuel French (n.d.)

Dynamo. New York: Duell, Sloan and Pearce, 1943.

Shifting Scenes of the Modern European Theatre. New York: Coward-McCann, 1928.

Rosamond Gilder

Enter the Actress: The First Women in the Theatre. New York: Theatre Arts Books, 1961.

John Gielgud's Hamlet. Oxford: Oxford University Press, 1937.

Susan Glaspell

Alison's House. In *The Pulitzer Plays,* Kathryn Cordell, ed. New York: Random House, 1935.

Berenice. London: E. Benn Ltd., 1924.

The Comic Artist. New York: F. A. Stokes, 1927.

Inheritors. Boston: Small, Maynard, 1921.

The People & Close the Book. New York: F. Shay, 1918.

Plays. Boston: Small, Maynard (n.d.).

The Road to the Temple. New York: F. A. Stokes, 1941.

Suppressed Desires. In collaboration with George Cram Cook. Boston: W. H. Baker (n.d.).

Emma Goldman

Anarchism and Other Essays. With biographic sketch by Hippolyte Havel. Port Washington, N.Y.: Kennitcat Press, 1969.

Living My Life. Vols. 1 and 2. New York: Dover, 1970.

Nowhere At Home: Letters from Exile of Emma Goldman and Alexander Berkman. Richard and Ann Maria Drinnon, eds. New York: Schocken, 1975.

The Psychology of Political Violence. New York: Gordon Press, 1974.

Red Emma Speaks. Alix Kates Shulman, ed. New York: Random House, 1972.

The Social Significance of the Modern Drama. Boston: Richard G. Badger, 1914.

The Traffic in Women & Other Essays on Feminism. New York: Times Change Press, 1970.

Martha Graham

The Notebooks of Martha Graham. New York: Harcourt Brace Jovanovich, 1973.

Lorraine Hansberry

A Raisin in the Sun & The Sign in Sidney Brustein's Window. New York: New American Library, 1966.

Lorraine Hansberry: The Collected Last Plays. Edited, with critical backgrounds by Robert Nemiroff. New York: Plume (New American Library), 1983.

To Be Young, Gifted and Black. Adapted by Robert Nemiroff. New York: Signet (New American Library), 1970.

Augusta Gregory

A Book of Saints and Wonders. New York: Oxford University Press, 1971.

Collected Plays. Vols. 1–4. Ann Saddlemeyer, ed. Gerrards Cross, Eng.: Colin Smythe, 1971.

The Kiltartan Books. New York: Oxford University Press, 1971.

Our Irish Theatre. New York: Capricorn Books, 1965.

Seventy Years: 1852–1922. Edited with foreword by Colin Smythe. New York: Macmillan, 1974.

Visions and Beliefs in the West of Ireland. Gerrards Cross, Eng.: Colin Smythe, 1970.

Fanny Kemble

Francis the First: An Historical Drama. London: John Murray, 1832.

Journal of a Residence on a Georgian Plantation. Edited with an introduction by John A. Scott. New York: Knopf, 1961.

The Journal of Frances Ann Butler, Better Known as Fanny Kemble. New York: Benjamin Blom, 1970.

Records of a Later Life. London: R. Bentley, 1882.

Eva Le Gallienne

At 33. New York: Longmans, 1934.

Eva Le Gallienne's Civic Repertory Plays. New York: Norton, 1928.

The Mystic in the Theater: Eleonora Duse. Carbondale, Ill.: Southern Illinois University Press, 1966.

With a Quiet Heart. New York: Viking, 1953.

Judith Malina

The Brig, A Play by Kenneth H. Brown With an Essay on the Living Theatre by Julian Beck and Director's Notes by Judith Malina. New York: Hill and Wang, 1965.

The Enormous Despair: The Diary of Judith Malina, August 1968 to April 1969. New York: Random House, 1972.

Paradise Now. Collective Creation of the Living Theatre. Written down by Judith Malina and Julian Beck. New York: Vintage, 1971.

Karen Malpede

A Lament for Three Women in *A Century of Plays by American Women.* Rachel France, ed. New York: Richards Rosen, 1979.

People's Theatre in Amerika. With a preface by John Howard Lawson. New York: Drama Book Specialists (Publishers), 1972.

Three Works by the Open Theatre. Karen Malpede, ed. New York: Drama Book Specialists (Publishers), 1974.

Gertrude Stein

Geography and Plays. New York: Something Else Press, 1968.

Last Operas and Plays. New York: Vintage, 1975.

Lectures in America. New York: Random House, 1935.

Lucretia Borgia, a play. New York: Albondocani Press, 1968.

Selected Operas and Plays. John Malcolm Brinnin, ed. Pittsburgh: University of Pittsburgh Press, 1970.

Ellen Terry

Ellen Terry and Bernard Shaw: A Correspondence. Christopher St. John, ed. New York: G. P. Putnam's Sons, 1931.

Four Lectures on Shakespeare. Christopher St. John, ed. New York: Benjamin Blom, 1969 (reprint of 1932 edition).

Ellen Terry's Memoirs. With a preface, notes, and additional biographical chapters by Edith Craig and Christopher St. John. New York: G. P. Putnam's Sons, 1932.

Index

ABOUT THE AUTHOR

Karen Malpede is a playwright, theater historian, and peace activist. Her first play, *A Lament for Three Women,* is included in the anthology *A Century of Plays by American Women.* Among her other published plays are a collection, *A Monster Has Stolen the Sun and Other Plays,* as well as *Better People* and *Us,* both of which premiered at Theater for the New City in New York. Her plays have also been performed at New Cycle Theater, in Brooklyn, which she co-founded; at theaters in New York, London, Rome, Boston, San Francisco, and Cleveland; and at colleges and universities, including Harvard and Smith.

Ms. Malpede has conducted theater workshops with battered women and recovering drug addicts, and has taught writing and drama at Smith College; the Tisch School of the Arts, New York University; and Lang College. Her writings on women and war and peace have been frequently anthologized. The editor of *Three Works by the Open Theater,* she lives in Brooklyn with her daughter, Carrie Sophia, and actor/producer George Bartenieff.